KV-193-953

The Library of
Sir Ben Helfgott MBE

CLORE

CLORE

The Man and his Millions

David Clutterbuck
and
Marion Devine

WEIDENFELD AND NICOLSON
LONDON

Copyright © Clutterbuck Associates 1987

First published in Great Britain by
George Weidenfeld & Nicolson Limited
91 Clapham High Street, London SW4 7TA

All rights reserved. No part of this publication may
be reproduced, stored in a retrieval system, or
transmitted in any form or by any means, electronic,
mechanical, photocopying, recording or otherwise,
without the prior permission of the copyright owner.

ISBN 0 297 79086 2

Printed by The Bath Press, Avon

Contents

Illustrations

Israel Clore (*Vivien Duffield*)
Charles, aged ten (*Vivien Duffield*)
With two of his brothers, Hyman and David (*Vivien Duffield*)
With his family at his sister Rosie's wedding, 1920 (*the Clore family*)
The two impresarios, Charles and Alfred Esdaile (*Mrs Esdaile*)
On horseback at Ray Court (*Mrs Clotz*)
Francine, aged eighteen, at her coming-out ball (*Vivien Duffield*)
Charles' and Francine's wedding picture, 7 June 1943 (*Mrs Francine
    Clore*)
Charles and Francine with Alan, 1944 (*Vivien Duffield*)
Alan and Vivien, *c.* 1950 (*Vivien Duffield*)
Checkendon (*Mrs Clotz*)
Charles relaxing in his study at Checkendon (*Mrs Clotz*)
Jack Cotton at a Norwich Union party with Aubrey Orchard-Lisle and
    Maurice Wohl (*Aubrey Orchard-Lisle*)
With his right-hand man, Leonard Sainer (*Vivien Duffield*)
Two tycoons together: Clore with Sir Isaac Wolfson (*photo: Be-Zvi;
    Vivien Duffield*)
With Meyer Weisgal, 1962 (*The Weizmann Institute*)
With Teddy Kollek at the opening of the Charles Clore Hill Gardens in
    Jerusalem (*Photo-Emka; Vivien Duffield*)
With Alan in the 1960s (*Mrs Esdaile*)
Farmer Clore at Stype (*Daily Express; Vivien Duffield*)
Shooting at Stype (*Vivien Duffield*)

Acknowledgements

The authors would like to thank the following for their great help on this book: Jarvis Astaire, H. Bart-Smith, John Bodie, Sir Nigel Broackes, Charles Clore Jr, Francine Clore, Leon Clore, Martin Clore, Mrs I. Clotz, Dr Arnold Cohen, Lord Delfont, Vivien Duffield, Mr Abba Eban, Rene Esdaile, Edward Footring, Jack Gardiner, Lord Hanson, President Chaim Herzog, Charles Hughesdon, Frederick Kay, Sidney Kaye, Lord Kenneth Keith, Mena Kohust, Joseph Levy, Geoffrey Maitland Smith, Janet, Marchioness of Milford Haven, Mordechai Mayer, Moshe Mayer, Sir Peter Millett, Aubrey Orchard-Lisle, Lord Rayne, Gerald Ronson, Leonard Sainer, Sir Patrick Sargeant, Vivienne Schuster, Lord Sieff, Ruth Solomons, Jocelyn Stevens and Meyer Weisgal. They would also like to thank the many other people who gave so freely of their time during the book's preparation.

Shares in shops and ships and shoes;
Takeover bids, prize bulls and booze;
Hotels and theatres, transport, mines
And other miscellaneous lines . . .
Your restless hands reach out for
more.
. . . But are you happy, Charlie Clore?

Evening News, 20 April 1961

1

The Making of the Man

'He was always interested in money ...'
Ben Hacker, Rochelle Street School

'In my judgement Sir Charles Clore was domiciled in England both in February 1979 and at his death on 26 July 1979, and I shall hereby declare so.' These sparse words, uttered by Mr Justice Nourse in October 1984, heralded the beginning of the end of one of the most controversial legal battles of the twentieth century in British courts. At stake were Charles Clore's world-wide assets, estimated at around £123 million, and his last ambition – some say obsession – to keep his fortune safe from the grasp of the British taxman. During the six-year case, every aspect of this remarkable man's personality and character was picked over. And yet, at the end of it, people who had been involved in it from the beginning could not truly say they knew the man.

Charles Clore was an enigma, a paradox. Regarded by many as a gauche *nouveau riche*, his was not by any means a rags to riches story. Although abrupt in his language, he was one of the most perceptive connoisseurs of art in his time and demonstrated impeccable taste in everything from furnishing to gourmet food. Parsimonious – even miserly on occasion – he ranks among the most generous benefactors of the arts and social causes in the post-war years. Indeed, almost all of the fortune in his contested will was intended for charitable causes. Vilified as a ruthless bounder for the manner in which he acquired ownership of Sears and other companies, he is none the less remembered by many as incorruptibly honest. 'He was', says the late Stuart Young, head of the BBC and a one-time business associate, 'the most honest man I have ever known.' The delight of society gossip columnists for his string of young companionettes and love of parties, he made no attempt to be a sexual athlete and drank very little. A man with a deep affection for the country of his birth, he exiled himself at the very time he most needed the companionship and security of friends and things familiar.

Perhaps the greatest paradox of all is that Charles Clore, who was by any test a remarkable success in business and commercial terms, should have been a failure in so many other aspects of his life. Clore's family life

1

was a disaster, from his acrimonious marriage and divorce, to an estrangement from his children that was only repaired in the case of his daughter, Vivien. His Herculean efforts to achieve a knighthood were thwarted for years, and there was never a serious chance of his achieving the peerage that his socialite ambitions led him to covet.

Above all, the misery and discomfort of his self-imposed exile proved worthless. Although cast-iron decisiveness and determination characterized every business deal he ever made, Clore's attempt to establish a foreign domicile was severely hindered by his inability to pick a single country as his home. Restlessly flitting between Monaco, Paris, New York and London, he never reached the point of finally abandoning England.

Mr Justice Nourse described the last two years of Clore's life in these terms: 'Able, restless, cerebral without being intellectual or cultured, dutiful in religion but not spiritual, sometimes on the edge of loneliness or boredom, the impression is of a final period of unhappiness and doubt.'

Rarely putting a foot wrong when he built up his vast property and retail empire, Clore made some obvious mistakes during his exile. These led directly to the reduction of his fortune by death duties of £67 million. The closest Clore ever came to committing himself to live permanently in Monaco was to spend £2 million buying and furnishing an apartment in Monte Carlo and to purchase a *carte de séjour* (a residence permit). Even then, he never severed his links with his home. He continued to visit Britain frequently for social, business, sporting and medical purposes, even though he knew that these trips severely weakened his claim to domicile in Monaco.

Another mistake Clore made was to be so slow in taking his money out of the country via his Jersey company Stype Investments, which was especially formed to avoid income tax and death duties. Only by establishing domicile abroad (a long process) or by having few or no assets in Britain could he avoid the two taxes. But, even after he made the decision that this was what he intended to do, he could not easily give up the things that tied him to England, and the sale of his properties was still going through when he died. This left the Inland Revenue free to seize taxes. At the same time, his son Alan froze the assets by contesting the will in an ugly confrontation. On all counts, the biggest deal Clore ever made was the one he lost to the Inland Revenue.

So where did this remarkable man come from? What mixture of environment and temperament produced such an enigma? Clore's roots, like so many others, stem from the huge influx of Russian Jews who were fleeing from the series of vicious and large-scale pogroms sweeping through Eastern Europe during the 1880s. Charles Clore's father, Israel

Claw, was the son of a butcher and was born in 1870 in Kovno, Lithuania. When he was sixteen or seventeen, Israel married Yetta Abrahams, who lived in Riga, in Latvia. One of the largest Russian cities, Riga had a sizeable Jewish population. The young couple married at a time of great political instability and volatility. The Jewish community was living under intense pressure, as the crumbling Tsarist regime in Russia desperately tried to channel revolutionary feeling into anti-Semitic expression. Hard-working Jewish merchants and artisans were branded as exploiters and the prime cause for Russia's economic ills. Officially-inspired rumours were spread accusing Jewish people of being anti-Tsar and the chief propagators of the revolutionary upheaval.

Oppressive and harsh anti-Semitic legislation gradually made the Jewish position more and more untenable. Jews were severely limited in the jobs they could take, the schools they could send their children to, and the towns they could live in. Israel and Yetta were among the 4,900,000 Jews (or 94 per cent of Russian Jewry) who were forced to live in the Pale of Settlement, a one million square kilometre area of land originally created to contain Jews, Poles, Ukrainians and any other ethnic group that threatened to compete with Russian merchants and artisans. A large proportion of the forty-three million people living in the Pale of Settlement were forced to work in a narrow range of occupations, so poverty was widespread. Despite this, the Jews in the Pale organized themselves and created 18,000 schools. From nine in the morning to nine at night, boys aged between four and thirteen attended *Cheder*. Twenty to thirty children would crowd into one room to repeat lessons aloud. Israel Claw was among the more fortunate to be able to attend *Yeshivah*, the academy for young men. *Yeshivah* students totally depended on the charity of local families and lodged with a different family every night while they attended the academy during the week.

While the average Jew was familiar with poverty, it was the new wave of pogroms which finally caused many families to think about flight from Russia. Anti-Jewish propaganda became increasingly inflammatory and a series of bloody attacks on Jewish towns occurred in Ukraine and the nearby provinces. The local police and Russian authorities both tolerated and tacitly encouraged these activities. By then, an intense sense of vulnerability had pervaded the entire Jewish community. Rumours abounded that the Tsarist Government was about to introduce yet harsher legislation. This was the final blow and many young couples, including Israel and Yetta Claw, determined that they would leave Russia regardless of the danger or difficulty. Until then, only a slow trickle of Jews had began to emigrate to the United States, but these people eagerly encouraged their families to follow suit.

3

Mary Antin, whose family left Russia in 1891, describes the hope which emigration offered. In her autobiography *From Plotzk to Boston*, she says:

> America was in everybody's mouth. Businessmen talked of it over their accounts; the women in the market made up their quarrels that they might discuss it from stall to stall; people, who had relatives in the famous land, went around reading their letters for the enlightenment of less fortunate folk ... children played at emigrating ... but scarcely anyone knew two facts about this magic land.

Israel and Yetta Claw were among the first great exodus of Jews to leave Russia and attempt to reach the United States of America. Although emigration without an exit permit was strictly forbidden, the Russian authorities did little to stem the flow. The Claws left Russia in 1888, leaving behind their home, their belongings and most of their family. Israel's brother and sister travelled with the young couple to England, while Yetta's family emigrated to the United States.

It is likely that the Claws believed that they were following Yetta's family. Charles' brother, the late David Clore, recalls: 'My father always used to tell me how he and my mother arrived penniless on the wharf at Liverpool. He only had 4d in his pocket. Like a lot of the emigrants he thought they were going to the US.'

Such an experience was not uncommon for the poorer emigrants, many of whom viewed their unexpected arrival in England as a temporary halt before going on to the United States. The temporary stay for many became permanent, however, as the emigrants received aid and shelter from various Jewish charitable organizations such as the Jewish Board of Guardians, now known as the Jewish Welfare Board.

Israel Claw soon found a job working for a cobbler and he and his wife lived with his sister for a year before they moved to the East End of London. They followed the example of many other Jewish families who had been attracted to the East End by the opportunities offered by the long-established clothing market – the rag trade. The immigrants, a large majority of whom were tailors and seamstresses, found a ripe market for cheaply produced clothes which, until then, had largely been supplied by German imports. Within a short time, with the aid of the precious sewing machine which he had brought with him from Russia, Israel established a thriving family business.

Chaim Bermant, Jewish historian and author, recalls these East End immigrants: 'Most of the Jewish people in the East End came from the Pale settlement. These families tended to be energetic, ambitious and great opportunists.' Familiar with hardship, oppression and exploitation, England seemed to be a dazzling land of opportunity. Unlike

4

Russia, England was a country where prosperity and security depended on hard work and shrewdness and not on race or religion. A spirit of hope and excitement filled the air, and was further encouraged by the obvious wealth and influence of the old Anglo-Jewish families. Every young family felt it had a reasonable chance of succeeding, an optimism clearly reflected in the 1895–6 archives of the Poor Jews Temporary Shelter. Of the 2,000 Jews passing through that year, 460 described themselves as merchants even though they were obviously paupers.

Nor did this optimism turn out to be an empty boast. A new entrepreneurial energy filled the East End of London and, in an extraordinarily short time, the area was injected with new life as Jewish families started their own businesses. The growth of these family businesses was so rapid that, according to Bermant,

> Londoners often resented the Russian immigrants because despite their early poverty and distress, they wholly transformed the face of the East End. There were kosher shops, Hebrew signs in shops, and entire businesses run by Jews. A Jewish community formed, closely similar to those in the Pale settlement, which was close knit and still religiously observant.

Harry Blacker, painter and author of *Just like it was – memoirs of the Mittel East*, vividly paints the scene:

> In those days, the Mittel East (as the Jews jokingly referred to the East End) was a conglomeration of narrow, cobbled streets, terraced houses, cat-smelling tenements and gas-lit cabinet-making workshops. In Virginia Road, a sawmill banshee howled through planks of wood. Across the way, Abrams the Goy . . . applied his oils and varnishes and when drunk on Saturday nights, beat his wife unmercifully. On the corner of Gibraltar Walk Jones' Dairy supplied milk direct from the cows they housed in an adjoining stable; it was ladled into the jug still warm. A minute's walk away, Mrs Rubin's grocery and delicatessen provided smoked salmon and schmaltz herring by the barrel-full. She recorded all non-cash purchases on the back of a blue-sugar bag with the stub of a carpenter's pencil.

Once in the lively environment of the East End, Israel Claw quickly succumbed to the entrepreneurial spirit. He anglicized his name to Clore, although there is no record of why he did so. He found another job working on leather uppers, but after a few months, despite his youth and inexperience, he started his own tailoring business. Israel first made garments at his home in Spitalfields, which Yetta would sell by standing on the pavement with the clothes in her arms. After a while he acquired a stall in Lambeth, then another in Bermondsey. It was a physically demanding job, with long, tiring hours away from home. When Charles was born Israel was absent on the Bermondsey stall.

5

Despite the long hours and poverty of those early days, the strong community feeling which pervaded the East End helped many families to adjust and thrive in their new country. Harry Blacker remembers that time with great affection. He says:

> The atmosphere in the East End was rich, warm and hospitable. When you visited someone, there was invariably a cauldron of soup over the fire. You were always offered a bowl, even though it often meant that someone in the family went without. No one felt poor because everyone lived in the same way. It was only after you left the East End that you realized how poor you had been.

In addition to the close community feeling, there was also an exuberant atmosphere, an air of expectation and a sense of pioneering. The poorer their circumstances, the further individuals seemed to go. They knew that if they were to achieve anything, they would have to do it themselves. They produced a generation, Clore's generation, which was talented, hard-working and ambitious. From these roots, some of the finest business empires were founded.

Most remarkable of the East End at that time was the dynamic upsurge from the first generation of Jewish émigrés. So many famous names, Bernofsky, Lord Grade, Lord Delfont and Clore, came from the East End. What they sought above all was economic independence. Such independence seemed a hopeless dream at that time, but many people in that generation refused to be defeated.

As their business and their family expanded, Israel and Yetta moved from Spitalfields to Whitechapel, then to Mile End, where Charles was born on Boxing Day in 1904. Before long, they moved again, this time to Bethnal Green, where David was born in 1907. Israel first bought a shop on Bethnal Green High Street, and the family moved into the apartment above. While Yetta sold boys' short trousers (known as knickers) from a stall in Brick Lane and Petticoat Lane, Israel continued to make clothes in his workshop and to serve customers in the shop. The late Leah Gelman, a distant relative of the Clore family and Charles' secretary at Park Street for many years, remembers the shop as small, the walls lined with piles of clothes and especially busy on Sundays. David Clore's only memory of that time is that 'Yiddish was spoken at home' and that, according to his sisters, Charles was an exceptionally quiet child who did not begin to speak until he was three years old.

Charles later told his wife Francine that he used to get up at 6 a.m., stoke the boiler and iron his shirts. He also used to have to make deliveries for his father. On one occasion, he was delivering a suit to Londonderry House. The butler threw him down the steps and sent him to the rear. In later life, Charles took immense pleasure in striding up those same steps as if he owned the place.

His idea of luxury as a boy, he told Francine, was a slice of pineapple from the market. In later years, he would always have a bowl of the finest fruit, wherever he was.

Once the shop in Bethnal Green was running well, Israel purchased a factory in Old Nichol Street. This was next door to a cane emporium in a broad street lined with respectable family businesses. In the factory (a large blackened Victorian building which still bears the name of Clore & Sons today) local Jewish employees cut and sewed men's suits and boys' clothes for sale in the shop. Just before holy days, Israel sold his boys' clothes at a cheaper price. On those occasions the shop became crammed as local Jewish families flocked to take advantage of Israel's benevolence. This charitable trust continued as Israel prospered and he began to send suits every Passover to the poor children who attended Hebrew classes in Bethnal Green.

By then Israel was an established figure in his neighbourhood; an intelligent, distinguished-looking man easily recognized by his goatee beard. Never forgetting his *Yeshivah* days, Israel started to meet regularly with other men for lively discussions about philosophy, religion and politics. He soon became well acquainted with Mark Cirkel, a forward-thinking, learned man. Cirkel quickly recognized that Israel Clore was one of numerous immigrants who were really intellectuals and scholars, but who were forced by economic necessity to become cabinet makers, tailors and cobblers. As the two men spent many long evenings together, Cirkel found the tailor to be a devout, intelligent, scholarly man, well educated in Judaism and politics.

Mrs Eva Pulvermacher, who was born in 1902 and who used to live in Old Nichol Street, recalls Yetta Clore. She was a well-built, reserved woman with a heavy Russian accent. She used to sell remnants as well as materials by the yard and would set up the stall for a few hours each morning in Brick Lane, before serving in the family shop on the High Street.

> Her stall would become very busy, because everyone knew she was there the same time every day. My mother always used to go to the stall because she knew she would get good quality cloth there. Yetta knew what my mother liked and always picked out some nice remnants for her.

In 1909, when Charles was almost five, Yetta died in childbirth. Charles took the bereavement badly. His sister, the late Rosie Cohen, who was nine at the time, recalls her brother's response to his mother's death. At the time, it was the fashion for women to wear Fair Isle shawls. Soon after the funeral, the little boy saw a woman with the same kind of shawl. He went up to her and pulled it off saying, 'That shawl belongs to my mother.'

Only a year later, Israel married Rebecca Crook, a distant relative of the family. Rebecca was a well-built spinster teacher, the daughter of a tailor who had died leaving her to provide for her mother. Rosie comments: 'My first step-mother was very kind. We all liked her.' David Clore describes her as 'a wonderful woman' whom he and Charles affectionately used to call 'auntie'. She was eleven years younger than Israel and moved into the Bethnal Green shop with her mother, whom Cirkel remembers as 'a shawled, silent presence, seated always by the fire'. Rebecca bore Israel two children, a baby girl who died at birth, and a boy, Bernard, who was born a year later. Bernard died of meningitis when he was five.

Soon after his mother's death, Charles started to attend Rochelle Street School, a pleasant middle-class school which was part of the new development scheme that London County Council had began in 1890. The old terrace slums around the school had been cleared away to be replaced with broad, tree-lined streets. At the centre of the estate was and still is a domed public garden and bandstand, with Rochelle Street School a hundred yards away. When Charles entered the school in 1909, it had been rebuilt as a tall, imposing, red-brick building with two stone signs indicating the boys' and girls' entrances.

Myer Blaiberg, who was a few classes above Charles, recalls: 'Rochelle Street School was a bit of a "khasi" school – old fashioned, but lovely. There was one woman teacher, who all the boys fancied.' Most of the English boys in the East End went to a Church of England school called St Phillips. There would be innumerable fights between the two schools, with screams of 'Yids' and 'Yocks' flying between the two camps.

While separated for most of the time during the day, with the girls housed in the upper part of the school building, the boys and girls used to meet at the bandstand after school. Mick Serlin, now a retired furniture manufacturer, recalls: 'We used to play every Wednesday evening around the bandstand with the other boys, and of course, it gave us the chance to talk to the girls.' The boys also used to play leap-frog with each other, although it ended in grief for Charles one day when he fell and knocked his teeth through his upper lip. He was taken to London hospital and soon patched up, but the scar remained with him all his life. So did his dislike for energetic games.

One of the key events during the week was the brass bands which used to play every Tuesday night at the bandstand. Many of the Jewish families living in the area used to attend, with the women clustered together, speaking in an assortment of Yiddish, Russian and English. All the local children used to bring sandwiches and drinks and listen to

8

the band. A toffee man would stand outside the boys' gate, causing long queues of children anxious to sample his special toffee with coconut, which he made himself.

At Rochelle Street School, 40 per cent of the children attending spoke Yiddish at home and were learning English as a second tongue. Despite this, many were exceptionally quick to progress. Lord Grade, for instance (then plain Lew Winogradsky), recalls starting school with no English, but by the time he was thirteen he had his own desk in the hall and was helping the headmaster, Mr Baldwin, to teach the other boys. It would have been surprising if boys like Charles Clore and Lew Winogradsky had not learnt rapidly. As one Jewish historian points out:

> The ethos of study has always pervaded the whole of the Jewish religion. Because the immigrants were often denied the right to attend Polish and Russian schools, there was an enormous hunger for education. When they arrived in Britain, they were determined that their children should make the most of their education. Every parent dreamt that their child would enter the professions.

Charles was in the class above Lord Delfont (then Bernard Winogradsky) and had already acquired a reputation in the school for his intelligence and interest in business. Because of his early concern with money, the other children nicknamed him 'Poppy', another name for money.

'Even as a boy, Charles had a reputation for scheming and for cleverness. He was different from the other boys and girls. He didn't tend to mix with other children but instead liked to spend time with the older Jewish business folk,' recalls Eva Pulvermacher. As she walked past the Clore factory in Old Nichol Street on her way to school, she used to see Charles standing at the door of the warehouse, looking out at the street. 'That was a favourite position of his. He would always be smartly dressed, looking as though his mind was on other things.'

After school every day Charles and David used to attend Hebrew classes. Harry Blacker describes the typical scene:

> Every afternoon following school we would be served a hasty tea and then run off reluctantly to *Cheder*. Here, in ill-lit overcrowded classrooms, short-tempered, yarmelke-covered rabbis would teach Hebrew, with a book in one hand and a cane in the other. Punishment was dealt out liberally. Woe betide the unfortunate who failed to grasp the meaning of a phrase, or did not readily recognize the shape of a letter. Tears and lamentations were threaded through the *Sh'ma Yisroel* like metallic thread through a Torah vestment. Despite this, we learned to read and write Hebrew.

Even as a child, Charles was lonely and reserved. It seems likely that he was affected by his mother's sudden death and the traumatic upheaval in his family life as his father married again so soon. Charles' loneliness was not lessened by belonging to a large family. He and David were substantially younger than Hyman (the oldest brother who was eleven years older than Charles), Fanny and Rose. Because of the age differences, Charles and David spent most of their time together and were very close. Even as a child, Charles was always very serious, always aloof and reluctant to join in the games of other boys. 'Chas was a loner but he never forgot his friends', says David. 'Even as a boy, his general knowledge was very high.'

Charles was also very close to his father with whom he developed a strong relationship, probably because he was very like Israel in many ways. Says David: 'Father had a temper. You had to do what he wanted you to do. Of the seven children my mother had by him, the one he doted on and had complete faith in was Chas. Whatever he wanted, Chas would get.' His father actively encouraged and supported him in all his ambitions and dreams about what he would do after he left school.

One of the ways in which Charles strongly resembled his father, even as a boy, was his vanity about his appearance. Cecil Elsom, of Elsom Pack & Robert Partnership, used to visit the Clore family with his father every Sunday afternoon. On those occasions Israel would be smartly dressed, wearing his characteristic trilby and waistcoat with a gold chain. When Israel married Rebecca, he told the registrar he was three years younger than he was, presumably to lessen the obvious age disparity between himself and his wife. David remembers that Charles would go to bed with his knickers (short trousers) under the pillow to make sure they had a good crease. Charles' childhood friend, Israel Clotz, also recalled this trait. On one occasion, as they were almost ready for bed, Charles amazed Israel by insisting he get out of bed. Then Charles solemnly lifted the mattress, carefully folded his shorts and put them under it so they would look smart the next morning. Even as a man, he never wore turn-ups because he said that they harboured dust and were unhygienic.

The Clore family's rise to prosperity was marked by their move to the middle-class suburb of Willesden in 1916. It was only then that the family saw a house with a bathroom. Before that the family either bathed in front of the fire or went to the council baths once a week armed with the stock equipment of a brown paper bag containing a towel, a face-cloth and a large bar of carbolic soap.

Charles was also close to his sister Fanny, who was eight years his senior and who worked as a cigarette maker. At eighteen, she married Abraham Davis, always known as Abe, a clothier, one of the first persons Charles went into business with. Charles used to spend a great deal of time at Fanny's house after she married. Eva Pulvermacher, who knew Fanny well, recalls playing cards one Christmas Eve with Fanny and Abraham. Charles used to need to escape from home quite often and on that Christmas Eve he arrived and watched the party play cards. The phone kept ringing, however, because Israel insisted on knowing where Charles was. Charles plainly did not want to go home and demanded quite strongly that Fanny refuse to tell them. Israel was by all accounts a strong-willed and domineering man. Charles' similar nature probably led to clashes of will as the teenager began to exert his own independence.

In 1919 Israel's young wife committed suicide by gassing herself, while 'temporarily of unsound mind'. Just what caused this traumatic event is unclear. Certainly the subject became taboo in the Clore family and none of the children had much idea of what had happened and why. There is little to suggest that the family was particularly unhappy or that Israel and his wife were at loggerheads. Nor was the family suffering from the depths of poverty like so many others around them. Israel contacted Fanny to ask her to take the two boys while he tried to sort out his affairs. For the next year Charles and David stayed with Fanny, who was by then living in Birmingham helping Abraham run a gentleman's outfitters shop. The following year Charles' five-year-old half-brother Bernard died of meningitis. In the same year Israel married Jenny Finklestein, with whom he emigrated to Palestine in 1929.

While Charles (now fifteen) was living with Fanny and attending a school in Birmingham, he went missing one evening. When Fanny and her husband went to tell the two brothers to go to bed, they found that Charles had been absent for some time. Becoming more and more alarmed, Abe left the house to see if he could find Charles anywhere. As he passed a local grocer's shop, which stayed open late into the evening, he briefly glanced into the window, only to see Charles busily helping to pack groceries into the shopping bags of customers. Entering the shop, Abraham discovered that Charles had asked the owner for a job there. Exasperated and relieved, he asked Charles why he was out so late. All the answer he received was: 'That grocery is what I call a business. He is taking money while your shop is shut. That is the difference between him and you.' Charles continued to work there in the evenings.

As a teenager, Charles did not outgrow his reserved nature. Harry Cash, a childhood friend, recalls that Charles was an introvert and had very few friends. 'He was quite a loner and didn't mix with his brothers and sisters. He was difficult to get to know.' Cash was his only close friend at that time. He often used to catch the number 8 bus from Neasden and visit Charles on a Saturday evening at his family's small, plain terraced house. Charles and Cash would sit in the drawing-room and talk, while the family sat around the dining-table, talking for most of the evening.

When Charles was fifteen or sixteen, he invited Cash to see around his father's factory. Although he himself did not visit the factory very frequently, he was nevertheless proud of it. Cash recalls: 'Israel was there among his staff, but he didn't take any notice of us.' The factory was an open-planned place with big Singer machines and about fifteen staff.

Although Charles did not go out very much, or play sport, he would go to the theatre or the ballet on his own occasionally. He would also go to the theatre or a dance with Clotz. The two youths were a strange combination: the one an extrovert, intellectual and gentle, the other essentially an introvert, practical and cynical. Although Charles enjoyed dancing and mixing with girls, he always asked Clotz to approach a girl to dance on his behalf, a curious shyness (some say haughtiness), which continued all his life.

After a dance, it was not unusual for him to turn up on the doorstep of his friend's house at three in the morning, demanding a place to sleep. Israel hated leaving his house unlocked into the early hours of the morning and was quite prepared to lock his son out, should he fail to appear at the agreed hour. Despite the unsociable hour, Charles would often greet one friend's sister with: 'Come on, make a pot of tea.' Used to him arriving in this fashion, she would tell him he was crazy but brew a pot of tea none the less.

As a young man, Charles became something of an enigma to his brothers and sisters. Clever, quiet, smartly dressed, with an insight into business that was already manifesting itself, he was quite obviously different. As David Clore describes it: 'Chas always had appearance and reputation. Even as a young man, he had white hair. He went white around the age of twenty-one. He used to go out riding in Rotten Row on Sunday mornings. It was a very unusual recreation for a middle-class Jewish boy.'

Charles began to show his flair and ability to recognize an opportunity when he was as young as twenty. At that time he went to stay in South Africa with his cousins the Sarembocks, who were pioneers in the fruit business and lived in Ceres near Cape Town. He quickly recognized the possibilities of the cinematographic industry, which at that time in South Africa was controlled by the Schlesinger family. It was there also that his interest in agriculture was awakened, although it was not until he purchased his Stype estate that he was able to put his innovative ideas to commercial use. Briefly returning to England, he managed to buy the South African rights to the film of the World Championship fight between Jack Dempsey and Gene Tunney and the film *The First*

Lieutenant. On his return to South Africa he toured around with the film, and on one occasion showed it to the Duke and Duchess of Athlone. He eventually resold the film at a profit.

For a short time Charles lived in Doornfontein. He mixed with a wide variety of people and so impressed Bernard Sachs, a well-known South African author, that he was included in Sachs' book, *South African Personalities and Places.*

His entrepreneurial activities did not go down well with his relatives, who were so incensed when he suggested selling off part of the farm for building that they telegraphed Israel to call him home. In the event, he left hurriedly when a property deal he was putting together went sour. A misunderstanding of South African law put him in the position of having agreed to buy before he had secured the wherewithal. He left the country via Mozambique and never returned, even though he became a director of a South African company in his sixties.

By the time Charles returned to England, his entrepreneurial instincts had moved out of first gear. Israel Clore was a particularly important influence upon Charles' business approach. He gave Charles some early selling experience by sending him to various West End companies with samples of men's suits. According to David, Charles was a good salesman for his father.

Charles gradually began to look at other areas of business. His interest in cinema, an interest his father seemed to share, had been whetted by his South African success. Together they purchased Walthamstow Cinema in partnership. They later acquired a cinema in Cricklewood and soon formed a company called Westminster Cinemas. In an extraordinarily short time Charles had established himself in business and seemed to have an uncanny knack for successfully turning his hand to anything. His sister Fanny commented at that time: 'Although Charlie goes from one thing to another, whatever he tries seems to turn out all right.'

Charles explored a variety of means of raising capital, although some ways were more short-lived than others. For a short time he had the idea of running a gambling party at the Cricklewood Roller Skating Rink and Dance Hall. He was on good terms with the management, who told him he could use the place discreetly. Because gambling was illegal then, Charles made arrangements in great secrecy. The gambling parties started around 11 p.m. and finished near dawn, with an average number of seventy men attending. He did not play himself, but charged table money instead. After five weeks, however, his foray into gambling came to an abrupt halt when the local police told him firmly that he had better stop.

One family story recounts that, in order to provide cash flow for the

13

various enterprises, certain members of the family would make use of the three or four days it would take for cheques to be cleared by the banks, paying money in and out among themselves without ever having any cash to support it. The account was in the name of 'Clarendon', the most English-sounding name that the family could think of.

At times Charles had no money in his pocket at all. He remembered with gratitude all his life the time when a friend lent him half a crown for a meal. Although the friend emigrated to Israel in the late 1920s, the two kept in contact for thirty odd years. He used to receive cheques from Charles in exchange for Israeli stamps, which he sent to England as soon as they were issued.

Charles also received a great deal of practical help from his family, both in the form of finance, encouragement and simple observation. His brother Hyman, for instance, played an essential part in Charles' acquisition of the Cricklewood Skating Rink and Dance Hall. While Hyman was travelling in a number 16 bus down the Edgware Road, he noticed a 'For Sale' notice outside the skating rink. Says Rosie Cohen's son Arnold: 'He took the proposition to Charles, which shows you how this young man was regarded by his brother who was ten years older.'

He was the stickler of the family. Even though he had no money and little experience, he was determined to own the rink where he had spent so much of his childhood roller skating. He knew that he could make a success of the venture; his only problem was how to impress this upon someone with some spare money. Charles approached Abe Davis, whose men's retail shop had become a lucrative business and who was the only member of the family who could raise money swiftly. Abe was persuaded, albeit reluctantly, to part with some money by selling his life insurance. Charles spent about two years building up the business and, although his family helped him run the rink, he was, in every sense, the owner and manager.

For a while it looked as though the venture would sink. The bank had approached the Clore family and demanded that the loan, most of which had been invested into the rink, be returned. Charles could not pay. He told the bank manager how he had spent the money and promised that he would repay the bank eventually. The manager finally agreed, although afraid he would lose his job.

Full of plans, ideas and ambitions, Charles' entrepreneurial enthusiasm was so great that he collected the entrance fees to the rink every day himself. Although Cricklewood was a humble beginning, it was the start of Charles Clore's accumulation of capital. It was indeed, the first Big Deal.

2

The Prince of Wales

'The key to Charles' success was the Prince of
Wales . . .' David Clore

The period after the First World War was a good one for Israel Clore. The
tailoring business was prospering and there was money to invest.
Israel's family was now off his hands, with most of the children in
steady jobs which, if unlikely to earn them a fortune, were at least
secure. The exception was Charles, who had acquired a strong taste for
business after his successful experience in South Africa. Restless and
ambitious, he filled in his time by working with his father.

To all appearances, Charles seemed set to follow in Israel's footsteps.
He had grown into a serious-looking young man, with premature grey
streaks in his hair. Rather small, he had a neat and trim figure which
showed to great advantage in the well-cut, smart suits that he always
wore. It was obvious to Charles' family that he had inherited both his
father's distinguished looks and practical intelligence; who better to run
the family business once Israel retired? Charles' strong streak of independence and hunger for success made him resist this safe option,
however. Unknown to his family, he had ambitions far beyond his
father's modest business. In the meantime, he encouraged Israel, a
cautious man, to invest his spare money in property. Charles, who was
also cautious in his way, had a much keener eye for a bargain than his
father. He rapidly developed a shrewd sense of what property could be
worth if it was made to work, and was prepared to take considered risks
if the potential gains were high.

It was only when Israel retired with his wife to Palestine in 1929 that
Charles was able to give free rein to his commercial instincts. Although
persuaded by his son to purchase several cinemas, Israel's scholarly
mind did not look to the world of entertainment as a source of property
potential. But Charles had already recognized that, if you could buy a
working asset for its development value or less, then the risks of the
business venture were already underwritten. He had also discovered
the opportunities in buying up bulk stock from bankrupt companies and
selling it on piecemeal.

A further encouragement to Charles was the flamboyant figure of Jack Phillips, the well-known entrepreneur, who dominated the property scene before the war. Through Phillips, Clore also met David and Joseph Levy, with whom he later began a long business association when they formed D. E. & J. Levy Estate Agents after the war. Joe Levy recalls vividly Clore's drive and ambition as a young man: 'Once Clore turned to me and said, "I'll be a bigger man than Jackie Phillips will ever be." It was an extravagant boast, but you couldn't argue with him. He aimed to be the biggest. He wasn't greedy, he just wanted to be the best.'

As the Depression took hold, the entertainment world seemed to offer Charles the best opportunity to prove that his words were not empty boasts. Although money was short, people's need to escape from the real and miserable world of poverty and unemployment was great. Everyday living became more mundane, yet the stage continued to recreate a world of elegance and aristocratic high living. The cinema, in particular, provided the opportunity to escape into make-believe worlds which were either extravagant and opulent or which provided a Chaplinesque happy ending.

To Charles, as to millions of other people, the cinema and theatre appealed to deep inner longings. Shy, aloof, a poor communicator at the best of times, the screen and stage beings represented many of the things he would have liked to have been. Not for him, however, the front stage or a performing career. Even in his later years he was nervous about appearing before an audience and would go to great lengths to keep in the background. An awkward, stumbling and often incoherent speaker, he was most comfortable operating on a person-to-person basis, or in a crowd. On one occasion in his sixties, at a dinner to mark the completion of a project he had funded in Israel, it took a request from the Israeli Prime Minister, Golda Meir, herself to bring him up to the top table. Wherever he could, Charles used other people to speak in public on his behalf, particularly his brother David, who was a natural speaker and raconteur.

To the people of Whitechapel and to many of those such as Charles who had left the area for less crowded suburbs, Charlie Chaplin was a symbol of how the entertainment industry could lead from rags to riches – their own local lad making good. Among those inspired by this example were the two brothers Winogradsky, for whom the theatre seemed the most promising escape route from the drudgery and boredom of clerical work. Poor and with little chance of improving their meagre lot as office-boys, it made sense to them to capitalize upon their acting and dancing talents. Starting at the height of the variety age as Charleston dancers, they appeared in innumerable dingy music halls in the East

16

End. Next came European bookings and a nomadic existence for a few years. Although dancing was a physically gruelling and badly paid job, the money at last started to pour in. It was a memorable day when Lew proudly displayed his new yellow car to his envious and less adventurous friends. By the time Clore started dealing with Lew and Bernard, they were theatre agents. Lew had formed a partnership with Joe Collins, a veteran with twenty years' experience in the theatre. For a short spell, Bernard worked for Collins & Grade before he, too, started his own agency business.

There is no doubt that when the Prince of Wales theatre came up for sale, Charles' interest was primarily in its property value. Placed in the heart of Piccadilly, the fundamental question in his mind was: 'Could the site be redeveloped and sold at a profit?' But there were other considerations too.

Firstly, he was particularly fond of the unique building, dating from just before the turn of the century: an elegant, tall Victorian theatre situated on Coventry Street. Relatively small, it had built up a reputation for friendliness and informality. The whole design of the interior facilitated socializing. The walkways around the auditorium were lined invitingly with settees and decorated with exotic ferns; the smoking-rooms and the stalls foyer were comfortable and informal with open fires, suites of furniture and refreshment kiosks.

The Prince of Wales theatre was a busy and colourful place and, to an unsophisticated young man like Clore with a taste for stylish comfort, it was alluring and welcoming. For him the theatre was a doorway into a gay, carefree world unlike that of the East End or Willesden. Clever but not intellectual, sociable but also shy, he felt at his ease there. Often dropping in with his friends and particularly frequenting the theatre bar, the informal nature of the theatre enabled Charles to get himself known, make useful business contacts and, not least of all, meet plenty of girls.

It was there for instance that Clore met Jill, a tall, attractive and self-confident redhead, who worked in the cloakrooms. Although she was his girlfriend for many years, there was never at any stage any serious thought of making the relationship permanent – much to the relief of the Clore family. When Clore met his future wife, he instantly lost all interest in Jill. 'She was furious at being cast aside so suddenly,' recalls Mena, a short, comfortable-looking Ukrainian woman who worked as Clore's cook for around seventeen years.

Secondly, there was a status attached to being a theatre owner that met his current social needs. To own a cinema or a few houses was simply to be another dull businessman; to own a West End theatre provided a reflected glamour he could relish. It also brought him into direct contact with the show girls and gave them a reason to take notice of him. As he grew farther and farther out of Israel's shadow, Charles allowed fuller reign to his sexual appetite. While he largely abandoned the chorus girls during the period of his marriage, he was irresistibly drawn back to them when the marriage broke up.

The sale of the Prince of Wales was not unexpected and he must have done considerable homework on the property before the auction date, although he claimed in later years only to have dropped in on the off chance. To someone as astute as Charles, it was obvious that the theatre was in trouble and had been so for the past two years at least.

During this period, the Prince of Wales had had a run of managers who had retired from the stage in order to direct their own plays. This form of management, however, was proving inadequate in the face of fierce competition from other forms of entertainment. Provincial repertory companies were enjoying a period of unprecedented popularity; radio was beginning to make an impact; the cinema was becoming a major form of popular entertainment; not only was the increasing success of the cinema taking away audiences, but it was also pulling up the fees of the stars.

Unaided, the actor/managers at the Prince of Wales did not have sufficient skill or business acumen to maintain the profitability of the theatre. Charles must have known that the Prince of Wales was barely surviving. In the two years before he became its manager, significant box office hits had eluded it. Its last outstanding success was in 1929 with R. C. Sherriff's *Journey's End*, which ran for seventy-two weeks and which was played in the same year by twenty-five different companies in sixteen languages. The exceedingly large box-office takings of this play enabled the Prince of Wales to keep going in the next year when it staged a quick succession of plays, none of which scored any notable success.

Most seriously, the Prince of Wales theatre seemed to have lost touch with the tastes and preferences of its audience. While never regarded as particularly sophisticated or avant-garde, it had none the less acquired the reputation for staging simple, straightforward entertainment. This type of play, however, became a rarity. André Charlot, the licensee for several years, frequently staged his own plays, to the obvious boredom of the audience and theatre critics. On several occasions he attempted to entice more people into the theatre by showing what were then considered to be more daring plays. All of these attempts failed disastrously. In 1930, for example, the theatre staged *Chéri*, a provocative French romantic drama adapted from a novel by the celebrated French authoress Colette. It was labelled as 'tawdry', a 'dust heap' and 'unpleasant' by the critics. Charlot tried and failed again with several more French romantic plays.

Overall, 1930 was a year of mediocrity for the Prince of Wales. It fared little better in the next year. Charlot's last play provoked one exasperated critic to say: 'If the theatre really has to fight the competition of the talking films, it must produce something more substantial than this play.' Finally beaten, Charlot put the lease of the theatre up for sale and, in September 1931, Edward Heath took over. His efforts were short-lived. He produced one play, then sold the lease of the theatre to Morris Benjamin two months later. After only five months, Charles bought the lease from Benjamin, who stayed on as theatre manager.

In the event, the purchase of the Prince of Wales was almost an accident. In spite of the theatre's poor commercial showing, Charles expected considerable competition for the site. There was none. He bought the lease for £700, an extraordinarily low sum for a large property in the centre of London but probably a fair price given the financial state of the theatre and the fact that the lease had only seven years to run. Such an opportunity could not have failed to appeal to a man who demonstrated all his life an extraordinary ability to recognize the potential value of a business or property and generate profit.

Having made his bid, Charles now had to find the money for the deposit, which he didn't have. In desperation, he turned to a friend who was a branch manager for the National Provincial Bank. The deal was that he would have to pay the money back before the end of the month when the accounts were checked. Charles kept his word and remembered how the bank manager had risked his career for him. Years later he provided the man with a sinecure at his issuing house, Investment Registry. Charles raised the money to repay the banker from Abe Davis.

The partnership did not last long, however. On the one hand, Abe, who was a nervous, cautious man at the best of times, was becoming increasingly concerned that he had been sweet-talked into a highly risky venture. He had little knowledge of finance and could never keep up with Charles' financial wizardry. At the same time, Charles felt that a partner who did not play a significant role in running the business was simply an encumbrance. After repeated nagging from Abe, Charles finally repaid him and dissolved the partnership. Days later, Abe learnt that Charles had managed to buy the freehold. He never forgave Charles for letting him withdraw just when the financial outlook for the theatre was on the upturn.

In any business venture, Clore was driven by a compulsion to feel in control. The disastrous partnership with Jack Cotton many years later was to bring this lesson sharply home. (Even Leonard Sainer, who handled every major deal after the Prince of Wales, was never treated as a partner. Their relationship was maintained on a professional basis, even after years of working together. 'It was Mr Sainer and Mr Clore till his divorce,' recalls Sainer. 'From then on it turned to Leonard and Charles.') Nor did Morris Benjamin last long. He took an instant dislike to Clore and was intimidated by him. They shared the same small office at the theatre. Benjamin was unnerved by Charles' silence and his habit of sitting for hours thinking and planning his business. He was thankful when Charles finally suggested he leave.

It was at that time that Leah Gelman came to work for Charles after her husband met with misfortune in his business. Small, brisk and very determined, Leah decided to approach Clore and ask him for a job. The interview did not start very encouragingly. Clore looked at her and grumbled: 'I don't like my family to know anything about my business.' When he heard that Leah had her own typewriter, he instantly brightened. Eventually the two reached the agreement that if Leah brought her typewriter along, Charles would employ her as his personal assistant. She worked for Clore until he died and was fiercely loyal to him. No uninvited person who tried to see Clore at Park Street would get past the formidable 'Miss Gelman'.

Charles believed it would be plain sailing once he had obtained the lease of the Prince of Wales. To realize the property value of the site, all he needed to do was to buy the freehold from Tonie Bruce, an ageing actress who lived in a flat above the theatre. His efforts were frustrated, however. He had not bargained on the fierce sense of loyalty which Bruce felt towards the theatre that her father had built, acted in and run for many years. Although Charles approached her on several occasions with an offer for the freehold, she refused to sell and it was several years before she finally accepted. Temporarily beaten and with mounting pressure to raise some sort of income from the theatre, Charles tried to rent it out. Such were his financial difficulties that during the months that he was looking for a tenant he was forced to remove the seats: without them he could prove that the site was not being used as a theatre, allowing him to pay lower rates. Herman Spector, who lived in Willesden near the Clore family, remembers that Charles offered a pound each to some of the young men in his neighbourhood to remove the seats in the theatre's auditorium. One of Spector's friends, now dead, always insisted that Charles never paid him the promised sum.

Charles failed to obtain a profitable rent for the building and in desperation decided to run the theatre himself. Confident in his own abilities and determined to make a fortune, he believed that he had as good a chance as anyone of succeeding in the entertainment industry. He had succeeded with his cinemas, his roller skating rink and his dance hall – why not with a West End theatre? There were plenty of people who, like himself, had had little prior experience or financial backing, but who had reached the top in the entertainment industry.

Thus he suddenly gained entrance into the hectic theatre world and found it more exciting than he expected. Always attracted by glamour and extravaganza, he was suddenly at the hub of the theatre world. His first production, a naval play, appeared in February 1932. The proceeds of the première were handed to the Lady Mayor of London towards her fund for the dependents of the men who lost their lives in the submarine *M2*. The choice of play strongly appealed to the audience. Suitably patriotic, it was a spirited and unpretentious tale of naval exploits leading to court martial, with intrigue, gallantry and peril interwoven. Besides being an excellent public relations exercise for the theatre, it was a financial success. Charles and Benjamin astutely announced that the play would run for six weeks only, ensuring that the actors played to packed audiences each night. This maximized the play's profit and minimized the production costs.

After Benjamin left, Charles had to decide what to stage next. Fortunately for him, Alfred Esdaile, who was 'one of the big impresarios of the time', approached Clore with the offer of building up the theatre by introducing non-stop revues. Clore agreed, recognizing that Esdaile had the vision and expertise which he lacked.

Esdaile was the general manager of the theatre until 1940, showing many of his own highly successful revues during that time. In the front rank of celebrated producer-directors during the 1930s and 1940s, he earned for himself the title 'the English Ziegfeld'. He was a pleasant and cultivated-looking man, with short, dark, smooth hair, a wide forehead and thin lips. He and Charles became good friends and lived together in a house in Clarges Street before Esdaile married. Although in after years Clore liked to say to friends: 'I was a better theatre manager than Esdaile ever was', it was his financial backing and business expertise and Esdaile's flair and experience which made the two such a formidable combination in the theatre world.

Rene Esdaile, Alfred's widow, comments about Clore and Esdaile's friendship:

The two men were totally different in character. Alfred was a showman through and through. He was a humanitarian with great zest for living who worked very hard. He was a friend to everyone and everything around him was gay. He had great admiration and respect for Charles. Charles was a very different character, moody and often morose. When he was with my husband though, he used to lighten up. They used to enjoy each other's company a great deal. But when he became rich, Charles discarded my husband.

Rene met her husband at the Prince of Wales when Leonard Sainer took her to see a play. When Esdaile caught sight of Rene, then a beautiful young woman, sitting in one of the theatre boxes, he immediately sent her a box of chocolates and asked her to go out with him one evening. In later years, Clore always used to claim that he virtually married the two.

A few months after Esdaile's arrival the first revue was staged. *The Jackpot*, which featured Marion Harris, a cabaret singer from the United States, included an Indiarubber tumbler, a tight-rope and trapeze artist, comediennes and dancers, burlesque and a potted newsreel. Marion Harris's daring bare shoulders were commented upon, as well as the show's modern tone of post-war malaise and world weariness. The show was simply pure, unpretentious entertainment, firmly announcing the new age of the 1930s. A miscellany of variety acts, it easily found a market and, while the critics sneered, the public kept asking for more.

For Charles, *The Jackpot* was something of a gamble. In a time of financial insecurity and fierce competition, he and Esdaile ran the risk of losing the theatre's already small following. Clore's budget was so limited that he had to persuade Marion Harris to appear free of charge so that he could pay the other members of the revue. Even taking on this professional singer was a gamble. While she was popular in her own country, she was virtually unknown outside the States and her appearance at the Prince of Wales was her first ever performance in Britain. On all counts, however, the risk paid off. *The Jackpot* played to packed audiences for months and Marion Harris' highly successful career in Britain had begun.

In June 1932, Charles and Esdaile introduced the idea of staging the West End's first continuous revue. *The non-stop revue* was played repeatedly from 2 p.m. to 12 p.m. Injecting a new degree of flexibility and informality into the theatre, this arrangement allowed customers to drop in and out whenever they wanted to. Wallace Parnell, who had a long association with the Prince of Wales throughout the 1940s and 1950s, was the producer of the revue. It featured tabloid plays, wonder midgets and an accordionist, with the intermittent appearance of 'the twelve beautiful Prince of Wales sweet young ladies'. Charles and 'Al' Parnell ran a competition inviting patrons to vote on which chorus girl was the most beautiful and graceful.

Charles had hit upon a winning formula and he knew it – and so did the theatre world. A national newspaper commented, albeit contemptuously:

> How splendid it must be for Alfred Esdaile and Charles Clore to know that, in a highly uncertain theatre world, they have hit upon an enter-

tainment recipe which can be relied upon never to fail. They have gained a steadfast and appreciative audience, and the producers have become expert in writing the pattern exactly to the audience's taste.

There were others who had noticed this success. Jack Buchanan, a theatre director and well-known singing and dancing star of the 1930s and 1940s, was indiscreet enough to discuss his plans to take over the Prince of Wales on the telephone. By a remarkable stroke of fortune, Clore overheard the conversation on a crossed line. He was incensed less by the takeover plan than by the blatantly anti-Semitic tone of the conversation. From that moment on Buchanan found himself frozen out of any dealings with the Prince of Wales and could never work out why.

As the box-office takings increased gradually, Charles was exhilarated to see his calculated risk paying off. Every evening he would appear promptly at the box office, to the dread of the three clerks there. He would ask frequently, 'What were your figures when you opened?' As one of the clerks fumbled with the books, Clore would tell her not to bother and would reel off the correct number. He would occasionally vary the question by inquiring about the preceding day's takings, but each time he displayed to his staff his remarkable ability to recall minute details.

He had an uncanny knack of cutting costs as well. Although most other theatres were forced to buy their cigarettes from a monopoly supplier, Clore discovered that the Green family, who were cousins of David Clore's wife, sold cigarettes at discount prices. David Clore would buy the supplies, despite fierce opposition from the monopoly holders.

From 1932 onwards the Prince of Wales theatre staged continuous revues only, with every show more glittering and spectacular than before. *The non-stop follies* in 1933 used French artistes and starred Yvonne Louis, the French film actress. 'Les girls' increased in number from twelve to forty and began to appear in ornate and spangled head-dresses and flimsy, sequined costumes. The revue *Paris* involved seventy artistes and ended in the grand finale, 'The stars of the night', in which the whole company paraded down a glass staircase. The revue was hailed as one of the most ambitious and spectacular continuous shows ever staged.

One year later Charles celebrated the first anniversary of non-stop revue by showing *Ça c'est Paris*. The whole show cost £20,000 to stage and was produced by Jacques Charles, the eminent producer from the Casino de Paris. In one year the Prince of Wales had been transformed from an unremarkable, slightly down-market theatre into 'London's equivalent of the Folies Bergère', a theatre considerably in vogue and the favourite meeting-place for the 'bright young things' of the 1930s.

The lavish use of chorus girls became one of the main reasons for the theatre's popularity. A description in a newspaper in 1933 reads: ' "Les girls" in almost every state of dress and undress carry out their garish manoeuvres. . . . Their sequins crackle and shimmer, they pant and pose and give the glad hip with unwearying good will.'

Charles enjoyed the company of glamorous women and was often seen out with his chorus girls. On one occasion he attended the wedding of his first cousin. The bride, Mrs R. Booklin, recalls: 'To the utter bewilderment of the orthodox assembled guests, Charles appeared with a bevy of uninvited chorus girls.' The guests at the wedding included Mrs Booklin's grandfather, 'who was not the least amused at the high-kicking display of the "gals". My grandfather remarked that Charles would never amount to anything in the future.'

As his theatre career took off, his family became gradually aware of changes within him. Gone was the young man who reluctantly helped his father run the family tailoring business. In his place was an energetic, affluent individual with an obvious taste for women and high living. Rosie Cohen's son, Arnold, remembers encounters with his uncle as a young boy. 'Even though he wasn't wealthy, Charles always appeared so to us. He was very particular about his appearance and took great pains to dress smartly. We children were terrified of him, even though he used to tip us generously with sixpence or a shilling.' Rosie remembers that Charles always came home late after the theatre each evening. His social life revolved almost entirely around the Prince of Wales and, if he was not to be found there, he would almost certainly be at the home of Fanny, his sister.

In 1934 the stage sets that were imported by the Prince of Wales became so complex and elaborate that they almost began to obstruct the running of the show itself. For instance, Clore and Esdaile were forced to postpone the showing of *Sourire de Paris* for one day because of the enormous quantity and elaborate nature of the French sets. The stage capacity of the Prince of Wales was taxed to its utmost because of the misguided enthusiasm of the director, Henri Varna. He was so anxious to create a spectacular opening night that he brought over his entire theatre sets, paying several thousand pounds to get them through customs. When the sets arrived, they had to be stacked in the passage outside the scene dock because they were so large. Some time passed before anyone could think of a way of getting them into the theatre.

For a man who religiously avoided the attentions of the press when he was a millionaire, Charles' career with the Prince of Wales was surprisingly controversial. In 1936, for instance, he became embroiled in an argument about who owned the front-of-house rights, the exclusive right to serve the public in the theatre's refreshment rooms, bars, cloakrooms and wine cellars. David Clore recounts: 'Chas was in dispute with Sir George Dance's company, which had the front-of-house rights. Chas turned the lights out, the water off. They sued. The result of the case – all law students have to read it now – was the end of house rights in theatres.'

Soon after the Prince of Wales had been built in 1896, the front-of-house rights were transferred to an independent party at a rental of £25 a week. Through a series of transactions, Theatrical Properties came to be the permanent assignees of the agreement. By the time Charles took over the theatre, the company was creaming off a substantial profit. Besides the use of the refreshment facilities, Theatrical Properties had the sole rights to sell theatre programmes, photographs, scent and flowers, and to hire out opera glasses.

The problem did not apply only to the Prince of Wales. Similar arrangements were found in many West End theatres and, although a great deal of dissent existed, most managers felt they could not change the situation. Clore and Esdaile, however, could not afford to let the situation remain unchanged. With production costs extremely high and the salaries of international stars escalating, losing such a large proportion of the total profit of a performance was a serious problem. A newspaper in 1937 estimated the cost of an average revue at the Prince of Wales: the production costs ran between £6,000 and £7,000, while the running expenses averaged £1,500 a week. If the Prince of Wales was to continue to stage spectacular events, Clore had to gain the front-of-house rights.

Besides the economic pressure of gaining the front-of-house rights, Charles also had his own score to settle with Theatrical Properties. He had come from an environment where any opportunity for self-improvement had to be fought for fiercely. If you wanted to get anywhere, you had to pull yourself up by your own boot-strings. In his view, Theatrical Properties was getting something for nothing; worse still, that 'something' was rightfully his. He felt personally cheated and unable to rest until he received all the profits from the theatre.

At that time Charles was using a number of solicitors – a practical approach in the days when they would raise cash – and at one firm he found a young lawyer, Leonard Sainer, who appeared to have the kind of innovative thinking he needed.

Sainer formed the view that it could be argued that the holding of the licence was a personal agreement between the original licensee and licenser. The day before, Evershed, the barrister representing Clore, had been barely able to speak, having almost lost his voice from a bad cold. 'We have a fair chance,' he told Clore and Sainer hoarsely. 'I'll be better in the morning.' It was not a promising start and Charles grumbled disconsolately to Sainer as they left: 'Hopeless. That fellow knows nothing about it.' In the courtroom, however, Clore's spirits rose as Evershed coughed and whispered his way through the day-and-a-half presentation. Clore's mood returned to despondency again as the other side made its case and elation as the court found in his favour.

Dance would not give up easily, however, and the case appeared before Lord Wright in the court of appeal in October 1937. The brief was over eighteen inches high. This time Dance's barrister presented first. Charles was plunged into deepest gloom, only to recover immediately as Evershed argued again that the front-of-house agreement, which the defendants claimed was a lease, was a licence. In that case, he insisted the rights of the licence were purely contractual and could not pass to any assignees even with notice. After much debate, and with some reluctance, based on the fact that Clore had been taking licence money from the defendants, the court agreed that the front-of-house rights were a purely personal covenant and therefore not binding to a third party. Years later, long after Clore had sold his interests in the Prince of Wales theatre, the precedent set by the judgement was overturned. But by then Clore had already made his first million. In David Clore's opinion: 'Without winning that case, there may never have been a Charles Clore.'

The result was to cement the business relationship between the entrepreneur and the young solicitor; a relationship which Sainer later described in the following terms: 'We discovered we made a good team. He had a lot of ideas and a lot of courage. I was the practical one; the technician who worked out the way to do the deals.' More and more of Clore's business was passed Sainer's way, until in 1938 Sainer set up his own partnership, Titmuss, Sainer & Webb.

When Clore approached Sainer to do some further work for him, Sainer was obliged to refuse, on the grounds that it would be poaching custom from his previous employer. Charles immediately approached the senior partner of that firm and obtained permission to instruct Sainer directly. Shortly afterwards, Clore found himself in an awkward position regarding the lease on a property he had not yet acquired, as a result of a failure of co-ordination between two solicitors dealing with different parts of the transaction. The experience convinced him that he should deal with one solicitor only. Sainer was subsequently to handle the legal side of every major venture Clore tackled.

Clore's experience in theatre management continued to be controversial. In the same year the Prince of Wales repeatedly clashed with the Musicians' Union over salaries and conditions of employment. While relations were often strained, out-and-out war sometimes erupted. On one occasion, for instance, sandwich-men from the Musicians' Union marched up and down Coventry Street demanding a boycott of the theatre. At the same time, a rival party brashly organized by a defiant Clore marched with similar sandwich-boards covered with the slogan 'Come in and see the happy band'. This incident took him onto the front page of British newspapers for the first time.

Towards the end of 1937 a new revue, *Les Folies de Paris et Londres*, appeared at the Prince of Wales. It had been in progress for twenty minutes only, when a man wearing a mackintosh in the stalls jumped onto the stage, which was full of bemused Folie girls, and shouted 'Why doesn't this theatre pay its musicians union rates?' The lead continued to sing while several attendants rushed on stage and hustled the man away. At the end of the show when the compère was asking the audience if they had any suggestions for the evening's performance, another man jumped up and said 'Pay your musicians union rates.' He, too, was ejected from the theatre.

Soon after this incident, Clore, who had obtained the names of the two musicians involved, was asked to comment by the press. Indicating that he did not intend to take legal action against the two men, he replied: 'Our relationships with the orchestra are perfectly harmonious.' This was probably because by that time he and Esdaile had been forced to employ non-unionized musicians after the Musicians' Union had ordered all its members to refuse to play at the theatre. The tension between the two sides intensified until at last Clore could no longer contain his irritation and frustration. Normally quiet and contained, he had a fierce temper when aroused. After a stormy meeting during which, according to Esdaile, the union side 'demanded domineering and impossible terms', Clore's temper finally snapped. He violently ejected the union secretary and was later fined £8 8s for his threatening behaviour. When he recounted this episode to his friends in later years he used to maintain, 'that was the best-spent money in my life'.

This was not the only brush with the law. Over another revue, *Sourire de Paris*, both Clore and Esdaile were again brought to court. This was because the two, as licenser and licensee, were held responsible for the inclusion in the show of a sketch which had been disallowed by the Lord Chamberlain. They were each fined £12 10s with £5 5s costs. They were also fined £4 4s each with costs for permitting an obscenity. The offending act? A comedian, whose script had been approved by the Lord Chamberlain, improvised by blowing a raspberry. In summing up, the magistrate said: 'The average Englishman is a clean-minded person. I should have thought that if there was one thing calculated to injure the house, it was this incredibly vulgar and disgusting stuff. I hope it will never happen again, or the penalties will be much more severe.'

The Prince of Wales came into the public eye again when it staged Sunday performances and ran foul of the stringent conditions of the Sunday licence. In one of the first Sunday performances the audience was treated to an impromptu comic display. Hats intended for a comic purpose had been banned on Sunday, hence the sight of a stage manager hurrying forward to snatch two actors' school caps. When the impersonator appeared in a top hat, the manager was seen to hover nervously as he tried to decide whether an ordinary hat breached the conditions. The same performance occurred when the actor took out an eye-glass. By the end of the performance, the manager, audience and actors were in a state of total confusion, to the obvious delight of the press.

In 1937 Clore decided that the takings of the Prince of Wales were too low, particularly considering the theatre's prime position in Piccadilly and its relative isolation from other theatres. With a much smaller seating capacity of 700, the Prince of Wales' takings were far lower than other theatres'. Clore's solution was to demolish the old theatre and rebuild one on exactly the same site with an auditorium capable of seating 1,200. After a farewell performance and an emotional round of songs by the actors and audiences led by Gracie Fields, the theatre was demolished. The total cost of dismantling the stage, demolishing the old theatre and building the new was £350,000. Gracie Fields returned to the Prince of Wales to lay the foundation stone of the new theatre in June.

The comfortable and informal old theatre had been transformed into a smart, modern building, and it took time for the old customers to become used to the change. According to Leah Gelman, the theatre did very badly in the first few months after it reopened. Clore owed a considerable amount of money to different tradesmen. 'I would say to him frequently: "You owe all this money, why not declare yourself bankrupt and start again?" But he never would, he was so honest and scrupulous.'

No wonder then that in 1938 Charles and Esdaile were anxious to cut production costs. Mrs Ann Sugar, a former actress called Ann Leigh, appeared in *La Revue du Bal Tabarin*, which Esdaile staged in the London Casino, a theatre which Charles had bought with some of the early profits from the Prince of Wales. Esdaile directed and produced the play and was probably receiving financial backing from Charles. Ann Leigh was offered a part in the revue. She refused unless the theatre paid for a car to take her to her home in Hendon. She explains: 'The play ended around 2 a.m. every night, which forced most of the girls in the show to take the workmen's trains home. I refused to do this, so the Casino made an appointment for me to go and see Clore and Esdaile at the Prince of Wales theatre.'

The morning appointment lasted about twenty minutes. Ann found the two men in a handsome office overlooking Coventry Street. She recalls:

> It was a very formal interview, so I went looking very smartly dressed wearing hat, gloves, handbag. I wanted to impress them. They asked me why wouldn't I give in and take the job without the additional pay? It was a prestigious show, brought from Paris. I made sure that I didn't appear too eager for the job. We argued about it and they didn't give in too easily. In the end, Mr Clore laughed and said I had good business sense and I got my rise. They swore me to secrecy in case the other girls asked for a rise too. I got my fully uniformed chauffeur. It was wonderful; he took me home all during the winter.

Ann also recalls rehearsing for the London Casino show with Esdaile in the Prince of Wales. She says:

> We looked down on the Prince of Wales, because we were only interested in appearing in the Casino. That was a more expensive and fashionable theatre. The Prince of Wales was very popular but less chichi. Compared to Esdaile, Clore was very much in the background. He was interested in the shows though, and would often come to watch us at rehearsals.

As war approached, the fate of London theatres became more and more uncertain. As soon as it was announced, West End theatres were ordered to close. A number, including the Prince of Wales, reopened quite soon and quickly adapted to the new restraints. The fear of air raids meant that theatres played matinées only, or gave performances that started at six o'clock. During the Battle of Britain, however, which began in August 1940, most theatres closed. While the Shaftesbury, Little and Queen's theatres were irreparably destroyed during the bombing, and the Duke of York, Old Vic and Sadler's Wells were damaged, the Prince of Wales and the Windmill continued to stage performances. The Prince of Wales staged two plays, *Present Arms* and *Revue des Alliés*. Performances continued throughout air raids. If the bombing became too disruptive, the audiences and theatre staff took shelter, with the actors often giving makeshift entertainment to everyone.

It was a determined gesture, but the Prince of Wales could not survive. As London took on the appearance and life-style of a city at war, actors, directors and musicians left the city and tried to join provincial companies. For the public, reaching a performance became increasingly difficult as public transport virtually ceased and taxi drivers became loath to risk driving to a theatre amidst a blackout. Finally, Clore closed the theatre and had the windows boarded up. As the doors on Coventry Street were locked for the last time, a dazzling and exuberant era of revue came to an end. With it, an era of Clore's life also drew to a close. Although he completely withdrew from theatre management, he continued to own the Prince of Wales until the mid 1960s, and retained a sentimental attachment to the theatre all his life.

From that time Clore channelled all his energy and skill into other business ventures. Although his concerns in the theatre ceased to be the life-blood of his operations, he was none the less always watchful for new opportunities. He built the Stoll Theatre with Sidney Kaye, the architect who worked with him on the London Hilton Hotel. In partnership with Jack Cotton and Lord Delfont he also made an abortive bid during the 1960s for Stoll Moss theatres, a huge corporation owned by Prince Littler. In both cases his interests were – as had originally been the case with the Prince of Wales – primarily in property values.

As he grew wealthier, Clore spent more of his time watching films than attending the theatre. He was fascinated with the big investments and the wheeling and dealing that went into film production. In the 1970s he became accustomed to attending the Cannes Film Festival every year with Jarvis Astaire, a long-standing friend and an entrepreneur with interests in property, bookmaking, films and boxing. Astaire would obligingly keep Clore amused by taking him with him to his film meetings at Cannes. There Clore would sit fascinated as new films were discussed. Characteristically, he could not resist butting in when he thought of a better way of doing a deal. At one meeting, Astaire's colleagues became deeply engrossed in their discussions and gave little thought to the small, silent man sitting to one side. They were startled when he interrupted suddenly. As they listened to the plan that he put forth – one that was far better than anything else they had yet thought of – their irritation turned to surprise and then to incredulity mixed with respect. When Clore finished, one of the film moguls turned to Astaire and asked: 'Where did you get him from?'

Sensing there was money to be made from films, Clore broke his usual rule of keeping business matters well away from his family. He decided to back a film that Leon Clore, his nephew, who had produced a number of successful films, was involved in. When it failed to generate the expected profit, Clore's foray into films came to an abrupt and somewhat bad-tempered end.

The failure rankled and some time later Clore astonished Astaire by a sudden frustrated outburst about his lack of success. At the time, Astaire was acting as Dustin Hoffman's agent for *Marathon Man*. On the flight to the Cannes Festival, Astaire handed Clore the book which the film was based upon. Clore sat engrossed throughout the flight, only pausing to occasionally dig Astaire in the ribs to tell him how good the story was. The two attended the première showing at Cannes. As they walked away from the cinema, Clore crossed the road and turned back to survey the crowded scene. The cinema was ablaze with lights and a long queue had already formed for the next showing; clearly the film was going to be a big box-office hit. Envious of Astaire and feeling totally excluded from the success and prestige of the event, Clore suddenly stamped his foot and exclaimed: 'It's not fair. You're going to make millions out of this. Nothing like that ever happens to me.' The bemused Astaire reminded Clore of his multimillionaire status, but he continued to curse his luck.

No matter how rich he became, Clore always wanted to be richer. Even as a young man running his own theatre, his mind was constantly preoccupied with strategies to make money. His insatiable desire for wealth drove him to look for larger and more spectacular deals, but as war approached, opportunities seemed to be rapidly contracting. How were his ambitions to be fulfilled in war-torn Britain?

CHAPTER

3

Wartime

'Opportunity is everywhere . . .' Charles Clore

Clore's involvement in the war effort was minimal. Because he was mildly diabetic and flat-footed he was never drafted. Even had he wanted to be, the forces would not have taken him. On the whole, the war was a nuisance to him, in that it disrupted plans and reduced creature comforts; but it was also an unprecedented opportunity. While most people were away fighting, for those who remained it was open season on the property and general commercial markets. Not that Clore's activities were against the national interest. On the contrary, his construction efforts on behalf of the Minister of Works won him commendation.

Yet Clore's financial position at the beginning of the war was by no means secure. He and Esdaile had for some time been playing on the American Stock Market on margin, a dangerous gamble as share prices began to sink. They would listen to Wall Street prices on the wireless after the performance had ended each night, but with the advent of war they saw their investments crash in value. Both lost considerable amounts of money and were near bankruptcy. Clore decided to retain the Prince of Wales, even though he could no longer rely on the theatre generating any significant income. He knew his small interests in property might pay off eventually, but in the meantime he had to look for other ventures. He was not dismayed by this; he was willing to look for opportunities in every industry and he knew that with his abilities he, more than anyone, was likely to survive the vicissitudes of the war. 'Opportunity is everywhere,' he was to say to the press after he emerged rich from the war.

It was his investment in 1939 in the Lydenburg Estate, a gold mining company in the Orange Free State, which changed everything for Clore. The deal not only made him a great deal of money but was also an indirect means of introducing him to Francine Halphen, a young Jewish refugee who would soon become his wife. Making the running in the Lydenburg affair was Teddy Marks, who lived at Bray. Marks was a director of Dorland City, the advertising agents who were later to handle all the share prospectuses for the Clore companies. Max Rose, who was a 'jolly and very human South African Jewish stockbroker', also advised Clore to buy some shares in the company. By 1941 the 5s shares had plummeted to 1s. In the Orange Free State gold boom, which followed the war, they rocketed to over £7.

Clore was the first to admit that the fortune he gained from that investment was pure luck. In an interview on his sixtieth birthday, the *Financial Times* asked him why most property tycoons lacked paper qualifications. 'Well, if you spend years learning the conventional ways, you keep to them. If you learn by experience, as I did, you think of new ways. And then there's luck.' Clore picked up a box with gold ornamentation. 'That was luck – gold from a mine. I didn't know anything about mining. I was just lucky.'

Clore became acquainted with Marks when he moved to Ray Court in Maidenhead shortly after war broke out. Built in the heyday of the Edwardian period, it was a rambling, ugly building close to the Thames. Near by was Skindles, the hotel famous for its assignations; Cliveden, originally the residence of Frederick, Prince of Wales, now the home of the hospitable and dynamic Astors; and a variety of homes built by rich Victorians for their mistresses.

The town's close links with the theatre had attracted numerous actors, singers and chorus girls. Clore found himself in good company as he rode home on the greasepaint special, the late night train from London, which took home squads of exhausted dancing girls. Besides 'the gals', the town was also filled with politicians, titled people, artists and military officers. Despite the war, the town retained its exuberant character and continued to have the occasional Venetian fête river regatta or pageant.

In residence at Ray Court was a group of people almost as colourful and theatrical as Maidenhead itself. Besides David Clore and his family and his sisters Mrs Cohen and Mrs Davis, the house was full of extraordinary characters whose only connection was their link with Clore over many years. As a member of the Clore family says: 'The atmosphere was very mercurial at Ray Court.'

Clotz (everyone was called by their surname), Clore's oldest friend, helped out in various ways by assisting Esdaile to run his provincial theatre shows. He knew the whole of Shakespeare off by heart and was fond of interlacing his conversation with quotations. He was also responsible for ensuring that on the eve of the Sabbath every week coffee and *Chola*, a specially baked loaf of bread, were ready for the assembled multitudes. As many as forty to forty-five people used to come. Ray Court would be alive with noise and life, crammed to the full with small children and groups of adults sitting around playing cards.

Also at Ray Court was Jack Zimmermann, an eccentric individual who claimed to be a film producer with important overseas connections. 'There was always going to be a huge transatlantic deal but he rarely did any sort of deal. He was mainly there to amuse Clore,' says a member of the Clore family. Zimmermann's only two ventures – both musicals – failed dismally. His wild claims led to one of Clore's rare flashes of humour. He phoned Zimmermann from another room at Ray Court and tricked him into thinking that MGM was calling from the United States.

Max Rose, an avid bridge player, was part of the entourage. Wherever Clore was, Rose was too. He always professed to know nothing of Clore's business, a reticence which Clore liked. Also there was Jill, who Mena recalls as being an unpopular figure with both servants and the family. Ruling the household with a rod of iron was Miss Gelman – no one would ever dare to call her Leah.

In the kitchen was Mena, then a parlourmaid, a Hungarian cook and two Romanian maids. An old gardener looked after the estate, while the kitchen staff kept a cow, geese, chickens and ducks. Mena supplied the whole household with cream and butter by making it herself. When she once threatened to leave, Clore decided he could not bear to miss these luxuries and promptly gave her a pay rise.

Clore once accused Mena of being obsessed with pay and, for several years, they had a running feud over the subject. One Christmas at Ray Court he walked into the kitchen and, with a characteristic grunt, gave her a pile of coins and pound notes. It was a Christmas box of £5 which he had just collected from the rest of the family and a few friends, including Sainer and Esdaile. Thinking he had done his duty, Clore returned to the dinner table to finish his meal. Suddenly an offended Mena burst into the room and slammed the money onto the table. All she would say in her broken English was, 'I leave tomorrow.' To her the small collection from such a large gathering seemed to add insult to injury. At that time she was earning 25s a month, a pittance compared to the normal rate. Clore finally raised her wage to 30s.

When Esdaile married, his wife Rene lived for a short time at Ray Court.

> My memories of Dunkirk, VE-Day or D-Day were totally outweighed by Charles Clore's frequent outbursts of temper and tantrums. He was a difficult individual to live with. He was a man of many moods, precise and meticulous in everything that he did. Everything had to be in order. Eventually, I told Alfred that he was married to me and not to Charles. We moved out and bought a small cottage.

Rene was not the only one to find Clore's moods difficult. To his staff he could appear harsh and moody. On one occasion, for instance, he entered the kitchen to find the farmer of the estate unknotting bits of string. Even though the war had caused a great shortage of string and the man was merely trying to conserve his supply, Clore shouted at him: 'Get out of here and do some work.' Another time, Clore shouted something abusive to his butler, causing the man to put down his tray and walk out. He went instantly to the cellar and consumed some of Clore's best wine before he filled the sugar bowl with salt and then left, never to be seen again.

Another time, after a word with Mrs Davis, Clore issued orders to Mena that she should dress formally and serve the children's meals. Already cooking several times a day for the gardeners, domestic staff and the family, this new arrangement appeared to her unnecessary and time-consuming. When she complained, Clore lost his temper and called her a lazy foreigner. Equally short-tempered, Mena promptly dropped Clore's meal into his lap, saying: 'I am a foreigner yes, but lazy, no.' She immediately started to pack her case and it took Leah Gelman, David Clore and his wife to calm the two down and achieve a truce.

With so many guests visiting Ray Court regularly, food was always in short supply. Clore took his staff's ration books and locked all the food supplies into the pantry. He also attempted to conserve food by cutting his staffs' supply. When he discovered that they all had a piece of toast and kipper for breakfast, he outraged the cook by telling her to give each person a piece of bread and a single sardine. The new menu did not last long. Clore finally crumbled under the barrage of complaints and the kippers appeared on the table once more.

Not even Mena, by then assistant cook, was allowed admittance to the pantry. After repeatedly requesting that Clore unlock the pantry, she was forced to serve strawberries without sugar during a dinner party and told him the reason loudly in front of the guests as she served.

Although they argued frequently, Mena still retains considerable affection for him and is fond of recalling how he approached her after a family wedding many years later. Exhausted after spending the previous night cooking for the wedding, she met Clore just as he had arrived in his Rolls-Royce. 'Everyone was pointing and saying "that's Charles Clore". He stopped, took off his hat and asked me how I was. Then he turned to Miss Gelman and said: "I always take my hat off to Mena."'

Even in those days Clore was secretive about his activities. He was expending most of his energy looking for cheap property or bankrupt companies which were selling off assets cheaply. He had already bought a few old country estates for their timber. One of his first wartime deals came through a former contact from the Prince of Wales. Clore had employed a clumsy but enthusiastic chorus girl. He gradually became acquainted with her father, a captain from the War Office. When the War Office began to look for property to store its arms and ammunition, the captain remembered that Clore had been acquiring small properties around Thatcham. It was to be the first of many profitable deals between Clore and the War Office.

He was also looking at bankrupt companies and quoted companies with depressed share prices. At the beginning of the war he bought a number of textile concerns. He gave textile manufacturer B. & J. Whitman a new lease of life by gaining a contract from the government to supply raw material for uniforms. He appointed his brother David as director of the wool merchant, Robert Whittaker. 'David ran the mill and the showrooms, but was often absent at the racetrack. Charles wasn't very interested. It was wound up eventually. But our family used to get some good suits from the company,' says a friend of the Clore family. He also bought the women's clothes manufacturer, designer and retailer Marjorie Chapman Ltd.

Other acquisitions included a controlling interest in Gillette Stevens, an engineering company which made weaponry for the armed forces during the war. John Christian Wegerif, a man greatly liked by Clore, ran the company. But for Clore, ever hungry for success, property appeared to be the key. In pre-war Britain, property had not offered him much opportunity. Property development was hindered by high unemployment and the recession which still held British trade in its grip. In that climate, industrialists and retailers were not willing to acquire or improve office premises. Clore had been involved with a small number of deals, some of which had nearly turned out to be losses. The Prince of Wales deal, for example, had nearly turned sour and almost ruined him financially. Even in the small number of cases when Clore had succeeded in developing and leasing property, pre-war rent restrictions and long leases had offered him little prospect of making any significant profit.

Despite governmental restrictions, which placed all land under interim development control after the start of the war, Clore judged that property development was about to become the key growth industry. Whether his decision to invest in property was due to his own foresight or to the advice of some of his business associates will never be known. In 1966 in a letter from Leah Gelman to Oliver Marriott, editor of business news at the *Sunday Times* and author of *The Property Boom*, Clore was reported as saying that his judgement was based upon 'the simple rules of history, when any form of restriction is followed by rapid expansion'.

There was, of course, the enticing memory of Jackie Phillips and his fleet of cars, lavish style of entertainment and mansion in Surrey, which made property particularly attractive to him. He had not forgotten his earlier intense envy of Phillips. But Phillips' sudden bankruptcy and death were also a stark reminder to Clore of the considerable risks attached to property, when high wins could be transformed suddenly into devastating losses.

He was ready to take the risk. He knew that if Germany won the war, his ambitions and plans would be brutally swept aside. But if Britain won, he would be sitting on plum property sites with what promised at that time to be almost limitless scope for redevelopment. He had nothing to lose and everything to gain.

He was not without expert advice. He had formed a strong friendship with David Levy who, with his brother Joe, was advising Clore and other clients to purchase as many bombed and blitzed sites in the heart of London as possible. Clore focused his efforts on buying stock and assets from bankrupt companies and investing in well-located bombed sites in the capital. After the war he was joined in acquiring and developing these sites by Felix Fenston and Stanislas Radziwill, a Polish prince who had fled his native country in 1940. Unable to return to Poland, he became a naturalized British subject and, in doing so, was obliged to drop his title. He was a renowned socialite, brother-in-law to Jackie Kennedy (now Onassis). A scholarly man and a strong supporter of Polish émigré causes, his social connections were a valuable asset when he began to deal in property.

Looking back at that time, Clore used to say to David Levy: 'We really had the world at our feet. We missed the opportunity of a lifetime.'

Clore also turned his eye to the provinces. With their expanding populations and growing high-street trade, they offered some rich pickings in property. He chose Tom Vincent, the owner of an estate agency and auctioneers in Reading, as the person most likely to have a sound knowledge of urban and country estates. Vincent was forthright, reliable and astute – qualities which Clore highly prized – but, more importantly, he had a sense of humour which enabled him to deal with Clore. 'Never talk to Clore before ten o'clock' became a favourite saying of Vincent after several unpleasant early morning encounters with him. Not only was he moody, but he was a demanding client, who expected Vincent to devote all his efforts into looking for suitable deals for him. Besides ringing Vincent at all hours, he would frequently disrupt his business by descending suddenly upon the estate agency in Reading loudly demanding attention. It was only an officious six-foot-tall female secretary who could inspire enough discomfort and embarrassment in Charles to make him sit down and wait more patiently.

Tom Vincent's son, Duncan, recalls Clore's style of business: 'He was a very difficult character to work for. He was cautious with his money and could never accept that you have to auction items at valuation. Clore would even count out the bean poles and price them separately.'

While a few far-sighted opportunists like Clore were quietly picking up property, a number of insurance companies were also starting to consider investing on a small scale. While the Wall Street crash of 1929 had put a sharp halt on investment for a few years, insurance companies were gradually beginning to look at property with renewed interest. They were beginning to accept that inflation had come to stay, making property an attractive long-term investment. With backing from an insurance company, Clore could raise the capital for the purchase of a site and sell it when the market was on an upturn.

It was backing from the Royal Bank of Scotland that enabled Clore to obtain two Scottish estates at Drumnadrochit and Bellmacragin in 1944. On Clore's instructions, Vincent had been combing Britain looking for undervalued estates. During one visit to Scotland he had hired a taxi for the day to visit several. By the time he arrived back at Glasgow station the taxi fare was between £70 and £80. Although Clore growled, 'What did you do, go and visit Hitler?', he none the less recognized the value of the two estates. He bought Drumnadrochit, which included Loch Ness, for £500,000. Although it was popularly reported that Clore, the unknown East Ender, had bought the estate for the philanthropic reason of making the rich man's sport of grouse shooting and salmon fishing available to poor people, he broke up the estate soon afterwards and sold it piecemeal at a significant profit.

It was also through Vincent that Charles began collecting antique furniture. He had long recognized the investment value of antiques. He had started obtaining *objets d'art* early in his career and had a small collection by the time he purchased the Prince of Wales. Fine glassware he bought from a shop in Soho owned by the father of Sylvia Sosnow, a long-standing friend of the family. Francine, his ex-wife, recalls that at the time of their marriage in 1943, he had acquired a creditable collection and knowledge of silver and Fabergé. Two Fabergé Easter eggs she bought him for £1,800 in 1944 recently fetched £200,000.

Although many of the purchases were made for their mixture of beauty and asset value, there was often an additional, more complex motivation. Charles envied those fortunate people, such as the Rothschilds, who had inherited ancient wealth. He would visit their homes and be greatly impressed by the visible evidence of privilege and inheritance. He wanted desperately to own what they owned, as if it would give him something of the same background, personality and social ease. So whenever one of the great families sold its treasures, Charles would rush to buy.

To this day Mena treasures an old steel fork and knife which were used at Ray Court before they were discarded for more elegant sets.

They are a poignant reminder to her of Clore's meteoric rise to wealth.

Such opportunities arose during a time when the war had been going particularly badly. An air of pessimism pervaded the country and many wealthy families had begun to convert their family treasures into hard cash. While most people were only thinking of self-preservation, Clore was looking for every chance to obtain items at prices considerably below their true value.

He would visit Sotheby's and Christie's occasionally. One day David Clore received a phone-call from his brother saying that he had just bought the Rothschild's collection of gold plate. David asked: 'What on earth have you done that for?' Charles replied: 'Well, if we lose the war, it won't matter. If we win, this collection will be priceless.' Clore told his brother to go to the warehouse and collect the plate. Although David thought the haste somewhat unnecessary, he none the less did as he was instructed. Only hours later the warehouse was bombed and the goods within totally destroyed.

Clore's interest in property had alerted him to the potential in the retail sector. He could see that the trend was away from the small corner shop to the high street store. His foresight was remarkable. In the years leading up to the war, many retail stores were sliding slowly into bankruptcy. Business deteriorated as people began to prepare to tighten their belts; any spare money was spent on basic commodities, many of which were already becoming scarce. For those shops which had emerged unscathed from the Depression, it was simply a case of hanging on grimly and surviving until the end of the war. Many of them simply didn't make it.

Clore saw his opportunity. Property prices had plunged; profit levels had sunk to an all-time low. A number of retail stores with valuable property assets were near bankrupt and hoped to improve their position by selling some of their sites. All Clore had to do was to look around and find the plumpest spoil. It did not take him long to find the right one.

Richard Shops was the perfect acquisition. It had a solid base of custom and assets, but had simply been badly managed. The company's American founder, J. S. Sofio, principal of a private bank with offices in London, New York and Turin, believed there were great opportunities in the staid British retail industry for a chain of fashion shops which aimed exclusively at the fashionable young woman's market. He formed the company in 1935 and bought over several American directors to develop the chain of fashion shops.

Although his business judgement was acute, Sofio's decision to appoint an American director to buy the merchandise proved to be his undoing. The director insisted that his buyers, Peggy Hope and Nora Gordon, two of the best in the trade, import American merchandise. As well as being too pricey for the less affluent British women, the styles often appeared gaudy and extravagant. Nora Gordon frequently declared to her colleagues that she never expected anything to sell in the stores.

Clore could see that, despite the merchandise problems, the market orientation of Richard Shops was on target. But better still was the large number of properties, around thirty, which had been acquired in the four years since it had started trading. These were in prime situations, often consisting of large, modern premises in the centre of towns with a rapidly expanding suburban population.

It was David Clore who first pointed out to his brother in 1942 that the company was in poor shape and about to go into the hands of the receiver. A number of suppliers were refusing to deliver merchandise to Richard Shops because of its dubious financial position. Sofio had left for the United States at the beginning of the war, most probably because his bank had run into difficulties. Richard Shops had proved to be too costly a venture for him; after losing £20,000 of his £100,000 investment, he had decided to withdraw his financial backing from the company. The other American directors had also disappeared home as it became increasingly obvious that Britain was about to enter the war. Sofio's wife, a lively and able woman but with relatively little experience in retailing, had been running the business for the last three years with the help of Rudolf Weyl, a young German refugee.

If Clore didn't snatch the opportunity quickly, someone else would, particularly once it became known outside the clothing industry that the stores were up for sale. Another Jewish entrepreneur, Isaac Wolfson, had already shown the way by snapping up the Drages chain. Even at that stage, a large group of manufacturing suppliers had gathered together to discuss how they could get the finances to buy the stores. Clore reacted faster though, by approaching the official receiver directly. He reached an agreement of £8,000 for the company. 'We were aghast when we heard about the absurdly low price,' recalls Weyl.

All Clore had to do was to find the money to pay the receiver and additional capital to inject into the business to get it running again. He correctly judged that with a relatively small investment and the right merchandise, the shops would quickly generate a profit. Partly through Francine's connections, he arranged to borrow the money from a French bank in the City. According to Weyl: 'The company was such an obviously good bargain that I doubt he had much difficulty in obtaining a loan.'

What gave Clore such confidence that he could make money where others all around him were failing? The answer lay, as so often proved the case in later deals, in his careful preparation. Richard Shops had some thirty leasehold stores. He and Sainer visited all the freeholders and attempted to persuade them to reduce the rental. Given the low probability of finding a new tenant, two-thirds of the freeholders agreed. These leases Clore acquired. The rest remained with the receiver. The lower rental costs immediately cut the company's overheads. With judicious management, it did not take long to turn it back to profit.

He made it clear to the management at Richard Shops that, if the merchandise was good enough and the price competitive, they should buy from his own textile factories. At the same time, he put pressure on the clothing designers in the factories to produce what Richard Shops wanted. This kind of dual pressure was highly unusual at the time, although it is now relatively common.

Once Clore was satisfied with the management of the company, he was reasonably content to allow the directors to decide how to best expand and improve the stores. He knew exactly how to draw in the customer and had strong notions about the image of his shops. Whenever he visited any of the stores, he commented immediately on the attractiveness of the layout and window display.

Weyl explains:

> Clore knew more about the promotion of retail than retail itself. His most clever contribution was his emphasis on advertising. He felt that if Richard Shops was to take off, its advertising had to rival that of the larger stores. Even though the business had little spare money, Clore insisted we use some of it for the services of a small advertising agency in London. In those days it was rare for a company of our size to advertise because the media network simply didn't exist. It immediately gave us a certain distinctiveness.

According to Weyl, who became a director of the company, Richard Shops never looked back after Clore's arrival: 'Clore brought a lot of new life to the business and was a pleasant man to work for. The stores shot right ahead with the additional injection of money. We made profits every year after he came.'

Clore's plans were beginning to crystallize. With so many companies ready to be sold, now was the perfect time to acquire a number of closely related businesses. Through Richard Shops he could build a vertically integrated organization, from manufacturer to retailer, with his textile companies.

In the same year that he had bought Richard Shops, Clore met Francine. On Christmas Eve 1942, he was invited over to Marks' home at Bray for pre-lunch drinks. Already there was Francine Halphen, a stunning young French-Jewish refugee. She exerted an immediate and compelling fascination upon him. She was all the things he aspired to but could not be: born and raised into ancient wealth and privilege, highly educated, vivacious and outgoing, a war heroine. She also shared several characteristics with him, being self-willed, impatient and never afraid to speak her mind.

Born in 1920, Francine counted among her relatives various members of the Sassoons and the Rothschilds, although her father, Henry Jules Halphen, was not spectacularly wealthy. He had emerged from the trenches after the First World War declaring he would never eat a cold meal nor do a day's work again – and kept his promise. Francine, her mother, her brother and her sister lived in a grand house on Avenue Foch in the centre of fashionable Paris. There were, she recalls, sixteen servants. Life in Paris was ordered, comfortable and happy. She saw little of her father. Although the Jewish religion did not figure strongly in their lives (her mother took them to synagogue once a year), Francine developed a strong feeling of Jewishness and an attraction to the ideal of a Jewish nation. Visits to London and an English nanny combined to give her a good grasp of English as a child. The nanny, Gertrude Beale, came from Whitechapel, not far from Israel Clore's tailoring workshop, which gave rise to one of those tales which is based on such remarkable concidence that it must have a grain of truth. At four years old Francine declared she would marry a man from Whitechapel, where Nanny Beale and Charlie Chaplin had both come from.

A determined individualist, Francine went to Sciences Po. (a rare event among French girls at that time) to study political science and economy, gaining her degree in July 1939. Even at university each day she was taken to and collected from classes by a governess. Passionately interested in the Jewish cause, she based her thesis on Hitler's *Mein Kampf*.

Then three months later came the war. Francine, just twenty years old, volunteered as a Red Cross ambulance driver. Along with twenty other rich Jewish girls she bought her own ambulance and even her own uniform, and was assigned a territory in the Ardennes.

The change in lifestyle was a rude awakening in more ways than one for the sheltered girl who had never before had to get up at six o'clock in the morning. As France fell, she found herself on a marathon drive transporting wounded soldiers to Arcachon (where the British consul arranged passage to England for an English girl companion but refused to help Francine), and finally to Pau in the foothills of the Pyrenees. Several times *en route* they were strafed by Stukas.

In the south of France Francine was taken care of by her old nanny, who had moved there some years before. But she soon became frustrated by inaction, donned her uniform again and began to deliver Red Cross food parcels to the troops in the prisoner-of-war camps. Passing messages between the Resistance and the prisoners became a natural part of this work, although Francine was never in active service with the underground. However, she relates that in her youthful exuberance she did cover the walls of Paris with victory signs the day the Russians entered the war.

Crossing in and out of the free zone and once even into Germany, no one questioned whether Francine might be Jewish. Then pressure was brought to bear on the French Red Cross. The Jewish volunteers, Francine among them, suddenly found themselves thrown out without any papers. A number of Christian women resigned from the organization in protest. Now penniless and without the all-important identity cards, Francine was smuggled to Vichy and from there over the Spanish border. The flight south was an ordeal, eased only by the many people who provided her with a place to sleep, where no questions would be asked, no papers demanded. Food, when available, was provided by the Salvation Army.

Even when she reached Portugal, Francine could not relax. Though staying with relatives, she still had no papers and ran the risk of being interned as an alien every time she made the trip to the British consul to secure an entry permit to Britain. Once again her family connections came to the rescue. The vastly wealthy Nubar Gulbenkian loaned her his Rolls-Royce for the six days of her stay. Naturally, no one stopped the driver of that vehicle to ask for papers.

On arrival in Britain, in a plane with all the windows blacked out, Francine had to spend several weeks proving she was the person she claimed to be. Although taken in by a great-aunt, and subsequently brought under the wing of her uncle, Victor Sassoon, she still had to support herself. She found some work with the BBC, but soon developed her own line of business, giving lectures to troops and factory workers about conditions in occupied France. She was constantly frustrated by the refusal of most people to accept the truth about the concentration camps.

Francine's sister also escaped from France. Desperate and frightened at the worsening situation for the Jews, she underwent a marriage of convenience with a young Catholic officer who was half-French, half-English. He helped to smuggle her out of the country. Francine's brother was less fortunate, being one of the last Jews to be rounded up and sent to Auschwitz.

Francine was awarded the *croix de guerre* shortly after the war, one of only 232 given to French women. The award was specifically for her Red Cross work.

Francine met Eileen Marks (*née* Petch) at the sauna in the Dorchester Hotel in July 1942 – the one and only time she entered a sauna. The two women found they had much in common and a close friendship developed. On that Christmas Eve in 1942, she pressed her only remaining suit and bought a yellow orchid with the last coins she had after paying the rail fare.

As Francine remembers it, Charles was immediately infatuated. 'Married or unmarried, you're going to be my wife,' he declared. Then, true to character, he broke the spell by telling her that her make-up was awful. Francine says she took an instant dislike to him and was relieved to discover he was not staying for lunch. She refused his invitation to dinner and described him to her hosts as a bore.

Charles, however, was used to getting his own way. Now polite but persistent, over the following weeks he continued to press the lonely young French refugee to have dinner with him. When she finally agreed, says Francine, he muffed the opportunity by suggesting in the taxi home that he should keep her as his mistress. She slapped his face and jumped out of the taxi. It was a precursor to the stormy nature of their marriage.

By her account she moved flats to avoid Charles' attentions – to no avail. Within a matter of days he was on the telephone to her, having obtained her number and address by bribing an official of the Aliens' Registration Office in Piccadilly with tickets to the Prince of Wales. Stunned – and at least a little flattered – by his refusal to give up, Francine's response was: 'Well, why haven't you sent any flowers then?'

An invitation to dinner at Ray Court was sealed by the promise of Francine's favourite food – caviar, cheese soufflé, chocolate mousse and champagne. David was sent to collect her from the station at Maidenhead and almost missed her in the blackout.

Clore stayed with Francine at her flat in London occasionally. She was living near Baker Street in what were then known as 'service' flats, where the entire building was serviced by domestic staff. All the residents would leave their shoes outside the door every night for the shoe shiner to clean. One morning Charles reached out of Francine's door to take his shoes. No shoes were to be found. Soon all the residents were loudly complaining about similar losses and it became clear that someone had systematically helped themselves to every shoe in the building. For the first and last time Clore arrived shoeless in his office in Park Street. It caused great hilarity at Ray Court, but everyone was sternly forbidden ever to mention the incident.

Another taboo subject was Clore's elocution lessons. Twice a week a man with an upper-class Oxford accent would come to Ray Court to give him a lesson. Gradually his Cockney accent was softened, but he continued to have lessons when he moved to Checkendon, in Oxfordshire.

The first time that Mena, then Clore's parlourmaid, met Francine was when the two became engaged. Clore brought Francine into the kitchen to meet the staff. He introduced her by saying: 'Here's a French young lady who would like some good French cooking.' Clore had already cleared out the rest of the family so that he and Francine could dine alone with candlelight in the large dining-room. When Mena entered to serve the next course, Clore called: 'Mena, I'm getting married.' Feigning surprise, the young Ukrainian congratulated Clore, although Mrs Davis, Clore's sister, had not been able to keep the secret and had already passed on the news.

The pressures on Francine to marry were considerable. She was determined to stay in England, close to the war, rather than retire to the Bahamas, where her uncle, Victor Sassoon, would provide a comfortable life and introduction to wealthy American Jewish bachelors. Yet she was desperately lonely. Most of her friends were either in occupied Europe, or dead, or fighting the war in some distant part of the world. Her brother was in a concentration camp; she had lost touch with her sister; her mother, still in France, had lost her reason. Her nearest available relative in England was a great-aunt. While she was able to earn a living, she had no prospect of regaining the lifestyle she had enjoyed before the war.

For all his lack of sophistication, Charles had much to offer. Almost untouched by the war, he represented a safe haven, a retreat from the realities of death, suffering and impoverishment, that was greatly attractive to a disillusioned young woman. Francine's disillusionment largely stemmed from the hypocrisy towards Jewish people shown both by the French and by the Allies. Her experience at the hands of the French Red Cross and the Vichy Government had left a sour taste. What she was not prepared for was continued treatment as a second-class citizen after her escape from France. For some time after her arrival in Britain she was half-suspected of being an enemy agent – a possibility the authorities could not ignore. Her attempts to join the WRENS had been frustrated by a British-national-only rule, while the Free French only wanted to parachute her back into occupied France as an agent. When she told de Gaulle she would not go back, he offered to drop her in Belgium instead. The final straw, however, was in spring 1942 when she applied to drive an ambulance for the Free French in Algiers and was turned down because there was 'a quota for Jews'. In her anger and hurt, she sought refuge in her Jewishness and turned to Charles. They became engaged on 18 April 1943 and married on 7 June. 'There was no time to think,' says Francine.

The marriage took place in St John's Wood with the signing of the register at Claridge's. Francine says that 'Charles was drunk, I was crying.' Rumour has it that at the wedding her aunt, Mrs Sassoon, asked her: 'Do you really know what you're doing?' Francine was said to have replied: 'At least there's money this way.'

The honeymoon lasted three days and was at Drumnadrochit, the vast estate around Loch Ness. (Charles boasted that he now owned the Loch Ness monster.) Francine started to show her independence from the start by spending much of the time fishing in the loch with a gillie. Charles, who was afraid of the water and hated fishing, stayed on shore.

Francine's attempt to escape from the horrors of war pushed her in the end into what was, from a personal point of view, a more harassing conflict. The two of them soon began to quarrel. Charles was unable to handle the fiery young French girl and, as always, lost his temper with anything or anybody he could not control. Francine became frustrated and frightened by his moods, sometimes loud and ranting, other times withdrawn and brooding.

She felt that Charles was using her for social climbing. In practice, however, it was Francine who gained the reputation as a social upstart – Charles was too busy making money to expend much effort on society flim flam. Charles was equally unhappy with Francine's flirtations. The young French socialite was used to and enjoyed the attention she received from other men. Charles, on the other hand, became increasingly jealous and possessive.

Francine's reaction to Ray Court was instant and negative. On seeing it for the first time, she took one step forward and two sharp steps back. It was, she recalls, 'a gothic horror'. Inside, the building had even less to recommend it to the Frenchwoman from the Avenue Foch. It was, she says, a hideous house, relieved only by the two panelled rooms where Charles' collection of *objets d'art* was displayed.

Francine had little time for the furnishings either, dismissing much of the antique furniture as nineteenth-century imitation. She was impressed, however, by the quality of Charles' collection of figurines.

Her own interests lay in paintings and furniture, and here at least they complemented each other. She influenced him to purchase several masterpieces, including a Renoir and a Caneletto. But even before this, Clore had begun collecting masters. When he became acquainted in 1952 with David Somerset, an art dealer (now the Duke of Beaufort), 'he was already an avid and skilful collector. He had natural taste and a very good eye, which he seemed to have developed as a young man.'

Francine's arrival made little change to the daily routine of the staff at Ray Court. To them she appeared 'a very superior lady, beautiful and refined. She had little to do with us because Clore continued to issue the orders and oversee the domestic arrangements. It looked to us as though she wanted to have nothing to do with that side of things.' Every morning Mena would bring Francine her breakfast in bed. It was always the same: a small bottle of champagne, some toast and an apple. Gradually Mena began to like Francine: 'She was jolly and enjoyed gossiping to me, although in many ways she was something of a mischief maker.'

From the day she moved in, Francine was determined that Ray Court would have to go. Within five months she and Charles had moved to the more imposing, beautiful house of Checkendon in Oxfordshire. The estate included a 400-acre farm. David Clore and his family moved out to his own home in Bourne End, and the rest of the Clore entourage was asked to leave.

It rapidly became clear that Charles and Francine were temperamentally ill matched. The glamour of night-club entertainment and of eating out every night began to pall. Francine could not make do with only three hours' sleep, while Charles flourished on it. She told him that, if he couldn't sleep, it must be because of a bad conscience. She also began to be bored by the constant talk about business. There were, after all, other things in life.

What Charles wanted in a wife was a decoration, a perfect hostess who would always look glamorous, would always be available for social duties, but would fade into the background when the important matter of business intruded. Francine, however, had a mind of her own and insisted on exercising it. The more stifled she felt, the more she rebelled.

Until the collapse of their marriage, Charles and Francine commuted between Checkendon and Park Street. It could have been an idyllic life, but the tensions between them were rarely far below the surface. The difference in their backgrounds, that was once part of the mutual attraction, now became a major cause of discord. The servants downstairs – among them, at the end, Albert Roux, the entrepreneur of Nouvelle Cuisine, who was chef for the Clore household at the time – learnt to keep out of the way during the frequent quarrels.

The bickering was not helped by Francine's pregnancy in 1944. Charles was not ready to be the proud father, finding it difficult at the best of times to communicate with his nephews and nieces. Only later in his life did he develop a real fondness for his own children and by then it was too late, for his relationship with his son Alan, at least. His liking and ability to be more comfortable (though still ill at ease) with children only truly emerged in his declining years.

Had they been able to share the enjoyment of the children at this stage, the marriage might have been saved. But Charles' concern was with the business. In 1946, the year that Vivien was born, Charles was rarely at home. Charles Wilson, who later became the managing director of Clore's finance operation, Investment Registry, remembers that

Clore was working so hard at that time that he would frequently leave dinner half-way through to go to bed.

By the end of the war, Clore was recognized as a rich man, although because of the extent and complexity of his business concerns the true extent of his wealth was only guessed at. His answer to the media was characteristically brusque: 'No man can say how much he has earned until he has packed everything up and put all his money in the bank.'

At no stage had Clore volunteered anything for the war effort that was not profitable in its own right. He was far from pleased when, towards the end of the war, Francine volunteered to work at St George's Hospital, looking after war wounded instead of looking after his household. Only on rare occasions had the war touched his private life. Francine remembers Clore's house in Farm Street being bombed: 'He told me one day that we were going to see his old home. I didn't want to go. When we got there all that was standing was the porticoes. It was his little joke.'

As far as Clore was concerned, the war had been a period of golden opportunity. The value of his inner city properties, particularly the commercial sites, had soared as victory had looked more and more certain. Douglas Tovey, an estate agent at Healey & Baker, commented: 'It was amazing how the boom in values started in the last eighteen months of the war once people could see that we were going to win.' It was at that time that Clore met Tovey. He had received many of Tovey's promotion letters, which were famous for their hard-sell line. Tovey had started as a rent collector on the Great Western Railway. He had joined Edward Lotery, the shop developer, in 1938. After Lotery emigrated, Tovey joined Healey & Baker, where he soon distinguished himself as a shrewd and talented commercial property agent. As Clore got to know Tovey, he started to pass increasing amounts of work to Healey & Baker.

And there were certainly enough development projects to keep Tovey busy. The values of sites were soaring, boosted by demand and the immediate post-war inflationary spiral. Property owners were enjoying capital appreciations of around 300 per cent and were able to borrow relatively small amounts of money at fixed rate cost, with a guaranteed profit always in sight. In order to expand his property interests, Clore created Prince of Wales Property Ltd, having bought in all the outstanding publicly held shares in the theatre.

The scope for development seemed unlimited; some three and a half million properties had been damaged or destroyed during the war and demand for all types of property was likely to outstrip supply for many years to come. But while the need for new offices was acute, particularly for those firms which had been evacuated to the country, rehousing the many governmental departments took first priority.

The government took the initiative and imposed stringent controls upon redevelopment: before any building took place, a licence had to be obtained. This created the situation where unlimited amounts of buying and selling could take place but where the ability to develop these sites was by no means certain.

Despite these controls the number of projects was considerable: in the twenty months to the end of 1946 licences worth £270 million were issued. The main way to gain permission to build was via the 'Lessor Scheme', the government's policy of leasing offices from a developer. In return for a licence, the developer was forced to let the government occupy the site and to allow it to choose the terms of rent. Although by no means a perfect scheme, it did at least guarantee the developer a profit and, with the government as tenant on completion, there were never any difficulties in borrowing the bridging money from a bank.

Clore became involved in numerous lessor schemes in the centre of London and, whenever he could, he would use Token Construction, his own construction company. For instance, Royalty House, the office block on the site of the old Royalty Theatre, was built by Token. So was a three-and-a-half acre office site adjoining Charing Cross Station, and St George's House, a 20,000 square foot site close to Holborn Circus, which was leased to the Ministry of Works.

One of Clore's earliest developments, in 1948, was Kensington Crescent in Holborn. The site had belonged to Olympia, and was bought by European Shipping, a company in which Clore held the chief interest. The three-and-a-half acre site took two years to develop, the finance being paid in instalments by Lloyds Bank. As security, Lloyds Bank took a debenture on the whole of the property and assets of Prince of Wales Properties.

In a letter to Marriott in 1966, Leah Gelman said: 'He was particularly proud of a development in Southwark Bridge Road, which was one of the largest office developments in London, but which was built in record time for the occupation of the Ministry of Transport.'

Clore also developed lessor schemes by joining syndicates. Adastral House in Theobald's Road, for instance, was developed by a syndicate including Clore, Sir William Threlford, a chartered accountant, Major Ash, an architect, and various estate agents. The syndicate put up a total of £5,000 in November 1947 and made a profit of some £340,000 when Land Securities Investment Trust bought the site in 1950.

In April 1949 the 5s ordinary shares of Prince of Wales Property Co., which had never yet paid a dividend, were quoted at the surprisingly high price of 12s on the Stock Exchange. Soon after, the Prince of Wales made a rights issue to increase its spending powers to £2,500,000 and a year later raised another £500,000. Once again the insurance companies were an essential part of the package Charles had arranged. The Legal and General put up the £11.4 million to take up mortgages on the buildings as they were completed.

Clore knew now the direction he wished to take. The fast-moving world of property satisfied his aggressive competitiveness; the vast gains that could be made excited him and drew him on. Other areas, such as shipping, were just about to take off and he wanted to be there when it happened.

4

Preparing for the Big Deal

'There are as many chances now as ever before
– more in fact. You have to find the
opportunity and then work. Work hard.'
                                        Charles Clore

After the austerity of the war years, the late 1940s and the 1950s were
like a massive release of tension. The war had not been kind to many of
that generation of tycoons and many business empires simply failed to
survive the conflict. Clore's mentor Jack Phillips died in poverty at the
start of the war after the sudden sweeping decline in the value of
property, particularly in London. Almost overnight, Phillips found the
value of his properties had heavily depreciated, tenants were hard to
find, and rent income was sharply reduced.

For those who survived the war, however, opportunities were suddenly everywhere and money was available for projects that would not have
been considered even in pre-war peacetime. Having learnt the tricks of
the entrepreneurial trade during the hard times, Charles was better
equipped than most to take advantage of a remarkable upsurge in
mergers and acquisitions.

The deluge of bids that began in the late 1940s came about as a result
of a combination of factors that produced exceptionally favourable
opportunities for the bidder. Most important among these were the
structural changes in Britain's economy, now so accepted that their
decisive impact is often underestimated. For the first time in living
memory, labour became scarce and therefore expensive; there were
swift changes in the market size of a whole raft of established industries;
and new industries such as aerospace, which had developed rapidly
during the war, began to expand along with growing world demand. The
assurance of full employment created a new range of consumer tastes
and attitudes, which had a major impact on the retail sector. People
wanted choice and convenience in their shopping. Multiple stores and
self-service groups took trade away from the less forward-looking
department stores and independent shops.

These changes were swift and far-reaching in their implications.

Overall, the differences between the most efficient firms and the also-rans became more glaring as many companies failed to adapt themselves to changed economic circumstances. This failure – often as much a matter of drained resources as of poor strategy – became the bidder's opportunity. Clore, like many others of his time, recognized that while many British firms were inefficiently run, their assets were basically sound. An injection of capital and sound management into these businesses could raise them to profit in fairly short order.

Another change, which made matters easier for the bidder, was the difficulty companies experienced in giving investors a real return on their money. Sharp rises in tax contribution to pay for the booming economy and welfare state had fallen heavily upon companies; for example, in 1956 tax took 56 per cent of gross trading profits, while in 1932 the figure had been only 32 per cent. Companies took the only course possible to preserve their cash flows and reduced the proportion of profits distributed to ordinary shareholders – from 52 per cent of gross trading profits in 1938 to 20 per cent in 1952. Growth in dividend payments failed to keep pace with the increase in profits and therefore with the growth of a company's profit-earning assets. Average profits in 1952 were 3.2 times the 1938 level, while dividends had risen only 1.2 times over the same period. The bigger the gap, the more incentive for the investor to cash in his holdings for a fair offer.

This dividend restraint hit Stock Market prices, too. Prices were determined primarily by historical and projected dividends rather than by profits, so there were numerous companies whose actual value, if realized, considerably exceeded their market quotation.

Another important factor which encouraged takeovers was the emergence from the war of companies with large liquid assets. Unable or unwilling to spend profits hoarded during the war years, or acquired as compensation for war damage, companies kept their assets liquid in order to replace premises and equipment, which had become expensive as a result of steep price rises after 1939. The increase in value of the assets the company still had often also added to its vulnerability to takeovers. Companies that failed to revalue their assets regularly risked attracting the attentions of people who recognized their true worth.

Pension funds and life insurance companies also played an important role in all this activity. Still a relatively new phenomenon for most people, pension funds were starting to accumulate vast sums of money that had to go somewhere. Earnings on the Stock Exchange being largely inadequate, they had to look for other investments that would show the kinds of relatively high returns and low risks they needed. Buying assets that would appreciate rapidly from companies that did not know what to do with them made sound sense from their point of view. The insurance companies could not realize those assets themselves. What they needed was an intermediary, a fixer who would shake up moribund, asset-heavy companies for them.

It was in this turbulent environment that Charles Clore burst into public prominence with a series of takeover bids. The fortune he had amassed during the war was now pressed into service as the seed corn for increasingly daring acquisitions that left a bemused British press wondering where on earth he had appeared from.

He had first attracted attention with the acquisition of the 50,000 acre Highland estate in Scotland. He also bought a coach builders – Park Royal Vehicles Ltd – for £650,000 from the Jaeger family. With the backing of Hambros, he floated it as a private company and made £50,000, less expenses, by selling his shares for £700,000. In 1946, he had also purchased Taylor & Lodge, a worsted cloth manufacturer, and Kaye & Stewart, a textile manufacturer. Taylor & Lodge had been a particularly good purchase. The company had built a world-wide reputation for quality worsted cloth. A shortage of operatives and worsted yarn had led to a slump in production during the war, giving Clore the chance to buy the business. The purchase price was partially recovered by floating 20 per cent of the shares shortly afterwards. In contrast, Kaye & Stewart's malaise proved more lasting. The company never recovered from its difficulties and remained near dormant for twenty-five years. No dividend was issued for twenty years. Despite the poor performance, Clore refused to sell the company. In the 1970s the Stock Exchange cancelled the company's quotes.

He was the first mill-owner to introduce the forty-hour working week, a gesture that, combined with the humble origins he insisted upon, caused much of the press to assume that he was a socialist. (In practice, he was more a humanitarian Conservative and made donations to the Conservative Party in later years.)

Other acquisitions included Wildt & Son, a Leicester hosiery machinery maker, which was subsequently taken over by Bentley Engineering, the dominant force in the British knitting machinery industry. In an unsuccessful partnership with Zimmermann, he also founded British Communications Corp. in the West London suburbs. Zimmermann had found a Polish electronic engineering genius, who thought he could create advanced radio products. When the venture proved a failure, Zimmermann disappeared.

Just after the war Clore had bought a night-club on Tagg's Island on the Thames. The island was reached by a bridge which had been festooned for the grand opening. Clore ordered food for up to 300 people and a superb floor show, with a big band and a cabaret. That night it poured with rain. While the floodwaters rushed past, the customers merely trickled in. Clore was appalled. He threw up his hands and had all the remaining food sent off to the local hospital. The following weekend he had half the staff and half the food. The queues of cars extended far along the river and most of the would-be customers had to be turned away.

The immediate post-war years also saw him add briefly to his retailing empire. He learnt from Vincent that Heelas, the ninety-year-old department store in Reading, was up for sale. Heelas seemed to have gone to sleep. Its management was lax and little had changed for the previous thirty years. But although the interior was out of date, it had none the less retained its note of quality and style. Clore immediately sensed the store's potential. Not only did it have an imposing frontage and excellent position in the town centre, but the area it covered could justify a large increase in turnover. Additionally, there was an excellent team of buyers and senior staff. It was an opportunity almost too good to miss.

All Clore had to do was to find someone with flair who could modernize and expand Heelas. Eventually he approached Fred Riceman, an experienced retailer who had just returned from the war. Riceman recalls a city gent in fur coat visiting him at Clore's request. It was not a name Riceman had heard of before. He recalls vividly his first impressions of Clore when they met at Riceman's workplace, Bealesons' fashion showrooms. The two walked silently through the store until Clore suddenly turned to Riceman and said, 'My store, Heelas of Reading, is a high-class store. What do you know about that class of business?' It was obvious Clore was trying to weigh Riceman up. He remembers that 'He did not miss a thing; everything he said was with a special purpose and it helped me to realize the importance of finding all one could about a person.' Riceman was quizzed about his marriage and children. It became obvious that Clore wanted to meet his wife and see his home setting. The two drove to have tea with her at Mudeford.

Although on the initial meeting Clore had not warmed to Riceman's personality and it was clear to him that the two would never reach a friendly footing, he decided the merchantman was the right person for Heelas. He and Sainer called on Riceman to offer him the position. Clore first asked: 'What do you think of Heelas?'

'A good store, but outdated.'

'Can you make a success of it?'

'Yes, on my terms.'

'What are they?'

'That I should be appointed managing director.'

'Agreed.'

'That I receive a salary plus bonus and share arrangements.'

Although Riceman's terms were high, Clore agreed without hesitation. Riceman comments: 'I can think of no one else in this country, in like circumstances, who would have agreed so readily to these terms. However, he was prepared to be what he may have felt to be generous, if by doing so he would get the person he wanted.'

Riceman was busy building up the image of a high-class store. In his usual abrasive way, Clore acknowledged Riceman's efforts in this regard while he was less than impressed by the store's financial performance. Riceman comments: 'Clore paid me the questionable compliment of telling me I was a good showman, even if I was not such a good merchant! I was never certain why he underlined the latter.'

Every Wednesday Clore would visit Richard Shops to check on progress and sign cheques. He met Riceman at Heelas every Saturday morning. 'He certainly knew how to look for results and I learned a lot from his visits.' Despite his obvious interest, Clore frequently seemed cold and aloof and, to some of his staff, he appeared more concerned with his assets than with them.

During Clore's ownership, the retail businesses had been transformed from unprofitable and stagnating businesses into thriving, expanding concerns. In four years, Heelas' annual turnover had increased to £2 million from near bankruptcy and the number of staff increased in number by over 50 per cent. Richard Shops was making similarly good progress and the original chain of twenty shops had been increased to forty-five. In some ways the challenge had gone and Clore was becoming restless.

Weyl recalls the uneasy atmosphere of change which permeated Richard Shops during that time, 'We could all smell something in the air,' he said. The opening of a new, prestigious store in Regent Street seemed to be a landmark to Clore. Weyl recalls asking him at the opening, 'Do you think the progress of Richard Shops is finished?' In a uncharacteristically reflective mood, Clore replied hesitantly, 'I don't think so, but I feel I want to do something else.' Weyl reminded him: 'We've made a profit every year we've been a part of your business.' Clore's answer was evasive: 'I don't know what the future will bring, but I'm thinking of moving on.'

Without warning, Clore announced the sale of Richard Shops and Heelas. Jo Collier, the managing director of United Draperies, had many times expressed his interest in Clore's retail businesses and it was an easy and speedy task for Clore to reach the mutually agreeable price of £1 million. Lord (then plain Kenneth) Keith was then a director at United Draperies. He recalls: 'Clore got one million for the deal. I think this was when he first touched cash.' As part of the agreement, Clore's group took one-sixth of the interest in United Draperies, which issued

55

900,000 shares worth £540,000, and £600,000 in unsecured notes.

Riceman recalls being suddenly requested by Clore to attend a special directors' meeting. On arriving he found the equally mystified directors of Richard Shops and quickly realized that 'the time had come when Charles Clore was going to realize his improved assets. It appeared to me that those concerned had never considered that I would be disappointed.'

The problem arose of what to do with the new Rolls-Royce Riceman had ordered. Clore was phlegmatic. The waiting time for a new Roller was two years; why didn't Sainer take it over? So he did.

Clore had no time for niceties. The stores had fulfilled their purpose, and he was more interested in acquiring interests elsewhere. It was in 1949 that he bought Investment Registry, a West End issuing house from a financier named Cousins, who had the distinction of also being a director of the *Daily Worker*. Through his involvement with Investment Registry and the dealing company, Princes Investments, Clore had a useful vantage-point from which to seek companies ripe for takeover.

While he shrugged off his interests in retail, Clore was rapidly making inroads into other, more profitable business sectors. He knew that he was ready to move on. Through his experience during and after the war, he had thoroughly learnt about every step of running a business; of making full use of assets; of spotting companies with undeveloped potential. He was also making considerable strides socially and, despite the domestic fractures which were beginning to appear, his hostess wife and graceful home were allowing him to establish numerous, useful business contacts. Clore felt he was reaching his peak and that it was the right moment to shift into top gear. He was determined to break into the big time, but he could only do this by taking on the City, which regarded him as a raw upstart and interloper. It was plain to him that takeover bids were the way forward. The quick profit, which he could raise by selling Richard Shops and Heelas, would be a useful first step.

The piecemeal acquisitions so far were a mere prelude, however – almost trial runs. There was little real pattern in them; they were purely opportunistic, rather than part of a grand design. Gradually, however, the need for a more coherent approach became clear. The management time involved in running disparate unlinked operations around the country was enormous and he was beginning to work all hours. As he told the press, in one of his few expansive moods: 'There are as many chances now as ever before – more in fact. You have to find the opportunity and then work. Work hard.'

His first takeover vehicle was a privately owned finance company, Princes Investments. It operated as a holding company, from which deals could be made. Its first major acquisition was Bentley Engineering, a company Clore now knew extremely well. Bentley was in the midst of rapid expansion. By 1951, Bentley's trading profits were £1 million and net profits were £250,000. The dividend was raised from 10 per cent to 12.5 per cent.

Charles, who owned about a third of the shares, approached the board and suggested they increase the dividend even further, but the board refused to budge. Princes Investment threatened to gain control to force through a higher dividend. Alternatively, the Bentley family could buy Clore's one million 4s ordinary shares for not less than 10s each. The latter was actually Charles's preferred option, but the Bentley family, however, refused to go above 8s.

From then on Clore bought Bentley shares in the open market and by private arrangements. In October 1952 the board defended itself by inaugurating interim dividends with a 7.5 per cent payment for that year. But it was too late. By April, Clore had the controlling interest, two million of the total 3.82 million shares. He and Sainer came onto the board. The dividend for 1952 was 20 per cent compared with 12.5 per cent of the previous year.

Three years later Clore made a bid for the Grosvenor House Hotel. Again, he first approached the board, then, when he was refused, indicated he was ready to go direct to shareholders. He already had a complex plan worked out, under which he would form a new company with Conrad Hilton's Hilton Hotels International. Hilton would operate the hotel on a profit-sharing arrangement with Princes Investment.

The Grosvenor House board dismissed the offer out of hand, but were forced to think again when Clore returned with rather more generous terms. At 6s a share, the offer was worth almost twice the 3s 6d quoted price. In addition, under the new offer, those shareholders who wanted to keep a stake in the business would be allowed to acquire an interest in the new business on preferential terms. From a short-term view the offer seemed reasonable; the current dividend was 6 per cent, having been cut from 10 per cent in 1947 and 8 per cent in 1948. But the true worth of the company, as reflected in the asset value of the site, was much greater than its Stock Market price suggested. Charles was offering £600,000 for a company with fixed assets of £1.8 million. Its balance sheet alone was worth 8s per 5s share, 2s above the bid price. If the Grosvenor House assets were broken up, the shares would be worth at least 12s each.

Clore's takeover bid put the directors of Grosvenor House, who included the influential Lord Balfour, in a difficult position with their shareholders. The only counter-argument they could put forward was to stress the true value of the company assets. Grosvenor House had been valued at £2.15 million, on a 'willing buyer to seller' basis, and £4.28 million on a replacement-cost basis. Naturally many of the shareholders wondered why the directors had allowed the share prices of the hotel to remain so low. The board's rather limp response was that the current price of shares had reflected general and unsettled stock-market conditions and that shareholders would soon see a higher dividend.

The situation had all the hallmarks of a classic Clore takeover – underused and undervalued assets, a moribund management and disgruntled shareholders. Then the bottom fell out of the bid. Hilton Hotels had entered the fray with Clore on the understanding that it would gain the support and services of the hotel's management. When the management contested the bid and showed no sign of weakening in its resolve, Hilton lost its resolution and withdrew.

The second and more powerful vehicle for acquisition was Investment Registry, a minor issuing house in the West End. The acquisition of Investment Registry was in itself something of a coup, because the ordinary shares were all privately held, with only preference shares being quoted. Only the ordinary shares carried voting rights and it was these Clore acquired.

The company had been running a brisk business after the war along traditional issuing-house lines, but had only flirted with takeover bids. Ironically, one of those bids was for Prince of Wales Theatre (Properties).

In 1951, Investment Registry launched a bid for Frederick Gorringe, the Buckingham Palace Road store, announcing that it intended to make an offer at a price substantially above the Stock Exchange quotation, for the 200,000 £1 preference and the 200,000 £1 ordinary shares. At the time, the preference shares (which unusually carried full voting rights) stood at 21s 9d and the £1 ordinary stood at 40s 7.5d, making a total valuation of £620,000. Gorringe warned its shareholders not to sell before a firm offer was made. Investment Registry revealed its hand with an offer of 25s for each preference and £3 for each ordinary share, valuing the company at £850,000. The offer depended on acceptance by 90 per cent of the shareholders.

The Gorringe directors reacted decisively by advising strongly against the offer. They argued that profits were rising, the company was about to benefit from the spending on development it had made in recent years, and, most crucially, the company's premises, should they be sold, would produce a sum considerably in excess of its balance sheet value. The board's arguments prevailed. Take-up of the Investment Registry offer was far below the required percentage and the bid lapsed.

The reason for the failure was clear enough. The offer for the preference shares was too low and the bid for the ordinary shares, while superficially attractive, did not look so beneficial after closer scrutiny. Moreover, Investment Registry had erred tactically by announcing its intention before naming the terms of the bid, especially as the shares it was after were not very active on the Stock Exchange. While the nature of the offer, with its focus on undervalued assets, had Clore's stamp written large upon it, it was an uncharacteristically clumsy campaign and it is likely that the company was not acting on his own behalf.

Investment Registry was to play a signal part in the Big Deal itself — the acquisition of Sears. It became registrar for Sears, for Butlins and numerous other companies. But it was never more than a convenient sideline to Clore, a useful tool but not a venture to invest great effort or money in for its own sake. He never seemed to be sure what he wanted to do with the operation other than keep it in store for use in further deals and make sure it turned in a respectable profit. Board meetings of Investment Registry were rarely particularly constructive. Clore would sit at one end of the table, Sainer at the other, with Clore invariably wanting to know why the company was not doing more business.

Although Investment Registry had moved from the West End to the City and was under a new chief executive, Charles Wilson, it was hampered in competing with other issuing houses by plain lack of financial muscle. It needed a heavy capital commitment behind major placings, as a precaution against being left with unsold stock. A failed major placing could bring the company down. So every issuing commitment by Investment Registry had to be cleared by Clore himself first, through his one-armed administrator, Boswell, at Park Street.

It was not surprising that Clore eventually decided to reduce his involvement with Investment Registry. By the early 1960s he had, after all, outgrown it, for Sears was big enough to handle future acquisitions on its own. A deal was struck in 1964 with M. Samuel & Co. and the company eventually lost its identity within what soon became the Hill Samuel Group. Clore remained a director until his resignation in 1975. The move greatly disappointed David Clore, who had been working for Investment Registry for some time. David had been at a loose end for some time and had been spending too much money on gambling. Several times Charles had to bale him out for large debts. In exasperation, Clore had offered his brother the job of identifying possible deals for the issuing house. Unexpectedly, David found himself in his element. His ability to mix and to gather information made him an invaluable asset to the company and his years at Investment Registry were among the happiest and most effective of his career.

Clore's brief but successful business relationship with Harold Samuel (now Lord Samuel of Wych Cross) began in 1953 when the Big Deal —

Sears – was under way. Samuel was chairman of Land Securities, a company he founded after the war when he ceased to practise as an estate agent. Through his skilful knowledge of the laws affecting property, Land Security's assets had grown from £19,000 in 1944 to £11 million in 1952. Normally something of a recluse in the property world, his short partnership with Clore proved a formidable arrangement. The two men had discussed the potential of the Savoy Hotel and its subsidiaries, which included Claridge's, the Connaught and the Berkeley, a number of times. Eventually Clore made an approach to the Savoy board, who rejected it roundly. Then ensued one of the most bizarre and sensational financial struggles of this century. Before it was finished, the takeover race between several unknown financiers ousted world crises from the headlines, led to a government inquiry, raised a public outcry about takeover methods, and inspired a heavily disputed and controversial defence scheme.

In late 1953 a mystery bidder started buying large quantities of the Savoy group shares and was obviously preparing for a takeover bid. The hotel company owned not only three of London's most prestigious hotels, occupying prime positions in the heart of the West End, but also the Savoy Theatre and Simpson's restaurant in the Strand. It soon became obvious to the Savoy directors that the Berkeley was the chief object of the takeover bid. Before the war the hotel's patrons were mainly the affluent 'young set', who particularly favoured the hotel's restaurant. After the war, custom fell away and profits plummeted. People were less well off, labour was hard to find and more expensive, and food supplies still strictly rationed. Eventually a ludicrous disparity arose between the value of the hotel site and the trading profits. By 1952 profits had dropped to £5,950, while the hotel building property and site were valued at £490,200.

For three months the identity of the mystery dealer became a matter of daily speculation. The chief suspects were Clore, Harold Samuel, Conrad Hilton and Aristotle Onassis. All denied their involvement. Clore was overheard at a racecourse remarking that he thought Savoy shares were undervalued.

It was Clore who gave Patrick Sergeant his first scoop for the *Daily Mail*, revealing that Samuel was the mystery bidder. What he did not tell Sergeant was that he had come to an informal agreement with Samuel some time before. Having been quietly buying shares for some time, Clore discovered that Samuel was also building up a holding. The two men met at the Café Royal, accompanied by Sainer. The two sides agreed that it was pointless to pursue a takeover separately and that one should buy the other out. Samuel gave Clore a commitment that he would not back down. Once the bid came into the open, Hugh Wontner, the Savoy chairman (who later became Lord Mayor of London), attempted to thwart the developers' ambitions by transferring all the properties to the staff pension fund, whose trustees would have the power to appoint their own successors. It was not a popular move and drew intense criticism in Parliament and in the City.

In the event, the combined shareholdings of Samuel and Clore, together with various pledges, would have been enough to seize control. But the blatantly anti-Semitic nature of the Savoy defence had wounded Samuel so much that he retired, disgusted, from the fray. Wontner's controversial share arrangement was enough to deter other raiders for thirty years thereafter.

Both Clore and Samuel came out of the affair with a healthy profit. Clore sold to Samuel when the shares were near their peak. Samuel took his revenge in the same way, netting between £150,000 and £300,000 by selling his shares to the board at his own price of 62s 6d. The considerable publicity afforded to his scheme to convert the Berkeley Hotel and restaurant into showrooms and offices helped establish his image as an innovative property entrepreneur. Clore, however, was publicly vilified as a treacherous schemer, 'the notorious West End financier'.

It was the Savoy affair that drove the biggest wedge between Clore and his wife, Francine. The unfavourable publicity was like a slap in the face to her. Society friends she had so assiduously cultivated suddenly turned cool; invitations to social events began to dry up; there were whispers when she and Charles appeared together in public.

Her behaviour towards him became increasingly shrill. His reaction was to bury himself even further in his work. 'He was a hard and abrupt man and often rude to people. I would only see him in the evenings; most of the time he was hard at work,' recalls Freddie Kay, the faithful butler, who doubled as chauffeur and valet to Clore till the day he died and who still works for the Clore family. Charles also sought protection in the regular routines he imposed to provide at least the semblance of an orderly life. At 8 a.m. sharp, he would go to the office, after saying goodbye to the children. He would return at about 5.30, then he and Francine would go out in the evening. Every fourth Thursday, Clore went to Leicester with Sainer. Every Friday the family would depart for Checkendon, the country estate, returning on Sunday evening.

'Everything was always a great ritual, always the same. Deauville and Monte Carlo in the summer. Gstaad in the winter,' recalls Clore's daughter Vivien.

For Francine the routine was stifling. She felt trapped and let down; her dream of an exotic and fast-moving life had faded like mist in the face of reality that was dreary and depressing. In an unguarded moment she commented to the press: 'Many people think that being in my

61

position is a life of winter sports and lying around in the sun. Not so. I stay here with my husband in the fog. He leaves every morning for work at eight o'clock and I don't see him again until night.'

The arguments continued in public and in private. At David Clore's house in Bourne End, the gathered children would look on in embarrassment as the two of them snarled and snapped at each other. In the end, almost anything Charles did was interpreted by Francine as a slight and almost everything she did seemed to him to be calculated to annoy. Francine's Gallic volatility and Charles' inherited temper made a highly combustible mixture.

Habits that at first had seemed slightly annoying now became a constant irritation to her; in particular, his apparent meanness. She claims he never gave a tip and she would have to resort to subterfuge to pass one to hotel staff. Every week she would go to Leah Gelman with a detailed list of expenses, in order to obtain an allowance.

On the other hand, Francine did like to spend money fairly freely, and this must have rankled with the young man who was always so careful with his pennies.

Sometimes Francine's free spending was wiser than he knew. On one occasion he had allowed her to buy some lithographs, although he said he was strapped for cash. She bought an antique table for £2,500. He exploded. Yet she claims that table is now worth in excess of £400,000. She also became irritated by his intensive secretiveness. Even when he used to talk business to her all evening, she felt he was holding things back.

The marriage might still have been saved, however, if they had not both been such strong personalities. Israel Sieff pinpointed this as the root of their problems. There was no room for compromise, no give-and-take.

On one occasion Charles had visited Bradfield College, where his nephews were boarding, to watch *Hamlet* performed in an open-air Greek theatre. He had promised to be home in time to greet Francine, who was returning from France. As he watched the drama, he became increasingly absorbed in it. Waving an occasional arm for another sandwich, he forgot Francine entirely and stayed to the end. The resulting row went on intermittently for days.

The task of bringing up the children was left to a nanny. Charles found it difficult to be a father – not least because he had come to it late: Vivien was born when he was forty. He had little conversation for them and never thought to discuss his work with them. The children did not figure prominently in either parent's lives and in this the Clore household was far from the typical Jewish family. The children would never have dinner with them, except at Christmas (his birthday), Passover and Yom Kippur. On the only other occasion they did so, Francine threw water over him as the ritual argument reached fury pitch.

Even on holiday the Clores took their personal animosities with them. Kay was originally employed as a chauffeur in 1948; his first task was to drive Clore and Francine around Europe that summer. Most of the time Clore dozed in the car, but when he was awake he would frequently argue with Francine and accuse her of being a back-seat driver.

It was hardly surprising that the tensions of public vilification and domestic strife should make Clore even more moody and uncommunicative than normal. Yet at the same time he was able to make some of his most humanitarian gestures. Leah Gelman telephoned Investment Registry one day to ask them to check out a letter Clore had received from an old man claiming to have worked in Israel Clore's factory. The letter explained he would shortly be evicted from his house and would have nowhere to go. The story was checked out. Clore was back on the telephone immediately. How much would it cost to buy the house? He gave instructions to purchase it and to allow the old man to live in it for the rest of his life. This act of generosity was too much for the old man, who promptly had a heart attack and died.

By 1953, Charles Clore had all the ingredients that were to make a success of his business life and a failure of his domestic life. He had a solid fortune in diverse areas of business; had learnt the hard way about winning and losing takeover bids; and had made his mark (if not in quite the way intended) on the financial scene. The rehearsals were now over; the stage was now set for the main act.

CHAPTER

5

The Big Deal – Sears

'I don't tear things down or break them up. I
build them up.' Charles Clore

It was Douglas Tovey, his friend and confidant, who brought J. Sears &
Co. (Trueform Boot Co.) Ltd to Charles' notice in 1953, waving an Extel
card and declaring, 'This is stuffed with property assets.' From the
beginning it was the attraction of the property portfolio (which had a
book value of £6 million, against a market value of £10 million) that
drew Clore to the stores group.

Sears was not entirely the moribund organization later commentators assumed it must have been. For the previous two years, for
example, the chairman, Dudley Church, had been able to report record
turnover and the number of premises was growing each year. (Sears
acquired the freehold of eleven sites and leasehold of another five in
1952, for example.) It was by any standards of the time a large and
successful business. It consisted of a substantial shoe manufacturing
operation and some 920 retail premises, mainly in the shoe chain of
Freeman, Hardy & Willis, and Trueform.

It was, however, capable of performing far more profitably, the whole
industry having virtually ceased to innovate in manufacture or retail
several decades before. There were, although the Sears' board seemed
largely unaware of it, good prospects of medium-term growth, Charles
deduced through his frequent trips to the United States. Having looked
at US shoe businesses, he knew that American women bought an
average of five pairs of shoes a year compared with the British, who
bought only two. It was only a matter of time, he reasoned, before the
British consumer caught up.

The key to Sears, as Tovey had suggested, lay in its retail properties.
Charles could see from the start that the value at which the high-street
properties could be sold greatly exceeded both the current value of the
shares and anything he was likely to have to pay for them. Like many
other shares on the Stock Market at that time, Sears still stood at their
1930 values, even though inflation had increased the value of their
assets. Tovey, full of enthusiasm for the deal, convinced him that he
would have no trouble selling the properties.

What Clore recognized was that the assets of these resources could be made to work *better*. Putting that same cash into improvements in the products and the layout of the shops, into new premises in better locations and into hiring better people, would show a far better return.

The idea of sale and lease-back was not completely original. It had been pioneered by Isaac Wolfson some years before and Charles had immediately grasped the potential of this form of asset management.

There were other additional reasons that attracted him to Sears. The shoe manufacturing side was potentially a close fit to Bentley, the hosiery machinery company, in which he now owned a significant proportion of the shares. The retail operation appealed strongly to the merchant in his blood. From his early youth, selling newspapers on street corners, through his days as a rep for his father's clothing factory, he had had an affinity for retailing. Nicky Mavroleon, of the famous shipping family, remembers how, when Francine and some of her women friends returned from a shopping trip, he rewrapped their purchases with an expertise that could only have been gained from long hours at a shop counter. Charles already had experience managing and building up a retail chain for sale in the form of Richard Shops. What he had done once, he could do again.

Charles sent Tovey touring around Britain to obtain a closer valuation of the asset value of its high street sites. Tovey returned enthusiastic and the bid plan was hatched. In what was to become the pattern for all future bids, the entire operation was kept a closely guarded secret. The only people in the know, apart from Charles himself, were Sainer, Tovey and an accountant, Jack Gardiner.

Gardiner was a relatively recent addition to the Clore business team. When Charles had bought British Oil Shipping, the auditors, Jenks, Percival, Pidgeon & Co., assumed they would lose the account. At the first meeting with Clore, Gardiner was expecting a fairly old man instead of the sprightly fellow who came up the steps two at a time. The two men got on well together immediately. The accountant remained with the firm and the relationship grew closer, especially after Clore and Sainer used him to assist in the acquisition investigation of the Furness shipbuilding business.

Leah Gelman was mysterious when she telephoned Gardiner about the new bid.

'Mr Clore would like to see you at two o'clock.'

'What papers do you want me to bring?'

'No papers. It's a new matter.'

That afternoon Clore and Sainer unfolded their plan. Gardiner was immediately struck by the novelty and simplicity of it.

It took a lot of late hours to put the scheme together. The deal had to be

attractive enough to win over the shareholders rapidly, yet still pay as
little as possible for Sears' assets. At the time, the shares stood at around
13s 6d. To quote Sainer: 'The City then worked on the basis that, if the
board didn't agree, you didn't accept an offer. So I had to think of a
gimmick.'

The 'gimmick' was to offer either 40s a share or, as an alternative, 32s
plus one non-voting share – both money now and a continuing stake in
the company. These non-voting shares could be cashed in one year later.
(In the event, many shareholders exercised the option to cash in.
Charles was only too glad to oblige, now having the cash from asset
sales. Those investors who sold out swiftly regretted doing so.) The
money – some £4 million – had to be found, too. The traditional British
banks would not support such an unconventional approach, but fortunately a brash young American bank was just opening its first British
office. For Bank of America, already used to contested takeovers at
home, the deal seemed tenable, if not copperbottomed.

The bid for Sears was announced in February 1953. The offer document, largely written by Gardiner and Sainer, with Clore walking up
and down as they tossed ideas back and forth, was one of the first for
years not to be affected by paper rationing. Yet Clore sent only the one
document to shareholders and advertising was relatively muted. The
offer, he felt, had to sell itself to the shareholders if it were to succeed at
all. Sir Patrick Sergeant, then a plain Mr on the *Investors Chronicle*,
dropped in to Investment Registry to find all of them with their coats off.
'We have to keep them off, roll up our sleeves and work,' insisted Charles
between telephone calls.

All this while Charles had been quietly buying Sears' shares. The low
share price was a reflection of the low dividends the company had been
paying for several years. The share price rose fairly rapidly to 21s 3d,
then more slowly.

To the board of Sears, the sudden attack was devastating. Its response
was confused and unconvincing. The idea that anyone would make such
an approach direct to the shareholders was unbelievable. Worse, it was
ungentlemanly. In panic, the board raised the dividend from 22.5 per
cent to 66.5 per cent at one go. In doing so, they lost all their credibility
with the shareholders, who rightly demanded why it had not been
possible to do that before. The main defensive measure turned out to be a
dangerous boomerang.

But the company was ripe for the plucking. The Sears' directors were
dyed-in-the-wool footwear people. They neither recognized the changes
that would have to be made if the British shoe industry were to remain
competitive, nor were they prepared to make them.

Charles had taken the idea of the contested takeover from the US and immediately recognized its logic. He had studied how companies in the US had gone about preparing contested bids and the pitfalls to avoid. The surprise is that no other industrialist had thought of doing it before.

The unprecedented bid created a furore in the City. The Sears' board cried foul. So did much of the Establishment. Charles and his team let the criticism wash over them. According to Gardiner,

> It didn't worry us. We ignored it. No one (apart from the board) was going to come to any harm. The shareholders would gain, because the bid price for their shares was much higher than the market price. The employees were protected, too, because we wanted to build the business up, not dismantle it. I didn't have any doubts that we'd get the shares.

In later years it was glibly assumed that Charles' aim was to asset strip the businesses he acquired (i.e. sell off all the valuable bits of a company and run with the cash). Yet this was far from the truth. When he released assets into liquid cash he did so to make them work. As he said when he took over Lewis' in 1965, 'I don't tear things down or break them up. I build them up.'

What offended so many people in the City was that Charles had broken the convention that acquisitions should be by agreement. It was felt to be the equivalent of being asked to dinner and stealing the silverware. It was unthinkable, an outrage, yet it was legal and it was done.

It was also, Clore argued with conviction, the right and proper thing to do from the shareholders' point of view. Convention allowed an idle or unimaginative board of directors to let valuable assets lie under-used or go to waste. There was an obligation upon the entrepreneur to exploit those assets to the full. 'In some businesses, the profits earned show that existing assets are not employed in the fullest capacity,' he declared. 'I maintain that neither this country nor any business can afford to have its resources remaining stagnant.' In the City today, there are few people who would dispute that view. *Plus ça change.*

In 1972 he became so incensed at the notion of asset-stripping that he felt obliged to make clear his own feelings on the matter, telling shareholders,

> It is not our policy to acquire a company merely to strip and sell its assets, since this rarely does anything to improve the profit-earning capacity of the assets and merely puts a once and for all profit into the hands of the company that breaks up a business and is so often to the detriment of the employees.

Gerald Ronson, a Clore protégé, sums up Charles' approach at this time succinctly: 'The business was built on the ethos of property. He was an asset man. The assets were the value and he ran a business on top of them.'

In reality, Charles Clore was a hoarder. He hated to sell anything he had once thought worth acquiring. Some of the businesses, such as Furness, he held on to for too long, because he could not bring himself to part with them. Like a squirrel with its acorns, he was so fiercely acquisitive that he had to be strongly persuaded before he would dispose of property, shares, businesses or even people, when they did not perform to expectations. 'Sell and regret' was one of his favourite mottoes. The majority of the shares, with which he established his foundation, are still within the portfolio producing solid incomes.

The inability of so much of the press to understand the difference between his approach and that of the asset-strippers, combined with a certain natural reticence about boasting of his business achievements (although he was quite happy to let his brother David do it on his behalf), caused Charles to have as little as possible to do with the newspapers and television. Even when he was interviewed, he was not impressive, both because he mumbled and because he came across as excessively cold and cautious. Although there were hundreds of requests for interviews, only a very small circle of favoured writers were allowed access to him. They, however, found they could ring him up at almost any time and that he might return the compliment. Charles needed to know what was going on and with those few journalists, whom he felt to be both knowledgeable and trustworthy, he was always willing to exchange both opinions and information.

The special relationship with these journalists extended to social life, too. Jocelyn Stevens, then managing director of Express Newspapers and another of the favoured circle, recalls:

> I inevitably used to arrive late for dinner at his country house, because I was never able to leave the office early. Someone once asked him: 'Why do you ask Jocelyn to dinner if he is always late?' Charles replied: 'Because he always brings me stories.'
>
> I knew I had to have at least three cracking good stories for him. When I arrived, he'd pull out a chair beside him and say: 'Right – what's going on?' As he listened, he'd say: 'I know that one.' If I could tell him some business news or scandal he didn't know about, he'd be delighted and he'd store it away. But he was not free with the gossip himself.

Another of those journalists was Patrick Sergeant, who recalls that Charles 'loved to gossip, to hear what was going on in politics and in the City. He liked nothing better than taking the mickey out of merchant banks.' Sergeant was amazed to find that the great man accepted an invitation to his housewarming:

I'd just become a City Editor and had moved into the house we still have. It was very poorly furnished. My wife was a little nervous at entertaining such a rich and famous figure. 'It's a good thing you didn't come yesterday,' she said. 'We didn't even have a carpet in the sitting-room then.'

Charles bent down and felt the pile of the carpet. As he straightened up, he replied with a twinkle in his eye, 'I hope you're here longer than this will be.'

Once Charles had promise of sufficient shares to achieve control, he and his team called upon the Sears' board to discuss arrangements for the handover.

'Well,' said Charles, not quite sure how to open the conversation.

'Well,' said one Freeman, Hardy & Willis director.

'Well,' said another.

The room relapsed into embarrassed silence until Sainer said: 'What are your plans now?' Charles sat waiting for somebody to say something. Eventually the Sears chairman, Dudley Church, gave in, saying: 'We never thought anything like this would happen to us.'

The departure of some of the Sears' board was an inevitable outcome of Clore's victory. E. J. Ward was paid off. Church was given a face-saving advisory post, to clear up loose ends in the handover. He had, said Charles in his first statement as the new Sears' chairman, 'arranged to give assistance to us in certain directions'. The two managing directors of Freeman, Hardy & Willis and Trueform also retired and were replaced by their deputies. Onto the new Sears' board came Clore himself, Sainer and Jack Gardiner. Gardiner retained his position at Jenks, Percival, Pidgeon & Co. for several more years until his senior partner retired, leaving him with the choice of running the practice or working full-time for Sears. He chose Sears, becoming the first (and for several years the only) executive director of the holding company.

The shock waves were felt far further afield than the Sears' board-room. As one newspaper expressed it:

In the City they are saying that the amazing Mr Clore has done it again. There is some envy for the man who can make millions, but there is another reaction, too, for Mr Clore has put directors of wealthy companies in a rare panic. Their fate, they feel, may be that of Mr E. J. Ward, chairman and managing director of Freeman, Hardy & Willis who, in the space of a few hours, found himself displaced as chairman of the company, to which he had devoted his life.

It sounds ruthless. Fights for control of big business houses are like that and millionaires cannot afford to be sentimental. But it means that Mr Clore is today the subject of discussion in every boardroom. In every company making fat profits he is pictured as a big bad wolf who might gobble them up.

The Sears family also took a dim view of the affair, selling up all its shares on the assumption that they would soon fall in value. In the event, of course, the opposite occurred and they could have sold them a few years later for thirty times as much. The name Charles Clore became anathema in the Sears household. Only once was it mentioned again. Charles' nephew and namesake, on holiday in Portugal, was invited to a house party. As he and his wife Sheila went in, the couple who had brought them whispered 'Don't mention your name.'

'Why not?'

'They're not very fond of the name Clore here. It's not anti-Semitism, just a family grudge.'

All went well in the early evening. Then the hosts organized a raffle for charity. Charles Jr was obliged to write out a cheque. Sears' face went white, then black. 'That joke is in exceedingly bad taste,' he thundered. 'Would you please sign your real name.'

'That *is* my real name,' replied Charles Jr, making his excuses and leaving.

For the first twelve months Charles made relatively little change to either the structure or operation of the group. He was, he declared, concerned to understand it thoroughly before making major moves. What he did not say was that, having acquired the business with the idea of building it up for resale, he was gradually becoming hooked by the opportunities it presented. 'Almost at the first board meeting you could tell he smelt the possibility of making the company a success,' recalls Gardiner.

The outgoing Sears' directors had regarded the shoe shops primarily as outlets for the production of the group's shoe factories. The shops were, historically, a result of vertical integration by the shoe producing business. Clore swiftly recognized that this was the wrong way round: that the real growth lay in making the shops drive the factories. In other words, to make what the customer wanted, rather than sell what the producer wanted to make. It is a lesson which many British companies have still not fully learnt.

The first step, however, lay in releasing the locked-up property assets. Sale and leaseback of high street properties to Legal & General raised £10 million. The deal involved a ninety-nine-year lease, with a fixed rental of 6 per cent per annum. Even when the main properties were sold, Charles reported to the annual general meeting in 1954, Sears still retained more than £3 million worth of freehold factories, warehouses and retail premises.

Of course, the leaseback deal meant that Sears would have to pay out considerable sums in annual rent – about £600,000 a year. But Charles saw this as just one more business expense. The freehold shop, he argued, was never really free because it was wasting cash that could be put to better uses and as such was really an opportunity cost. The successful business was one that could cover all its expenses, including the real cost of selling space, and still make a healthy profit. In his terms, he was making the shop managers face up to the commercial realities of their small operations.

But what was to be done with this cash windfall? In the annual report for 1953, Charles felt obliged to give an uncharacteristically lengthy statement of philosophy to the shareholders:

> The first call on this money will be the requirements of the footwear business to enable it to carry through the programme of improvements and expansion already mentioned. I do not anticipate, however, that this will absorb more than a small proportion of the total available.
>
> Now the policy that I have always had in mind has been based on my belief that it is not in the interests either of the shareholders or of the National Economy, for a Company such as ours to retain vast sums locked up in freehold properties effectively earning only a modest rental return. It is the investing institutions, such as the Insurance and Property Companies, Pension Funds and the like, who should be, and are, ready to provide the capital for this purpose. Our capital should be employed primarily in our own business of making and selling boots and shoes and if we have too much capital for this purpose we should seek some other outlet for our surplus resources where risk capital will be adequately rewarded and where benefits will accrue from the managerial skill which we believe we are able to contribute towards the conduct of any suitable undertaking or undertakings.
>
> It is, therefore, our intention to retain any surplus funds and to seek suitable employment for them by investing them in sound and progressive businesses. I do not wish to imply that it will be easy to find such businesses. We already have certain ideas in mind but it is too early to say anything about them yet and if they do not mature we may have to wait a long time before a suitable opportunity is presented. If necessary, we are prepared to wait a long time and meanwhile the money will earn only deposit rates of interest, so that shareholders must be patient if I cannot forecast increased dividends yet awhile.

The latter statements were not entirely true. Having now decided to keep the business rather than sell it off, Charles was already developing plans for what he was going to do with much of the money: he would use it to free the capital invested in his other interests. Accordingly, in September 1954 Sears acquired Haverton Holdings, the parent company of Furness shipyards. Sears also absorbed Bentley Engineering and a number of other Clore companies. Bill Bentley, chairman of Bentley and son of the company's founder, came onto the main board, as did Robert Boardman, the managing director of Furness.

71

Bentley had been acquired only a couple of months after Sears. This particular takeover was the result of a complex transaction. Charles had bought control of another knitting machine company, Wildt & Son, in 1949. But he did not get on well with Wildt himself, so an arrangement was made under which Bentley's larger firm absorbed Wildt and Bentley took over the management of both. Charles ended up with one-third of the Bentley shares and a seat on the board, then gradually bought up most of the remaining shares. By the mid 1960s the Bentley Group consisted of seventeen companies, most of them engaged in one aspect or another of the knitting machine industry. For a considerable time, Bentley was one of the stars in the Sears firmament. Bill Bentley, who had stayed on under the change of ownership, was determined to keep the atmosphere of the family business and largely succeeded.

A year later, Clore boosted Bentley yet again with the acquisition of another Leicester hosiery and textile machinery manufacturers, Mellor Bromley. This was a Sears bid in miniature. Clore made a bid of 11s 6d, for shares priced in the market at 9s 3d. His valuation was based on the fact that the company was earning 117 per cent annually on its ordinary shares, yet paying a dividend of only 36.5 per cent. The Mellor Bromley board advised shareholders to reject the offer, so Clore upped it to 15s, equivalent to £2.25 million in total. Investment Registry stressed the advantages of the merger with Bentley, in particular that research, servicing and sales promotion could be shared. Still the board rejected the offer, proposing to increase the dividend to 55 per cent accompanied with a 100 per cent script issue. The ploy failed to boost share prices to the level of Clore's offer because investors recognized that it was a ploy. Investment Registry played fair with the shareholders by allowing them to keep the board's unusually large final dividend. When the acceptances were totalled up, they amounted to 87 per cent of the equity. Clore then raised the cash to pay off the shareholders by issuing twelve million new shares in Bentley.

A flamboyant character (he drove a Bentley, of course), Bill Bentley established close links with Eastern Europe, which became a major market for his products. In a fiercely competitive international market, he increased the proportion of its output that went to export from 60 to 80 per cent between 1950 and 1960.

Bentley was his own man and was not prepared to kowtow to Charles, even if he had bought most of the company. Keeping Bentley under control was John Wegerif, who had been hired as joint managing director of Wildt & Son by Clore, and who had become assistant managing director of the Bentley Group when Wildt was taken over.

When Bill Bentley finally left the board in 1966, after a series of disagreements with Clore, the company was not performing well. One factory in Nottingham had had to close, prompting questions in the House and worker marches complete with banners declaiming 'Clored to death' and 'Gently Bentley'. The reason given for the closure was competition from the United States and the Continent in a saturated world market. Wegerif took over and immediately appointed his son Christopher to manage the sickest of the three divisions, seamless hosiery machinery. With Charles' encouragement, they invested in a separate development company and hired engineers from other disciplines, such as aviation, who introduced techniques previously unheard of in the industry, such as computer-aided design and high-speed photography. These investments put the company's technology far ahead of the competition and restored the sales fortunes in less than two years.

The Wegerifs were not content with technological innovation, however. They recognized that it was not enough to sell machinery on its technical excellence alone. So they persuaded major retailers such as Marks & Spencer to put samples through their rigorous consumer tests. With the endorsement of the retailers, the pressure on the manufacturers to buy the new machines was wellnigh irresistible.

The euphoria was not to last, however. Gradually the bottom dropped out of the knitting machinery market. Although the signs were clear that engineering was unlikely to be a growth sector again for many years to come, Charles hung on to the group. After his death, much of the engineering division, including the William Cotton factory in Loughborough – where the knitting machine industry started – was closed out of financial necessity. Today, not one of the Bentley companies remains within the Sears group.

By the time Haverton was incorporated into Sears in 1954, the group had been restructured into a holding company (Sears Holdings Ltd) and a subsidiary company, Freeman, Hardy & Willis. The latter now included all the shoe manufacturing operations as well as retail and operated through two divisions – FHW and Trueform. Much of the cash released by the asset sales went into improvements in the appearance of the shops and training of staff.

Some money also went into wage rises, of course, and here something of the man beneath the miserly image showed through. While other footwear manufacturers and retailers were complaining at having to increase wages, Charles, who knew what it was like to be poor and working class, wrote in his 1955 annual report:

> ... the increases which have been granted in the footwear manufacturing and retail trades have been no more than sufficient to keep them in step with the rising cost of living and with the increases granted in other industries such as transport and engineering.

During 1954, as all this reconstruction was taking place, FHW acquired Fortess Shoe Co., a down-market shoe retail chain. This was more than an addition of thirty high-street outlets; it was a deliberate attempt to introduce more dynamic retail management. Charles had watched Harry Levison put together his chain of footwear shops and had admired the young man's drive and imagination. This, he decided, was the kind of person he wanted to run his shoe empire. Levison, too, was keen to work with Charles, sensing the opportunity to create a much larger empire within Sears than he could on his own.

Once again the moving force behind the acquisition was Tovey and characteristically the deal was struck rapidly. Tovey brought Levison to see Charles at Park Street and the outline of a deal, under which Levison would take over all the standard shoe retail activities and Sears would buy out his business for £250,000, was quickly agreed. Gardiner refused to consider a higher price for Fortess. Levison said to him after the negotiations: 'You were too clever, you hit my bottom price.' That same evening Levison met with Gardiner to settle the financial details while Sainer worked on the legal side.

H. Bart-Smith, the solicitor who worked on the details of the transaction, recalls:

> We set up a scheme to avoid paying stamp duty. We sent a bill to Clore and mentioned what we had done. He telephoned to say: 'Just because you've saved me paying the state, it doesn't mean I've got to give it all to you.'

Later Fortess was renamed Curtess (the new name was chosen to cut the cost of repainting the whole of all the shop signs) and, shortly afterwards, FHW also acquired Philips Brothers Character Shoes Ltd for £700,000. The deal was much the same. The two Philips brothers would expand the fashion shoe side of Sears as Levison grew the standard shoes. Inevitably, this meant that they and Levison would have to work closely together. But Levison, a forceful man, clashed frequently with them. The uneasy relationship lasted six years before the Philips brothers (one of whom achieved notoriety from the frequency with which he pranged his private plane) quit and Levison took over the whole of the shoe retail business.

Then, in 1956, came Manfield and Dolcis, adding two further strings of shops. Within the space of four years, the footwear company had grown to encompass six major factories, a number of smaller factories and 1,500 retail shops. Like the Freeman Hardy shops, some were sold and leased back at a fixed rent, to be reviewed in fifty years. Dolcis also brought with it a half-share in a Canadian shoe retail chain, later sold at a profit. The shoe operations were now so large they needed an identity of their own, so Charles formed the British Shoe Corporation as an umbrella company. Our objective, he told shareholders, 'will be better quality, greater variety, more attractive styles and lower prices'.

Charles thus consolidated his hold on Leicester's two traditional businesses – shoes and textile equipment. When it was decided that British Shoes needed a home base, the Sears' board selected Leicester rather than Freeman Hardy's headquarters at Northampton.

Aware of the competitive advantage of modern, well-equipped warehousing, Charles determined to build the largest warehouse in the country. The first site selected was Freemen's Common. But negotiations with Leicester Corporation, which was to have built a dual carriageway across the common for access, broke down. Work eventually began at another site near Leicester, the forty-five-acre Braunstone Aerodrome which Levison had found. The one million square foot warehouse complex and six-storey office block contained the latest in automation and had seven miles of conveyor belt. Every shoe box that left the building contained a punched card, which the shoe shop would return for instant reordering. It was the kind of system Clore loved: original, effective and a great saving in time and effort.

Other acquisitions in these early stages of growth included Parmeko Ltd, a manufacturer of transformers for the electronic and electric industries. It was rapidly followed by Scottish Motor Traction and its subsidiary Alexander Findlay, a Scottish steel construction business.

SMT was cash-rich because its principal business, running Edinburgh's bus services, had been taken over by the city council. Its board had cast around for a new line of business and fastened on Vauxhall dealerships. The highly positive cash flow and relatively low overheads of this venture were just what Charles needed to finance further acquisitions.

Clore's bid for the company aroused all the passions of Scottish nationalism. It also brought him into conflict with the late Hugh Fraser (later Sir Hugh Fraser) of the House of Fraser. As usual, it was Tovey who brought the prospect to Charles' notice. He also floated it to several other clients, Fraser among them, to see who might be interested. Clore was first off the mark, offering a straight exchange of shares. Even if Fraser had not been strongly motivated to acquire SMT himself, the clamour of his countrymen would have been hard to resist. Many Scotsmen were strongly opposed to the idea that a Sassenach – let alone a Jewish Sassenach – should take over one of Scotland's most important enterprises.

The campaign was conducted from his home at 95 Park Street, where Clore was confined to bed with backache. Forced to lie on a board, he was obviously in pain and considerable discomfort. Sitting round the bedside at the regular meeting each morning were Gardiner, Tovey and, of course, an attractive young nurse. Being ill was a great frustration to Charles. Determined to carry on as usual, he had all calls diverted to his bedside, so the meeting was punctuated by conversations with people all over the world. Each time the telephone rang he would stretch out painfully to take the receiver. The tableau in the room would freeze as he listened, grunted and gave a brief yes or no to each caller. As the telephone went back to its rest, the conversation picked up where it had left off, as if the interruption had never happened.

The offer was a good one and the majority of the board were in favour of recommending it. However, the chairman, Sir John Primrose, was not. He was eventually replaced, on a formal vote, by another director, Sir Andrew Murray, but by this time the campaign was beginning to falter. Charles upped the stakes by offering to pay an extra 1s cash on all shares pledged within the week. He also blunted many of the nationalist objections by announcing that he would appoint the Earl of Elgin and Kincardine to the board. Fraser, who had been buying up all the shares he could muster, tipped in with an equal offer in House of Fraser shares.

Nationalism was no match for financial avarice, however. The shareholders were firmly convinced that the Sears' shares would be a more valuable buy. The day after Clore's improved offer, Sears was claiming more than 50 per cent acceptances. Fraser, unwilling to admit defeat and with 30 per cent of the shares either promised or in his hands, exercised his right to contact every shareholder in an attempt to persuade a sufficient proportion of those pledged to Sears to change their minds. However, it was now all over bar the shouting. Primrose had already issued a guarded statement congratulating Clore on the ingenuity of his bid approach. Murray had described the acquisition as 'quite remarkable'. In the press grudging acceptance turned to cautious welcome, with headlines such as 'Bonnie Prince Charlie comes to Scotland'.

It was preparation and forethought that won the day. As the retiring chief executive expressed it: 'The chips were stacked against us. Obviously Mr Clore has had his campaign mapped out for some time and his intelligence service exceptionally well-placed to give him inside information.'

The shouting did not stop, however. At the next annual general meeting in Edinburgh some eleven months later, the small shareholders launched a tirade of abuse at Clore. Sainer, as spokesman, sat in the chair. Charles sat sphinx-like at the side, refusing to comment as shareholder after shareholder denounced him for having taken the company over. The minority shareholders even voted against the dividend. One irate Scotsman referred to Charles as Ali Baba. With 62 per cent of the shares in Sears's pocket, however, every resolution was carried. Sainer and Clore then exited by a side door, leaving an excited and angry gathering behind.

Used to rushing through AGMs (ten minutes was the normal average for Clore companies) and acquiescent shareholders, Clore was both furious and resentful. Only on one other occasion did he suffer such calumny at an AGM, when shareholders of textile manufacturers Kaye & Stewart, which had not made reasonable profits for years, were up in arms about mismanagement. They had something to complain about. Charles had given the business to his brother David to run, in the hopes that it would keep him out of mischief. David, however, had little idea of how to manage a complex business and even less interest. He would much rather be on the racecourse, running up debts that Charles would occasionally have to settle. Charles lost his temper – all the more so because he knew the shareholders were right – and issued instructions the next day to buy in all the outstanding shares. Kaye & Stewart finally sank without trace in 1972, a victim of David's mismanagement and Charles' unwillingness to interfere.

The solution to the SMT affair was much the same. Charles negotiated with Fraser, the holder of the largest block of minority shares and agreed a price of 15s 3d. Fraser declared candidly:

> I don't say I am completely satisfied with the terms, but they are the best I can get in the circumstances. Being a minority shareholder, I am in a somewhat weak position. I am satisfied that, as things stood, Mr Clore did the best he could.

This deal gave Charles 90 per cent of the shares, allowing him to call the rest in automatically. Surprisingly, the contest and its aftermath did not create any bitterness between the two men. On the contrary, it brought about a close friendship that lasted until Fraser's death.

Over the next few years Charles collected nearly fifty Vauxhall distributorships around the country. Shaw & Kilburn was the first major such purchase south of the border and it was shortly followed by Carmo, which held distributorships in Wales. The car dealerships were intended to become a third arm of Sears.

The results of all this activity became clear by 1956, when Clore was able to tell shareholders:

> Until three years ago Sears was dependent wholly on the footwear trade for its prosperity and in 1952 the trading profits amounted to £1,135,000. Today the diverse interests of Sears cover basic industries, wide manufacturing activities in both capital and consumer goods and a large retail organization. By 1955 the group trading profits had increased to almost £4,300,000. In 1952 the amount of net profit retained in the business was under £100,000. Last year, although the proposed ordinary dividend is 20

per cent, compared with an effective 12 per cent in 1952, the undistributed profits retained in the business (excluding pre-acquisition profits) amounted to over £1,000,000.

Only a year later, profits of the shoe operations alone had trebled compared with the year of the takeover and the group profits exceeded £6 million. (By 1984, Sears' dividends per share had reached seventy-three times their 1953 value, while the value of the shares had grown by more than 100 times.)

One significant aspect of this acquisition spree was that most of the deals were by agreement. Most businesses that were worth acquiring had good management; after all an absence of good management is the first stage of decline. If there was good management in place, then it made sense to keep it. Although he enjoyed the rough and tumble of the contested bid, Charles usually tried to get the board of the target company on his side first.

For the next few years, Sears concentrated on internal growth rather than growth by acquisition. There were still acquisitions, of course, but none of any great size. The group was on the verge of indigestion and needed time to consolidate and improve the businesses it had.

By 1962, however, more opportunities arose in the shoe business, in the form of Saxone and Lilley & Skinner. Both were long-established businesses. Saxone had been started by two brothers, Frank and George Abbott, at the beginning of the century. They had the idea of providing mass-produced shoes in a sufficient variety of fittings to suit the individual's foot – then a complete novelty. They joined forces in 1928 with a Scottish shoe manufacturer, George Clark of Kilmarnock, who had built up a considerable export trade in quality shoes. Thomas Lilley started business in 1835, and it was his son who brought into the company his brother-in-law William Skinner in 1881. Like Saxone, it had substantial interests overseas, in the English-speaking Commonwealth. These two companies were clearly suited to each other. As Clore began to build up British Shoe, they saw their best chances of independent survival in pooling their interests, which they did in 1957. The merger created the second largest UK shoe retail chain, with 475 shops and five factories.

Independence did not last long, however. Charles, in now characteristic fashion, bided his time as he acquired a 25 per cent stake in the merged company through nominees. When the time was ripe, he launched his £30 million bid – and gobbled them both. Aubrey Orchard-Lisle, of Healey & Baker, accompanied the chairman of Lilley & Skinner, Jack Abbott, when he visited Park Street for the first time. As they left, Abbott, who was very much the Scottish laird in character, turned to Orchard-Lisle and said: 'You took me in to see a financier, but I found myself talking to a merchant.'

That same year Charles was invited to become president of the Boot Trade Benevolent Society and, to the surprise of many people in the trade who were unaware of his charitable activities, he accepted. *The Shoe and Leather News* obtained a rare interview on the strength of the appointment, but the interviewer came away with little more than a series of monosyllabic replies to his questions. The conversation went like this:

> *How can the public be said to benefit if shoe prices remain stable but quality is downgraded to meet rising costs and also to provide higher mark-ups?*
> The questioner misunderstands the facts.
> *The immense buying power of the British Shoe Corporation now has an almost terrifying influence on some sections of the manufacturing industry, due to its capacity for placing or withholding contracts and exerting downward pressure on prices. Do you think it right that prices should be depressed below a level of profitability for the producer?*
> Being large manufacturers on our own account, we are able to gauge a fair price for our purchases and all keen manufacturers are able to do profitable business with us and are glad to have the long runs of manufacture we are able to give.
> *Should the buying power thus occurring be used to jeopardize the economy of other sections of the trade?*
> No and it is not so used.
> *With a large proportion of footwear distribution under its control, is not the BSC in a very strong position to influence fashion trends and public taste? Could not this power be used creatively to stimulate British designing?*
> We do not seek to influence fashion, but prefer to supply our customers with what they want. So far as possible we do, in fact, seek to stimulate British designing.
> *With the prospect of Britain entering the Common Market, do you contemplate BSC opening a chain of shoe stores on the Continent? Or entering into merger arrangements with European shoe multiples?*
> I cannot discuss our possible plans under the circumstances indicated.

In truth, being outside the trusted circle of journalists, the interviewer was lucky to have received any comments at all.

Had he dared, the interviewer might have asked about Charles' own shoes. Made of expensive crocodile skin, for some reason they attracted more press comment that summer than his business activities. Quite what he would have made of this cold, unmovable man a few weeks later, had he seen Charles taking lessons in the twist from a twenty-six-year-old cabaret artiste can only be imagined. Said the twist expert: 'He is quite good, but has a very conservative approach to it.'

One major shoe chain did escape his net at this time. In September 1964, Charles launched a bid for W. Barratt & Co., an independent shoe retail chain, whose board rapidly made it clear that they preferred to remain independent. Its motto, appropriately, was 'Walk the Barratt Way'. When it became clear that complete independence was not possible, the board opted for a lower bid by Stylo Shoes, on the grounds that a merger of this size was more palatable than being swallowed up in the Sears' machine. The Barratt directors and the pension fund managers, who controlled around 48 per cent of the shares, pledged their support to Stylo and advised other shareholders to do the same, even though the discrepancy between the two bids was high. To finance the acquisition, Stylo had to make a new rights issue. Charles took the unprecedented step of appealing to the Stock Exchange to refuse to allow the Stylo shares to be quoted. The request was rejected. A High Court application also met with short shrift. Charles admitted defeat and refused to make his offer unconditional. It was not a good week for him. Only a few days later shares in his property firm, City Centre, plunged to an all-time low of 29s 6d. Even shares in Sears Holdings, with record profits in prospect, were down nearly 40 per cent.

This failure left British Shoe with cash to spend on acquisitions. Unfortunately, there was nothing else left to buy at a price Charles was prepared to pay. 'We have not found anything, which fulfils the essential requirements of not being overpriced, of being suitable for integration within the British Shoe Corporation and being capable of improvement and expansion,' he lamented, suggesting that the cash would probably have to be spent on other sectors or on acquisitions overseas.

Charles' buying spree in shoe shops came to a halt in 1972, when his bid for William Timpson was referred to the Monopolies Commission. In this case he was acting as a white knight, the Sears' bid having been prompted by an unwelcome and not particularly generous bid for Timpson's by United Drapery Stores. UDS had recently been rebuffed in an attempt to buy Debenhams. It had also tried to muscle in on the mail-order business by acquiring the firm of A. & S. Henry, only to be elbowed out by Sir Isaac Wolfson of Great Universal Stores. The UDS board, however, was not fainthearted. Having looked at the retail scene, it saw that the boom in shoe sales that Charles had long predicted was well under way and decided it would try to build up its own nationwide chain of shoe shops on much the same lines as British Shoe.

UDS opened the bidding at £17.3 million and was quickly forced to increase its offer to £26 million as Sears began to buy at whatever price it could, forcing the market price well above the UDS initial offer. Having acquired 16 per cent of the equity, Charles weighed in with an offer worth more than £29 million. It looked as though UDS had met another brick wall. But then the Monopolies Commission stepped in, on the grounds that British Shoe's turnover was the equivalent of a 29 per cent share of the whole British retail shoe market, and 44 per cent of the shoes sold through multiples. British Shoe's actual share of the market was rather less, for the turnover figures included all shoe manufacture and distribution. British Shoe might well have gained Monopolies Commission approval in due course, but for the time being was unable to proceed with its bid. The field was therefore left clear for UDS.

Sainer was livid, having expected both companies to be referred. From here on, he made it clear, the Sears group would not be seeking to expand its British shoe interests. Charles echoed the same theme at the extraordinary general meeting he had called to gain shareholders' approval to increase the equity by 20 million new shares, worth £30 million. The shareholders approved the motion to raise the cash anyway, on the grounds that it would not take Charles long to find something else to bid for.

By this time the nature of the British shoe industry had changed. Cheaper imports were putting all but the most efficient shoe manufacturers out of business. British Shoe, too, was reducing its emphasis on own production, to the extent that only 12 per cent of the women's shoes its outlets sold came from its own factories. The decision was clear. Sears would stay in the business, but the days of rapid growth and expansion of shoe interests were well and truly over.

Moreover, the interests of the group were now widely diversified, with shoes accounting for only about 40 per cent of group turnover. The engineering business had continued to expand during the late 1950s and 1960s, as had the car dealerships.

One of Clore's boldest attempts to diversify was his foray into the brewing industry through the abortive and contentious bid in 1959 for Watney Mann. The brewing industry was a sleeping giant, with vast, underused property assets and enormous potential. It was also a bastion of the industrial establishment, a symbol of everything solid in British business. Charles dared to challenge the cosiness of what was known as 'the beerage and the peerage', the tight-knit clique of families that had ruled Britain's pubs from oak-panelled boardrooms. He did so with at least a twinge of revenge, for only shortly before had he been incensed when Colonel Whitbread, of Whitbread Breweries, referred to him as a 'financial marauder'.

As a significant shareholder in the company already, Charles had taken a keen interest in the Stag Brewery site, which was ripe for redevelopment. The Watney management seemed disinterested in the value of the assets it was sitting on, although it had in fact commissioned a property revaluation. Charles also saw great potential in brightening up pubs and breaking the monopolies that many brewery chains exercised against independent suppliers of soft drinks and snacks. 'We feel that pubs should be modernized – not turned into enormous gin palaces but into a comfortable lounge and bar,' said Sears. Modernizing shops with good lighting, carpets and attractive decor had been good news for the retail trade, so why should the same not work for pubs? It was an idea ten years ahead of its time, although many of the public instantly sympathized with the aim of 'making the pub a place to take the wife'.

Simon Combe, the Watney chairman, was a crusty individual, a snob of the first water. An old Etonian and war hero (he served in the Guards), his was the fifth generation of the brewing family. The establishment closed ranks around him to beat off Clore's 'preposterous and deplorable' approach. Was nothing sacred? This time the impertinent Mr Clore had gone too far. There was even a special poem of protest composed for the occasion:

Lines on a Take-Over Bid

All agree that Mr Clore
May be quite within the lore
In insisting there's no roombe
For himself and Mr Coombe.
See how Watney's shares all boombe,
See the market prices sore
In this mighty tug-of-wore.
But the more they rise, the more
Boozers gloombe.

Mr Watney! Mr Reid!!
Do, we beg you, inteceid!
Pray prevail on Mr Coombe.
Horrible perspectives loombe!
Every pub a drawing-roombe?
If the Clore Plan should succeid
Watney stalwarts are agreeid
In a body to seceid
From this doombe.

Whitbreads, Charringtons or Meux
Will not offer mute rebeux
With loose-covers of glazed chintz
Which make every toper wintz.
Do accept these friendly hintz.
Be we Dustmen be we Deux
Every elbow-lifter peux
At the thought of beer and jeux.
So don't mintz

Any words with Mr Clore.
Keep things as they were before!
Let Red Barrel be the sign
Of a place where men may dign,
Sip their bitter, gin or wign.
Let's have sawdust on the flore
And let hearty tapsters drore
Honest liquor, then no more
We'll repign.

In the end, it was the market itself that defeated the bid. At 60s a share, Charles had calculated that it would be possible to make a good return on investment. The assets were quite clearly undervalued. But the punters had learnt some lessons from his earlier bids. They also looked at the assets. By the time the 13,000 letters to shareholders arrived for posting from Sears' head office, speculators had pushed the shares up to 75s. Indeed the rise, by just over 20s, took place in seconds after the bid was announced as the Stock Exchange floor seethed with buy orders. 'We are not going to pay a preposterous price,' said Sainer. 'We know what Watney's is worth. But it may be that we shall have to review our offer when the stock markets have settled down.'

Eventually a truce was arranged by Lionel Fraser (known as 'the bishop' because of his white hair), who was an influential banker with Helbert Wagg and a trustee of the Tate Gallery. Fraser acted as neutral chairman for a meeting between Charles and Simon Combe. Fraser told Clore bluntly that unless he raised his offer well above 60s, he would not win. Charles insisted that his valuation of the assets was correct and that he would not go higher. An 'armistice agreement' was issued that afternoon, signed by both Clore and Combe, announcing that 'Friendly discussions have taken place and Sears Holdings Ltd have decided now not to proceed with their proposed offer to the Watney Mann stockholders.'

Charles' anger came to the boil later that week when he attended the film première of John Osborne's *Look Back in Anger*. Accompanied by a woman six inches taller than himself, he found the way to his seat barred by an irascible cinema attendant, who insisted 'You can't come in here, Sir, you'll have to go down the stairs and round the other way.' To Dan the attendant it mattered not that Mr Clore was about to be presented to Princess Margaret. He had his orders. To Charles, being brooked twice in one week was too much. Theatre officials were called and the irate little man barged his way through to his seat. 'I don't think I've enjoyed a fight so much for years,' wrote the *Daily Herald*'s Henry Fielding, who had been observing the exchange with unconcealed glee.

Disappointing as it may have been, Sears none the less came out of the affair richer than it went in. Having forced the Stock Market to revalue the shares, it was now able to resell those Clore had bought at 50s or less for a very substantial profit. For Simon Combe, victory was dearly bought, for he now had to justify to shareholders the extra value they placed upon the shares.

It was about this time that the story arose of the young man in the Savoy, who appealed to Clore's better nature. Would Clore pretend to know him as he passed by? It would be most helpful in sealing his own first big deal. Clore agreed. He dutifully stopped by the young man's table as he got up to leave, only to be sharply rebuffed with: 'Get lost, Charlie. Can't you see I'm busy?' The tale, since adapted to fit a wide range of notables, circulated widely.

What would Charles do with the £10 million he had set aside for Watney? The length and breadth of the City, company chairmen began to make preparations in case they were next on the list, revaluing properties, reassessing dividend policy and looking for ways to stream-line their operations. The beer barons in the Brewers' Society met in secret session and instigated plans to modernize some pubs, using the money from selling off others. They also arranged a complex series of interlocking shares that would act as a defence against future attacks from outside and examined how they could increase efficiency by amal-gamations of their own. Charles, however, was no longer interested in brewing.

The brewing industry could never be the same again, however. Where Charles had led, others followed. Amalgamations, mergers and take-overs over the following years changed the face of the industry entirely. 'Brewery shareholders should be grateful to Santa Clore,' remarked the *Evening Standard*. 'He has done them a service. He has shattered the complacency of the industry. I expect to see this reflected in future dividend cheques.'

Many speculators expected Charles to pitch into the fierce struggle for Harrods, between House of Fraser and Debenhams. Again, he refrained, for the contest was pushing the shares too high for his liking. Instead, he won a different prize, the jewellers Mappin & Webb, which fell into his lap later that same year. The snob appeal of owning this particular business roused his interest, but the commercial prospects were what influenced his judgement. Not only could the shops be made to turn in a healthy trading profit, if well managed, but there were substantial, underused property assets.

The Mappin & Webb acquisition came about through Edgar Astaire, the stockbroker brother of Clore's friend Jarvis. Jarvis was married to the daughter of a wealthy property developer called Oppenheim, who had owned the majority holding in the jewellery firm. Jarvis and his brother had been slowly acquiring shares. When they owned the majority, they invited Clore to buy the business.

This was one of the few occasions, however, when news of the impending bid for the rest of the shares leaked. Even though Mappin & Webb announced trading losses, its price continued to move up, shooting in one day from 28s to 38s and eventually reaching 47s 6d. But Charles, having already secured the majority of shares he needed, wasn't playing that game. He obtained his revenge and dumbfounded the speculators by offering only 20s for the A-shares and 27s 6d for the ordinary shares. For once, instead of deprecating his behaviour, most observers warmly approved. The *Evening News* commented on 'this new bid technique':

> The Stock Exchange gamblers who specialize in buying shares likely to be in the takeover news in the hope of being able to make a quick turn have been shocked by the new tactics. It has hit them where it hurts most – in their pockets.
>
> But I find little sympathy for them among my broking friends. Without exception, they applaud Mr Clore's action and take the view that he has done the House a service by giving the 'in and out brigade' a lesson that will not be forgotten for a long time.

The *Financial Times* added: 'Mr Clore has proved . . . that hanging onto his coat-tails in a bid situation is a dangerous occupation.'

Of course, that didn't stop people from trying. On one occasion even the upright Miss Gelman could not resist the opportunity to buy a few of the shares that Charles was investing in heavily. Breathlessly, she rang Charles Jr, then a stockbroker, and asked him to buy a considerable quantity, in her terms, of the same shares. Charles Jr and half the rest of the family jumped on the bandwagon. All of them lost money, for when the tycoon himself unloaded his holding at the top of the cycle, the price of the shares collapsed.

Having obtained one chain of jewellers, Charles started looking for others. He swiftly focused on Garrard, the Queen's jewellers, and added it to his collection.

Charles now had a solid portfolio of blue-chip businesses, but he was still looking for the jewel in his crown. He found it in 1965, in London's prestigious department store, Selfridges.

6

Selfridges

'Nothing's too big. If we are going to start
thinking like that, we might as well shut up
shop now.' Charles Clore

As a keen observer of the US business scene, Charles was sure that the retailing boom there would sooner or later make its way across the Atlantic. In particular, he could sense the move away from traditional high-street shops towards the big stores. This led him, in the early 1960s, to eye the major stores and store chains. Undoubtedly the most prestigious of London stores was (and still is) Harrods. But Harrods was unavailable, having already been snapped up after a fierce battle by the Fraser family, so Charles fixed his eye on the next most valuable retail property, Selfridges. It was a property he already knew well, having been thwarted in an attempt to buy it some years before, when Gordon Selfridge died.

Selfridges had been founded in 1909 by Harry Gordon Selfridge, a Canadian, who learnt his storekeeping in Chicago, where he opened his first department store. The famous London store that bears his name was built on what was considered to be the 'dead' end of Oxford Street. Selfridge aimed to make his store 'the third biggest attraction for sight-seers in London' (the first two being Buckingham Palace and the Tower) and arguably succeeded. Until his death he held a friendly rivalry with Harrods. He even wagered the chairman of Harrods a silver model of the loser's store that he would outstrip Harrods in sales. He never did, but the wager was honoured by his son.

Gordon Selfridge, who used to walk the floors of his store every day, was a fearsome character with a soft heart. One morning, as he made his rounds, he noticed a young man waiting outside the buyer's office. With him were samples of the trousers from his father's workshop. That day and for many days previously, he had tramped the stores of London, waiting to be seen, struggling to obtain orders. An hour and a half later, Selfridge passed by again. 'What are you waiting for?' asked the great man. The young Charles stood up and explained. 'How long have you been here?' Charles told him. Selfridge sent for the buyer. 'Give this young man an order,' he instructed him and swept away. It was the only order the Clore tailoring business ever got from the store.

In 1947 Gordon Selfridge died. Four years later the company was run down and making a loss. Charles had his eye on the site as one of the most valuable property developments in the West End and asked the Selfridges board for a list of names and addresses of shareholders. Although there were severe restrictions in force concerning redevelopment, it was rumoured that Charles wanted to leave only the basement and ground floor as sales areas and turn the rest of the building into offices. In fact, what he had in mind was to rebuild the store, making it much larger and extending, as Gordon Selfridge himself had once planned, all the way to Wigmore Street. In addition, there would have been a car park on the top and two office blocks on the site. Clore and Sainer visited the Selfridges board on Friday afternoon, shook hands on a deal and left under the impression that all that remained was to settle the details and make the announcement to the press.

He was so confident that the deal was agreed that he told Sainer not to draw up the contract until the Monday. In fact, the Selfridges board members were so horrified they began to look for a rescuer. Lewis' Investment Trust Ltd (no relation to the John Lewis Partnership), which owned a number of provincial department stores, had flirted with Selfridges during the war. Over the weekend the Selfridges board visited Lewis' chairman, Lord Woolton, and managing director Rex Cohen, at their office in Liverpool.

The two sides agreed on the spot to a deal, under which the store remained intact, but some of the land to the north was to be sold off for development. (Charles pitched hard for this contract, too, but the Selfridges board would have nothing to do with him and the deal went to Max Rayne instead.)

The first that Clore and Sainer knew of the new deal was the announcement on Monday morning that Selfridges had agreed to be sold to Lewis'. Clore's reaction: 'Never let me shake hands with anyone again on a deal.' He felt totally betrayed. Always a patient man in such matters, he opted to bide his time until the opportunity emerged to extract his revenge.

Selfridges was also attractive because it was in Oxford Street. Although he never joined the Oxford Street Association, Clore owned a substantial proportion of the premises along what he believed to be the premier shopping street in Europe. With good management, he was convinced, Oxford Street could become the top shopping area in the world.

Over the following years, Charles kept buying small amounts of Lewis' shares until he had 8 per cent. Then Sainer went in with a firm

87

proposal. Cohen reacted angrily and almost threw Sainer out. Lewis' had belonged to his family since 1864 and he had no intention of relinquishing control now. The £63 million bid, which gave shareholders a variety of choices of cash and British Shoe shares, was launched a few days later. The offer document compared the performance of the two companies, pointing out that, whereas British Shoe Corporation's profits before tax had risen 48 per cent between 1963 and 1965, Lewis' had only gone up 1 per cent. The warning signs had been out for Cohen since 1963, when the *Sunday Express* drew unfavourable comparison between Lewis' results and those of Marks & Spencer and Great Universal Stores and suggested that it might do better under Wolfson or Clore.

For a while the bid hovered on the edge of success. Charles extended the deadline for acceptances by a week and added another 1s as a sweetener. Even Cohen had to admit the offer was fair. On 23 November, British Shoe announced it had gained control. Three days later Cohen met the victors at Lewis' London office in Duke Street, and showed them into the boardroom. He then shook them by the hand, said goodbye and drove off, leaving the family business behind him.

It was when Charles took over Lewis' that he made his famous statement: 'I don't tear things down or break them up. I build them up.' And this he set out to do, budgeting £1 million for improvements to the store alone.

To Charles' eye there were several obvious ways in which Selfridges and its site could make an increased return on investment. The first was the store itself, which had been gradually run down over the preceding years. It needed brightening up, the energies of staff rechannelled, the asset made to pay its way more effectively. Charles set to with a will. Selfridges was immediately 'my shop' and he was a frequent presence on the sales floor, making a tour almost every afternoon when he was in London. For many of the staff, the presence of this dour little man, asking questions, was unsettling. But it demonstrated that he was truly interested in the store and what happened to it. Charles wanted Selfridges to be the best of its kind and was determined to make it so.

While tackling some of the obvious improvements, Charles was looking closely at the land around the main store building. There was a garage, run under a management contract with the Lex company, an extension in Duke Street to which Selfridges staff gave the unattractive name of SWOD, the dilapidated food store and a relatively small amount of surrounding land, which could only be used for minor purposes, such as a small garden centre.

A clause in the garage contract allowed Selfridges to bring the operation back under its own control by paying a reasonable recompense to

Lex. This was done swiftly, on the grounds that anything with the Selfridges name on it should be managed by the store itself.

What could be added to the Selfridges formula to bring young people back through its doors? After much discussion, Clore and his team decided it had to be fashion. It was Leonard Sainer who came up with the new name, as he and Charles were walking outside the Miss Bonwit store in New York. 'What about Miss Selfridge?' he suggested. 'Done,' said Charles. And it was.

In selecting who should run this new venture Charles had another of his brilliant character insights. It needed a woman, one with fashion sense, drive and an ability to do what she knew was right. The ideal person was already working for the John Lewis group, having joined the company as personnel assistant to the managing director of Peter Jones. She was Winifred Sainer, the younger of Leonard's two sisters.

Winifred Sainer's impact upon Selfridges was swift and extensive. Her approach to fashion retailing was imaginative and innovative. Her target audience was young girls aged sixteen to twenty-one. To bring them in, she set her stamp upon every aspect of the new department, from the decor and the music to the selection of both buyers and suppliers. This was the first store to have piped music.

One of her coups was to bring over the French designer Pierre Cardin to London. She worked with him personally in selecting materials and styles that would appeal to fashion conscious British women. Cardin was contracted to produce four Selfridges collections a year, to sell within a set price range.

The new department had to be both part of Selfridges and yet have a separate entrance, so that customers did not have to troop through the perfumes and pens to reach it. The SWOD, an area bounded by Somerset Street, Wigmore Street, Orchard Street and Duke Street, made the ideal site. Originally built in 1933 as part of an ambitious plan to extend the store, it had never been fully completed. The basement had been used as a communications centre during the war, while the ground floor had been taken over by the Post Office for a sorting area when its local office was bombed. The building was finally vacated in 1965 and the old Lewis' management looked at turning it into a carpet shop.

Charles thought this was a waste of valuable space. There were, after all, specialist chains of cheap carpet shops springing up across the country. It made much more sense, he concluded, to introduce something really new. Winifred Sainer spent lavishly but carefully in making the most of the inherited building, insisting from the start that Miss Selfridge, as a separate operation, should have its own stockrooms, staff and administration.

Charles gave me [she recounts] a completely free rein to develop the idea
and I was soon convinced that it was a winner. It was the first time anyone
thought of using a big store in this way, to attract the free spending young
shoppers by offering them everything under one roof.... Fashion moves so
quickly and our stocks are changing all the time, so we need the freedom to
act swiftly without being held back by the traditional methods of mer-
chandizing usually adopted in big stores.

It was a lesson that other parts of the company needed to learn, as the
incident of the square-toed shoes demonstrated. In 1962, Charles
ascribed a 4 per cent fall in British Shoe profits to what he called the
'square toe débâcle'. The problem arose because British Shoe had seen
what it thought was a new fashion trend, in the United States and on the
Continent. But the trend proved to be no more than a short-term fad and
British Shoe found itself with an unsaleable inventory of 200,000 pairs.
Charles blamed the fashion writers, who had enthused over the new
style, predicting that square-toed shoes would be all the rage during the
summer. The fashion writers hit back, pointing out that British Shoe
simply moved too slowly. By the time it had the shoes in the shops, the
fashion had moved on. Charles was not amused.

The incident had its silver lining, however, in that it demonstrated
how swiftly British Shoe had to move to keep up with the fashion
business. New systems were rapidly introduced, which allowed the
company to have new styles in stock within six weeks.

After twelve months' trading, the Miss Selfridge store on the ground
floor in Oxford Street had made a £1 million turnover. It had also
contributed significantly to a 12 per cent increase in fashion sales in
other departments in the store. A year later there were seven Miss
Selfridge departments in Lewis' stores across the country and plans for a
high-street chain of Miss Selfridge shops. The contrast with the rather
stuffy, traditional flavour of the stores was instantly noticeable. That,
said Charles, was a good thing: 'It gives everyone something to live up to
and is a faster way of goading people into action than nagging.'

Selfridges' London rival, Harrods, was forced into a 'me-too', in the
form of a fourth-floor department named 'Way In'. These departments in
the two stores were the distant forbears of today's high fashion chains
such as Next and Top Shop.

Winifred Sainer, described as 'the only tycoon in the rag trade, who
can still take dictation at 120 words and type at eighty words a minute',
stayed with Sears for seven years. Then she got bored. The whole
operation simply grew too big, she explained, so that responsibility was
shared between a host of executives. 'That's when the job lost its excitement, its challenge. And that's when I decided to quit.' After a two-year

break, travelling the world, she returned to the fashion business to run Britain's largest blouse manufacturer.

The food store had to be rebuilt, it was clear. But could a better use be made of the site? On investigation, Sainer discovered that there had previously been a hotel there and that it should therefore be possible to obtain planning permission for another. Selfridges Hotel was soon under construction and, in spite of a pay strike by the site workers in 1972, was completed by the middle of that year. The unusual building retained a food store in the ground floor, with the hotel facilities above.

Alan French, as chairman of Selfridges' buyers' council, was the only middle manager to meet Clore, Sainer and Gardiner as they toured the store for the first time under Sears ownership. The four stood and discussed the store's problems among the pots and pans of the hardware department, which French ran. Having left three years later for a job elsewhere, French was brought back by Selfridges' managing director, Edward McClean, as his successor designate. French stipulated that he wanted Clore's approval first. This time they met in the more sombre surroundings of the Park Street office. He recalls:

> It was not a formal interview in any way. Miss Gelman showed me in and I suppose we talked for ten minutes. None of it was memorable. I think he was more interested in my personality than my experience. We shook hands and two or three days later I got the offer letter from Mac. I restarted in Selfridges on 1 February 1971.

The decision, so far as Clore was concerned, was McClean's. He just needed to feel sure about an important appointment.

During the next five years the two men had to deal with each other frequently. Here is how French describes Clore's management style:

> Charles Clore appeared to be hard and ruthless, a man of few words and essentially shy. Although many of the managers of the store avoided him, their fear was entirely misplaced. He was essentially a much kinder man than he got credit for. In my entire time in Selfridges I was not aware that he sacked anybody. Over the years he and I had substantial arguments about Selfridges' tactics: we always agreed about strategy. The argument was always in his office or mine – no witnesses. I never argued with him at meetings or in public. I think we respected each other. He certainly did not want 'yes' men. I believe he accepted my views because I and my team gave him the results. If I was able to talk to Sir Charles direct there were no problems. On one occasion when he thought I had been a bit intransigent he patted me on the shoulder and said 'Let me talk to you like a father.' He gave me a little lecture about not upsetting people, but I don't believe I ever upset him.

Selfridges' sixtieth birthday came round in 1969. For Charles this was an opportunity to celebrate in extravagant style. Here, for once, he became directly involved in the detailed planning. The theme, of course, had to be diamonds, he insisted. The shopping halls were hung with hundreds of cascades of silvery diamond shapes and there was a major exhibition of expensive glitter by de Beers. Also on show was the famous silver model of Harrods, won by the rival store forty years before. (It should have been a model of Selfridges, but the winner requested it be of his own building.) Into the celebrations were drawn a host of the talented and the famous, from Mary Quant to Clement Freud.

The store came to mean a great deal to Clore. His pride in it almost matched that of Selfridge himself. On one occasion, when he was dining with a number of friends, including his frequent companion, Max Rose, the bachelor stockbroker from South Africa, Rose leaned across the table and asked, 'Did you know that Selfridges' coffee is the dearest in London?' Charles said it wasn't. Rose repeated that it was. A slanging match began to develop across the table. Suddenly Charles pushed back his chair, asked for his hat and coat and stalked out, leaving behind a stunned silence. The incident was never mentioned again. Yet the next morning the price of coffee at Selfridges had fallen appreciably.

William Hill, the bookmakers, which then had a chain of 550 shops, came into the stable in 1971, shortly after the death of Hill himself, at a cost of £21 million. Considering the keen interest that both Clore and Sainer now had in horse-racing, it was not a surprising acquisition. Moreover, it was attractive to Sears because of its positive cash flow. This was an expanding business area, which could finance other group activities and, indeed, both Ladbrokes and Coral were using their excess cash flow to diversify into hotels, property and casinos. The impetus, however, almost certainly came from Jarvis Astaire, whose own betting company had been absorbed into William Hill not long before. Yet only ten years before, when a change in the law had permitted the establishment of legalized betting shops, Clore had angrily rejected the idea that Investment Registry should handle the flotation of Joe Coral's bookmaking business, declaring: 'I don't want to be involved with bookmaking. It's a terrible business. It's not respectable.'

Now clearly respectable enough, the bookmaking business was expanded with the acquisition of Windsors (Sporting Investments) only six months later. The agreement to buy a second chain of betting shops caught the market on the hop. A Clore classic, the deal involved buying 66 per cent of the equity of Windsors (Sporting Investments) from the chairman, Jim Windsor, and his family trusts for £2.9 million. Only when this deal was signed and sealed did the news break to the small shareholders, who were advised by Windsors' stockbrokers to sell out. Coral Leisure and Ladbrokes, the main rivals of William Hill, were greatly angered at this coup, for their previous offers to the seventy-five-year-old Windsor had been rebuffed.

By the mid 1970s the Sears Group was established in four major sectors of business, each supporting the other: shoes, engineering, vehicle distribution and general retail.

In so far as the shoe business was concerned, the strategy was clear – to dominate the marketplace and achieve economies of scale. For Sears as a whole, however, the strategy was to create a diversified group where a downturn in one area of business would be balanced by the well-being of the others. In practice this worked fairly well. For a while, for example, engineering supported the retail side. The Bentley interests had a number of exceptional years, due at least in part to their good relations with Eastern bloc countries, such as Poland, from which there were frequent large orders. Charles' friendship with Dr Armand Hammer, of Occidental, one of the few American industrialists to be *persona grata* in Moscow, was helpful here, although Bentley already had close relationships with Eastern bloc countries dating from the 1940s. Later, when the roles were reversed, retailing took up the slack as the engineering companies felt the blast of international competition. This diversity meant that no business area was safe from the predatory Sears. Moreover, Sears was in so many businesses that there were always opportunities for dramatic acquisitions to reinforce an existing area of business as circumstances made it more interesting.

On one occasion, Clore asked the present chairman, Geoffrey Maitland Smith, 'Why don't we take over Boots?'

'It's too big,' was the reply.

'Nothing's too big. If we are going to start thinking like that, we might as well shut up shop now.'

In the event, many of Charles' ideas never came off. In the early 1970s, for instance, Sears held secret discussions with British American Tobacco and Commercial Union, but nothing ever came from either talks.

In effect, Clore created the first true industrial conglomerate in Britain. He was the first to demonstrate that good management, in the form of effective leadership, sound financial controls and a high degree of autonomy for major operating units could be the glue to hold a variety of disparate companies together. Although the conglomerate theory has increasingly been questioned in recent years, it certainly worked for him. Those conglomerates, which ran into serious problems in their diversifications in the 1970s, did so primarily because the leadership failed to identify the true value of the assets they were buying and because they lacked both the flair to choose the right person to run the business and the confidence to leave him to it.

Many conglomerates were simply managed into ineffectiveness by top managements who thought they knew more about running a business than people who had worked in it for a lifetime. Charles was one of the few industrialists who frequently *did* know more about the industry than those who had grown up in it – he acquired an almost encyclopaedic knowledge of whatever business he became involved in, by reading, by listening and by observing – yet he left the running of those businesses to a handful of people in whose competence he had absolute trust. With few exceptions, that trust was amply justified.

While some of the acquisitions had overseas subsidiaries and interests, Sears itself made no serious attempts to expand abroad until 1964, when it suddenly launched a £6 million bid for Consolidated Laundries, a New York linen hire company. The money was to be raised from New York banks, who charged more competitive interest rates. Consolidated was hardly in a growth sector of the economy and, in comparison with its major US rivals, it was certainly not a dynamic performer. In spite of the speculation over why Sears should buy such an uninspiring business, Sears A shares shot up 4s 5d. There was a tenuous link with the existing group – Brown & Green, a Bentley subsidiary, manufactured dry cleaning and laundry equipment – but the main attraction was the chance to be quoted, at relatively little cost, on the New York Stock Exchange. Sears was careful to bid for only 75 per cent of the shares, to ensure it retained its listing. This, to the investment community, was a clear sign that the acquisition was to be a springboard for more exciting ventures.

Sears' interest in the United States was prompted to a considerable extent by the lack of acquisition opportunities in Britain at the time. Charles had declared some time before that the prices of the more progressive firms had now risen so high that they 'fully anticipated the likely improvements in earnings in the next few years'. To interest Sears, any takeover target had to be capable of showing an increased contribution relatively quickly. The problem was, suggested the *Birmingham Post*:

> Mr Clore's career as a takeover bidder has encouraged imitators, pushed directors into paying more generous dividends and increasing their companies' efficiency and alerted the Stock Exchange to the possibilities of greater profits concealed in many firms' balance sheets.

The search for suitable acquisitions led Charles to Australia, where he was entertained by the premier. The pickings were not sufficient, however, and Charles disappointed many of the pundits by refusing to snap up any of the property or hotel white elephants that were dangled before him.

Alas, the good intentions of the US deal never came to fruition. Consolidated remained a low growth and low share business, in spite of heavy additional investment and a great deal of top management time. Other activities were introduced, in knitwear, for example, under the umbrella of Sears Industries. But the profits were never exciting. After Charles' retirement Sainer divested himself of the laundry business, freeing cash to invest in more dynamic opportunities.

Although – perhaps even because – he remained so aloof from them, the King of Takeover won the admiration of the City. His popularity with the City pundits was at an all-time high at this stage. The *Investors' Guide* wrote that

> Of all the shares one could choose for future growth, Sears Holdings is without doubt one of the best .... To presume that future profitability by Charles Clore was definitely on the cards would be like supposing that dawn will break tomorrow ... over the past five years the profit has gone up by 55 per cent and Charles Clore's passing shot on his last chairman's statement was that he saw no reason why growth over the next five years should not be at an even greater rate.'

Throughout the 1960s and early 1970s, whenever a share price began to rise unexpectedly, rumours began to fly that Clore was about to make a takeover bid. Was he going to take another crack at Watney's? Would he bid for Debenhams? Or Army & Navy Stores? When Charles was invited to join the board of the Ritz, the news sent the share price rocketing from £11.50 to £16.50. Until then no one knew that he had for years held 25 per cent of the company's shares, having bought in with the takings from the abortive attempt to take over the Savoy with Harold Samuel. The punters automatically assumed that a redevelopment of the site was on the cards. It wasn't.

Clore and takeovers became synonymous and were the butt of numerous comedians. One London revue had a brusque Clore snapping at a harassed secretary, 'Get me New York'; then having to explain, 'No, I don't want to buy it – I meant on the telephone.'

Charles' ability to retain absolute secrecy on bid plans – and indeed on most aspects of his business – became legendary, so much so that, in 1970, a parliamentary investigation into insider dealing asked Clore to appear to explain how he had been so successful at avoiding leaks. Could his approach be a model for other companies, asked the Jenkins Committee? On such a delicate mission, Charles naturally brought along Sainer. There ensued a strange three-cornered dialogue in which the committee would ask a question and Clore would turn to Sainer, saying, 'Tell them what I'm thinking, Mr Sainer.'

Not even the closest of friends or family were allowed the slightest hint of Charles' plans. Indeed, surprise was an essential part of the rules Charles played by, for once news leaked out, the market price was liable to shoot up above the value he had calculated for the company. Hope springs eternal, however, and whenever Charles attended a family function, all his relatives would try to remain within earshot, just in case the great man let slip some hint that might permit them to make their fortunes.

Only once, in the 1950s, did news of a deal leak, when the family was gathered for Passover. In the midst of the chatter Alan, then about nine years old, suddenly announced to all and sundry that his father was about to acquire Dolcis. In walking past one of the Dolcis branches, Charles had stopped and told Alan, 'Tomorrow, this will be mine.' The room fell silent, as if by magic. Charles' face was thunderous, growing more and more so as the room split up into small syndicates of relatives discussing how they would raise the cash to buy in before the deal was announced. 'The excitement and intrigue were immediate and intense,' recalls Charles Jr. But it was shortlived. At nine o'clock the next morning, as the Stock Exchange opened for business, the announcement of the Sears' bid for Dolcis was made. Once more, the family's dreams of making their fortunes were dashed.

Even at the peak of adulation, however, the first cautionary notes were being sounded in the City. The *Daily Express* was the first seriously to pose the question of succession. 'At sixty-eight next Boxing Day, the question growing in many City minds, though there is no sign the master has lost his touch or his bid appetite, is – who is heir to the Clore throne?' The *Express* pointed out that Alan Clore had little interest in the business and suggested that the new heir apparent might be Pat Matthews, chief executive of the giant First National Finance Corporation. Certainly, the rumours were strong that Charles had been talking to Matthews about taking Sears into banking. Why else, asked the stockbroking community, would Sainer be on the First National board? The Clore team remained close-mouthed.

The major stumbling-block to this plan was the nature of the Sears' share capital. A regular trickle of criticism was becoming a torrent. The major shareholders of First National made it quite clear that they would not consider taking non-voting Sears shares in return for their First National shares. At the time, the non-voting shares stood at 158p versus 180p for the voting shares, most of which were held by Clore family members or trusts.

The flirtation with First National rapidly came to an end, not least because speculation had forced up its market price. There was, indeed, no evidence from either side that any kind of deal had even been seriously contemplated. But the press comment raised the temperature over the Sears shares issue and stirred up the minority shareholders.

All through the 1960s Charles had kept a tight rein on the group by the simple device of owning most of the voting shares in both Sears and British Shoe. This led him into hot water twice. The first occasion was when the minority shareholders of British Shoe took exception to the fact that dividends of their company were lower than necessary because BSC cash was swelling Sears' profits. The highly embarrassing argument became public when Charles attempted to buy these shareholders out in 1964 and was beaten off by a shareholders' protection committee that included the Prudential and Scottish Widows insurance companies. The second was in the early 1970s, when holders of Sears ordinary voting shares complained that control of the company (amounting to only 5 per cent of the total capital) was in the hands of Charles himself or in family trusts. Charles enfranchised the ordinary shares in September 1972, to stem the tide of criticism. His decision was influenced by the refusal of some institutional investors to support companies that had both voting and non-voting shares.

The effect of the move was not what Charles or his advisers had expected. Instead of rising, the Sears shares suddenly dropped and kept dropping till nearly 30 per cent was wiped off their value. Isaac Wolfson, who was strongly committed to the concept of non-voting shares as a means of retaining control, took great pleasure in saying: 'I told you so.'

Part of the reason for the fall was the perception that Charles was no longer truly active in Sears' affairs. Certainly, during the 1970s, he spent less and less time in running Sears and more and more on other activities, such as his Israeli involvements. He now had such a smooth machine and such efficient lieutenants, who knew his way of thinking, that there was not that much for him to do. Not that he had lost interest. 'Mr Clore may no longer be as much in evidence at Sears as he once was,' commented the *Observer* in 1973, 'but he is in daily contact with the managers of his four main divisions (engineering, retailing, footwear and betting shops) no matter in what part of the world he happens to be.'

The structure of the organization that Charles built up reflected a pioneering management style that has become a model for other major conglomerates. Nowadays, one of the key differences between the successful and unsuccessful British conglomerates is that the successful ones have very small headquarters. The people – and the money – are used out in the market, where they can have most effect.

The whole empire was run out of what must have been the smallest head office of a conglomerate anywhere in the world. Apart from Clore himself and the ever present Miss Gelman, his office at 22 Park Street housed only Boswell, accountant and second in command, a couple of bookkeepers, a secretary and a tea girl.

Direct interventions were truly rare. More typically, Clore would digest the dozens of ideas for major improvements brought to him by Sainer and others, then suddenly make a decision involving millions of pounds of investment. From then on it was up to Leonard to make sure it happened. While Charles would keep a close eye on progress, he would not interfere unless he observed something radically wrong. 'He spent a lot of time just thinking,' recalls Gardiner, 'picking out, from a host of ideas thrown at him, those that were best.'

'Clore put together the systems that enabled his companies to grow from the bottom,' says Maitland Smith. Picking the right person and letting them get on with it made sure that the right things got done; having good information systems meant that he knew that things were being done right. As Charles himself put it succinctly: 'Why should I put together a business where I have to go to the office every day and worry about it? I want other people to worry about it.' Eventually the business was running so smoothly that he required an average of only two hours a day on its detailed affairs, although his executives had all become used to working six and a half days a week.

That is not to say that Sears was not occupying most of the rest of his time. Whether he was in or out of his office, Charles would always be thinking over one business proposition or another. 'He was a great person to collect ideas from other people and reshape them,' says Geoffrey Maitland Smith, the current chairman and chief executive of Sears. 'There would always be three or four new ideas at every meeting.' These would be investigated, refashioned, re-examined and, in most cases, found wanting. Those that passed the Clore test, however, would be given instant approval, on the assumption that, one way or another, Sainer and his colleagues would find a way of implementing them. That frequently meant a lot of research, which had to be boiled down to two concise pages for him to consider.

The fertility of his brain was a problem for his colleagues, however. Sometimes there were just too many ideas for them to cope with. The Sears' headquarters in Duke Street – itself of only four people – was deliberately set apart from Park Street so that Charles would not be tempted to keep dropping in with more suggestions. The office was above the Hastings & Thanet Building Society in Thrift House. Gardiner chose 'thrift' as his telex answerback, a touch that Charles greatly liked.

At Park Street was a big switchboard for world-wide connections, but Charles retained a wind-up telephone – a direct line to Sainer. He would call Maitland Smith promptly every morning and several times later in the day to enquire: 'What's new?'

Once a month there would be a board meeting of each major subsidiary. First Gardiner and then Maitland Smith would attend as the financial advisers. The holding company acted as a monitor and as a source of advice. The key questions were always, what are you going to do, and what resources do you need to do it? 'Build from the bottom; put the money into the subsidiaries,' Charles insisted.

One penalty for giving people their head is that mistakes are inevitable. Charles recognized that mistakes are a necessary part of the learning experience for managers, that anyone who has not made a mistake has not made anything. 'He didn't mind if someone had made a mistake and said so,' recalls Maitland Smith. 'But he wouldn't forgive anyone who had done something wrong and wouldn't admit it.'

Before forgiveness, however, often came the Clore temper. Inherited from their father, all the Clore sons had a wild, flaring temper. Once released, it would soon subside and all would be forgotten, by Charles at least. The hapless recipient of the tirade, if he did not know Clore well, could remain devastated for days afterwards.

When someone had done something right, however, there was rarely, if ever, a word of praise. 'I never heard him congratulate anyone,' says Maitland Smith. 'They'd have dropped dead if they had heard him say "Well done".' A nod and a grunt were the best that anyone could hope for.

The hands-off approach did not mean that Charles did not want to know about the detail of his companies' operations. Far from it. He made a point of visiting the operations as frequently as he could, and in particular the retail branches, because that was where the customer interface occurred.

He visited Selfridges every afternoon when he was in London and made a point of talking to the staff. In particular, he liked to drop in on the photographic department. As Harry Shacklady, the photographic buyer, said: 'He became a regular visitor to my department. He was a keen photographer. He used to go through cameras like most men go through clean shirts. He was a keen enthusiast and determined to keep up with the new technology.' And that meant that Selfridges, too, had to be bang up to date.

These frequent visits to the customer floor helped Charles take the pulse of the market. 'He used to talk to me like an uncle,' recalls a former sales assistant in one of the shoe shops. 'He was always interested in everything.'

'He used to amaze the buyers,' says architect Sidney Kaye, who designed much of the Leicester complex. 'They would show what they were buying for the next season and he'd tell them: "You can buy that shoe for 10s less in so-and-so's." And he'd always be right.'

These visitations left behind their own legends. On one occasion, when visiting one of the shoe shops in Maidenhead, the manager complained that he needed more staff. Customers were walking out rather than waiting to be served. No problem, observed Clore: 'Wherever they go from here, they'll still be buying from me.' Another presumably apocryphal tale concerns a young lad whose own shoes were in such poor repair that the sole was hanging off one of them. Charles called him aside.

'How dare you serve customers in my shop wearing shoes in that state?'

'I'm sorry, sir,' replied the lad, 'but I've only been working here a short while and I haven't been able to afford any new shoes of my own yet.'

'That's terrible,' replied Charles. Digging in his back pocket, he pulled out a thick wad of notes, held together by a rubber band. 'Here, wrap this around it to stop it flapping,' he continued, peeling off the rubber band and stuffing the notes back in his pocket.

The image of the penny-pinching millionaire was strengthened by a number of such tales and by unfortunate incidents such as the thief of Kilburn. The manager of one of the Sears' stores in Kilburn was horrified to see a customer try on a pair of shoes, then run out of the shop without paying. As the manager ran after him, the man attempted to weave through the traffic, slipped in front of a bus and was killed instantly. While waiting for the ambulance, the manager carefully retrieved the stolen shoes, assuming that this would be in line with company policy.

'To my mind, Charles' greatest skill was as a merchandiser,' recalls Gardiner. 'We'd go down to Leicester sometimes and the first thing he would do was look at the window of the local Freeman, Hardy shop. "Tell the manager it's not quite right. Put those shoes there ..." he'd say. We used to go up to Leicester by train from St Pancras or by car and spend a lot of our time looking at the shops and the factory (although he found that less interesting). He wouldn't stop talking shop until we got back to London. Then he'd turn round and say: "I did enjoy today."'

In 1953, at the end of the very first meeting after Sears took over, Alfred Butlin, the managing director of Sears, produced some shoes that they were manufacturing. 'Very nice,' said Clore, 'but can you sell them?' 'You know, sir,' said Butlin, 'that's the trouble.'

Anyone who showed an interest (and a good many who didn't) would find themselves accompanying Clore to inspect his shops. Orchard-Lisle recalls walking down Oxford Street with Clore and Tovey around 5.30 p.m. to inspect a branch. While they were inside the store looking at the window display, the lights suddenly went out, although the store was teeming with people. Charles stormed off to find out why and was told that it was 'to save electricity'. An edict was soon issued ordering that the lights stayed on as long as there were customers either inside or passing the shops.

Soon after taking over Sears, Charles dropped into a Dolcis store in Reading one Saturday afternoon. He was appalled at the inefficiency he saw. The reason, he discovered, was that the manager only had eighteen months to retirement. He brought the subject up at the next board meeting and insisted the manager left that day on full pay until his retirement date. The message came through loud and clear right from the start – poor performance would not be tolerated.

The Dolcis chairman, a small man whose job had been part of the acquisition agreement, drew himself up in his chair saying: 'It will be done, but what business have you got visiting the stores? We have inspectors to do that.' Shortly afterwards a new chairman was appointed.

As Gardiner grew near to retirement, Charles began to cast around for a replacement. He fastened on Geoffrey Maitland Smith, then a partner at chartered accountants Thornton Baker, where he had been involved in a number of Sears' projects with Investment Registry. Sainer invited him over for lunch just before Christmas 1970. As Sainer described all the constituent parts of the group, Maitland Smith began to wonder what on earth he was there for. Eventually Sainer came to the point. Did Maitland Smith know of anyone who could take over as executive director of Sears, when Gardiner, who was then sixty-four, left? Did that mean that the job might be open to him, asked Maitland Smith? Yes, replied Sainer. Would he see Clore within the next two or three days?

Over lunch at Park Street, Clore chatted to Maitland Smith about anything but the business in hand. He was taking his time measuring up the man who would have to take over the day-to-day operations of an empire. Eventually Maitland Smith asked how many people worked for him. Charles replied: 'About half.' (Some years later, he was asked how many handicapped people he employed and responded 'Pretty well all of them.')

Maitland Smith was hooked. Sitting facing Canaletto's *Bridge of Sighs*, beside one of the most successful entrepreneurs in Europe, it was difficult to refuse anything.

'What do you think you are going to do for me?' Clore eventually asked. Maitland Smith explained how he saw the group and what could be done with it. Charles grunted, as near to an expression of agreement as he would normally give. Maitland Smith joined six months later, working in tandem with Gardiner for a year.

There were, of course, further acquisitions. In 1973, for example, Clore bought Edgar Pickering of Blackburn, a tufted carpet manufacturer, for £6 million, and a Dutch shoe retail business, Hoogenbosch, for £1.75 million. Pickering was not a success and was sold off again a few years later. Hoogenbosch was a more typical Clore deal, in which most of the initial outlay was recovered by selling a large warehouse. In 1975 he bought Galliford Estates, a highly successful housebuilders for £3.7 million. Even the good buys (Galliford made £7 million pre-tax profit in 1984) were only small beer compared with the larger acquisitions of the earlier days. The fire that drove Charles Clore was dying down noticeably. The only sizeable deal that came on the horizon was a £44 million deal with Nottingham Manufacturing in 1974. Though agreed, the merger came to nothing, once it was referred to the Monopolies Commission.

After Charles' retirement in 1976, Sainer was given the task of dismantling those low-performing parts of the conglomerate that should have been cut away earlier, but which Charles could not bear to let go. Bentley was one of the first to go, on the grounds that engineering was no longer either a close fit with the rest of the group's activities or a dynamic business to be in. The US laundry business has also been scrubbed from the Sears' portfolio while other businesses have been brought in. The result: a highly efficient, highly conservative and very profitable business machine.

Of all the major companies in Britain, Sears remains the most fiscally prudent. Clore's dislike of owing money to anyone led him to reduce Sears' debts to nil as rapidly as possible and that same philosophy applies to the company today. All acquisitions since the bid for Sears itself have been financed by cash flow. Annual borrowings rarely exceed cash in hand by significant amounts. Profits since the takeover have grown from £1.1 million to £185 million, while the value of the company has soared from £4 million to £1.8 billion. Moreover, Sears – in spite of its sale and lease-back origins – has one of the largest property portfolios of any company in Europe.

Yet Sears in the 1970s and 1980s has lost something that only Clore himself could give it: its sense of aggression, innovation and ability to do the cheekily unexpected. It is, perhaps, all part of growing up. The massive takeover bids in Britain during the late 1970s and the 1980s have somehow passed Clore's empire by, although the opportunities were there. (The group has, none the less, continued to expand through acquisition in the United States, particularly through the successful $100 million offer for a major US shoe retailer, Butler Shoe Corp.) Ironically, as we write, speculation abounds as to which of numerous potential contenders will attempt to acquire Sears itself. Could any of them emulate the special entrepreneurial flair of the 'King of Takeover'? Probably not.

CHAPTER

7

Boats and Buildings

'Clore had a fascination for making money
quickly.... He couldn't bear to see success and
not be involved....' George Grant

For a man who hated the thought of getting on a boat, and was invariably seasick the moment he did so, Charles Clore's attraction to shipping was remarkable. It also exposed one of his principal weaknesses – the jackdaw side of his nature, which made him pour money into unsuccessful businesses, which the more prudent side of him would have severed long before.

Unlike in his property and retail interests, Clore lacked the Midas touch in shipping. For once, he was a clumsy amateur, an inexperienced outsider who had rushed in and then found himself poorly equipped to deal with the caprices of an unfamiliar industry.

Riding high on the shipping boom, Furness shipyards and British Oil at first looked highly profitable to Clore, but for once his judgement went disastrously astray. His shipping concerns eventually turned sour and became financial deadweights. This might not have happened if he had been able to swallow his pride and sell the businesses at the right time.

Why did he commit himself so heavily to an industry he knew almost nothing about? His property and retail interests were thriving; the capital that he was releasing from the leaseback of sites belonging to Sears promised to be a lever to finance further expansion within the footwear industry. Why spread himself thin by diversifying his concerns to such an extent?

Clore saw shipping as a natural diversification into manufacturing and a useful base for expanding into other areas of industry. It was a constant irritant to him during his early contested deals that the media insisted on calling him the 'West End financier'. He considered himself an industrialist, not just a property investor or retailer – and as an industrialist he intended to build an integrated business spanning manufacturing, property and retailing.

The glamour and romance surrounding shipping was, of course, an important sweetener to Clore. Immediately after the war the industry was doing well and had rapidly gained a high profile. With the navy and merchant fleets scrambling to replace lost tonnage, shipyards had full books and were even turning clients away. The government was giving shipping top priority and, with most European yards still out of action, the way was clear for British shipbuilders to win most of the world's shipping contracts.

Regardless of later events, the time was right to invest in shipbuilding and shipping. Charles could see acquaintances like Stavros Niarchos and Aristotle Onassis amassing vast personal profits; why could he not do the same? His associates and friends were aware of his envy of the extravagant life-styles of the shipping magnates. 'How do they do it?' he would ask in exasperation.

'Clore had a fascination for making money quickly and shipowning seemed to offer him the chance to do just that. He couldn't bear to see success and not be involved. He decided that he wanted a piece of the action,' comments George Grant, a tall, cheerful individual and the founder director of Stephenson Hardy, the shipping agents to British Oil.

Clore's first interests in shipping came through the oil tanker industry, which at that stage was very slow to recover from the effects of the war. He was acquainted with Harold Rappaport, a wealthy ship owner and owner of British Oil, an oil tanker business. Rappaport's fleet of oil tankers had been destroyed by the war. He was disillusioned with the state of the industry and did not believe that things would improve. It was not hard for Clore to persuade him to sell the company and he obtained 90 per cent of the shares. Although Rappaport had no tankers left, he handed over to Clore £300,000 worth of shipping entitlement, issued by the government to replace lost tonnage. Such papers allowed shipowners to rebuild or to buy secondhand ships.

George Grant explains: 'Clore got the company for a low price because oil tankers did not look very promising at that stage. The world market was very slow to recover.' Charles recognized the bargain and was prepared to wait a year or two for his profits.

The market for oil tankers, however, was just about to take off as oil steadily replaced coal as the main source of fuel. Although British Oil's profits were only small in the beginning, averaging around £200,000, they began to grow considerably as the demand for tankers rapidly increased. For a short time Clore's company flourished, before the onslaught of world competition caused freight rates to plummet. Rappaport's paper enabled Clore to acquire a ship he renamed the *Vivien Louise*. This diesel-powered vessel's engine was in poor condition and proved to be a constant source of problems. He also built the *Alan Evelyn* at Furness shipyard.

A substantial part of the early profits from British Oil came through selling the tankers at the peak of the shipping boom. Clore sent Grant, who had become a director of British Oil, to New York to buy a turbo-electric-powered ship. The States had started to produce these expensive and powerful ships soon after the war. For a few years they were sold to the Allies only. Clore used the remaining value of his paper and some of his own capital to purchase a ship which he renamed the *Francine Clore* for around £200,000, a figure which was even more reasonable because of a good exchange rate.

Shortly afterwards and just before the shipping industry slumped, Grant sold the *Francine Clore* for a huge profit. He recalls: 'Clore was reluctant to part with her at that point because he was convinced that tanker prices would continue to rise.' He kept worrying Grant while he was looking for a buyer until finally the director turned around exasperatedly and said: 'It's no good saying you don't like the thought of the sale. She's sold.' Grant sold out at the top of the market, for a price of £1,200,000.

'Clore was never a shipowner and he didn't understand the way the market worked. I was very unpopular in his office for a while. We didn't talk to each other directly for a month.' About six months later the market collapsed and then Clore said finally: 'Good sale.' It was the first time he had ever congratulated Grant.

The money from the sale of the *Francine Clore* helped Clore to buy Furness shipyards. He sent Gardiner to take a look at the yard. The investigation was the beginning of a business relationship between the two which lasted for thirty years.

Clore then set about expanding into shipbuilding. At the time, his eventual choice seemed excellent. Furness was a private company owned by the Furness family, consisting of a shipyard on the banks of the Tees. Although not a classic Admiralty yard, it was known as a good commercial yard with extensive facilities and plenty of space to build large ships. In 1951 it was one of the most modern yards in Britain.

'The Furness family was not terribly interested in hanging on to the yard,' recalls Gardiner. The family held the share capital of £600,000 and a debenture of £1 million, issued on the terms that the company could repay it whenever it chose. The yard had a full order book and demand was so strong that the only way clients could order a ship was by putting down a very large deposit. Furness held enough deposits of this nature to repay the debenture on the spot, if it also wished.

Sainer arrived to discuss with the family the terms of the deal. Eventually they settled on £1 million for the whole business. Clore then repaid the debenture and topped up the cash flow by concluding a major deal with shipping magnate, Basil Mavroleon, a matter of weeks afterwards.

Mavroleon's London & Overseas Freighters ordered three new 25,000 tonne turbine-driven tankers, estimated to cost around £3 million. Part of this cash was used to acquire the majority ownership of Bentley Engineering.

The deal was all the more surprising in view of the unpropitious start to his acquaintance with Mavroleon. While he was expanding his shipping interests, Charles had marched unannounced into London & Overseas Freighters and stated that he wanted to see the chairman. Without waiting, he strode into Mavroleon's office and said: 'I've come to buy you out.' He was politely but firmly shown the door.

The Greek dismissed the incident. A few months later he found that the mysterious Mr Clore had become the owner of Furness. Because Furness was his main supplier, he decided that it was wise to become better acquainted with Clore. It did not take long for the two to become friends. A good-natured rivalry sprang up between them, with a great deal of camaraderie about their Jewish and Greek roots. They would attempt to outdo each other by claiming they started in greater poverty than the other. Both were self-made men. As a youth, Mavroleon had come to England from Greece to join a cousin employed by a shipping agent. He had worked his way up the company and then established his own business.

Mavroleon was an outgoing and generous man, with a sense of humour and a preference for the quiet life. Although he was only a year older than Clore, he used to call him 'Charlie boy'. Although Clore was inexperienced in shipping, Mavroleon grew to respect his independence and determination to do things his own way.

The night before he bought Furness, Clore threw a party. Most of the guests had close connections with the shipping world. 'It was his way of saying he had arrived,' recalls one of them.

Clore enjoyed the ceremony and tradition of shipping events. When he was launching a new ship, he would arrange for a train to bring his guests from London to Teesside. Thirty to forty guests would be given lunch and drinks on the train, 'with Clore marching through the train saying hello only to the people he liked'. David Clore attended sometimes. On one occasion he stumbled accidentally into the ladies WC, muttering 'Are there any drinks here?' He listened while one lady explained solemnly that there was only water available and then engaged her in a long conversation.

Clore would occasionally visit British Oil to inspect the company's ships. He frequently brought Vivien and Alan, then two small, smartly dressed children, who were held tightly by their nurse all day. Clore would attempt to talk to the captains of his ships but, because of his technical ignorance, he frequently lapsed into an awkward silence. 'Our employees never thought of Clore as the owner of British Oil. They identified more closely with Stephenson Hardy,' comments Grant.

During the Coronation, Clore used the offices of Furness, which were on the corner of Bennet St and St James's, to celebrate the occasion. Francine saw to the decoration of the building, from which invited guests could watch the royal procession. As she swept around the building, Charles trailed behind, causing at least one observer to wonder how such a powerful man could appear so henpecked.

As Furness went from strength to strength, Clore's property concerns, which were carried out through the Prince of Wales Property Co., took an upward leap. The new legislation in 1954, which abolished the need to obtain building licences from the government, caused the value of land to shoot up overnight by 70 per cent. The new legislation initiated one of the most profitable booms ever known.

In addition to the end of all controls, Macmillan's government abolished development charges, which had been previously nearly 100 per cent. The pace of development accelerated dramatically from then on. The need to replace old buildings was only one aspect of the boom: the balance of industry was moving from manufacturing to service; companies were forming into larger units, many of which selected London as their headquarters. In 1952, planning permission reached 2.4 million square feet of space. Three years later, it had increased to 5.9 million.

Clore could not lose; he owned a number of properties with soaring values, which he had purchased by borrowing money at a fixed rate. With inflation steadily increasing and demand far in excess of supply, the property owner often had a capital appreciation of 300 per cent. According to a number of friends, it was Clore's property interests above all which led to his becoming one of the richest men in Britain.

Despite his successes, Clore was never satisfied. He was always driven by the desire to be the biggest and best and the thought of how he might have played a better and more profitable game often gnawed at him. Years later, when he drove around the City with Janet, Marchioness of Milford Haven, he would point often to a building and say: 'Do you see that, my girl. I could have had that. I was a fool.'

Clore was gradually passing more of his business to Healey & Baker. The talented Douglas Tovey, then one of the senior partners, was acting on behalf of several store and property magnates such as Fraser and Lord Thomson. In 1959, Clore changed the name of his property company to City & Central Investments, a more appropriate title for a company so active in the capital.

He was still a client to Joe Levy. Despite their long acquaintance, the relationship between the two men was cold and brittle. They preferred not to meet socially. Both were strong-minded, stubborn men. Clore had fixed notions about property development and would brook no argument on the subject, an attitude which was beginning to chafe with Levy. He was becoming impatient of handing over important sites to his clients when he could, in many cases, develop them just as well himself.

The chance for Levy to venture into development came at Clore's expense. In 1952, Levy was approached by a Mr Young, the owner of a one-acre site in Euston Road. He offered Levy the site for £400,000. Levy had Sidney Kaye draw up plans for City & Central and successfully applied for planning permission from the London County Council. A last-minute tax problem for the owner meant that the sale never went through. Four years later, Young approached Levy asking for the same price.

Levy took the offer to Clore, who naturally gave the go-ahead. With Kaye, Levy approached the LCC to discuss the development plans. The LCC dismissed their overture, telling them the site was needed to build a main road. The council's consternation was great when the four-year-old planning permission for an office block was produced. If it went ahead with its plans, Clore could claim compensation for the loss of development rights, totalling around £1 million.

In the event, a compromise was reached, which presented Clore with a huge development opportunity. Besides the road project, the LCC dreamed up a unified plan to redevelop the whole run-down area to the north of Euston Road. It had never had the chance to realize the vision because it had no chance of raising the required finance. But if the money came from a private developer willing to fit in with the LCC's plans, then the council would issue the building permission.

If Clore went ahead, he would pull off the biggest single private redevelopment deal since the war. The only question was whether all the owners of the individual sites – most of which were ramshackle and seedy – within the 13-acre area would sell up.

The uncertainty worried Clore. At the eleventh hour he delayed signing the contract and sought a second opinion. To Levy's annoyance, he turned to Tovey, who usually handled most of Sears' business. Levy complained to Clore that Tovey's advice was appropriate for shops but not for office blocks, an area that was Levy's domain.

After looking at the fragmented 13-acre site, Tovey advised Clore not to buy. Setting commercial reasons aside, the development would obviously require a great deal of patience for a number of years before all the owners would sell. 'I knew that Charles Clore couldn't stand the strain of such a long-drawn-out speculation. He would never have given me any peace. I would have had to comfort him for years. It wasn't worth it,' recalls Tovey.

But for Levy it was worth it. He was not going to let such an opportunity slip and approached two large contracting firms for the finance. As predicted, it took many years of secrecy and much persuasive effort before the site could be developed. Seventeen years after the deal with the LCC, Levy and his investors owned every single crumbling shop, bomb site and derelict house on the 13-acre site. The resulting office complex, one of the biggest in London, earned Levy and his partners around £11 million.

Joe Levy's account of the project is somewhat different to Tovey's. He recalls that Clore pulled out of the deal before the notion of the 13-acre development arose. Whichever recollection is correct, Levy's move into development was a constant irritant to Clore. It even irked him to see the estate agent buy small properties. Levy recalls: 'Once he was on his way, Clore went for large deals only. He always criticized me for acquiring small properties.'

The two men once had a heated conversation over a site Levy was planning to buy. Clore asked impatiently: 'Why do you want such small pebbles?' 'If I want to pick up a small pebble, I will. I know and you know that the moment I stop doing my job properly, I'll be through that window and on the street. But what I can do for you, I can do for someone else.' Clore admitted reluctantly that he was interfering but went on to say: 'There's a lot of common sense in what you do, but what annoys me is that every time you walk through this door you're wealthier.'

Once Clore started in the property world, he wanted to be number one. He had developed a formidable property portfolio with innumerable sites around Piccadilly, Holborn and Oxford Circus, yet he still begrudged the good fortune of others, particularly when they worked for him. When Clore heard of Levy becoming a director in another property company, Stock Conversion Ltd, he turned to him during a meeting at Park Street and complained that he was picking up more property for himself than anyone else.

The key to Clore's skill in property was his ability to recognize the potential of a site; such an instinct was often based on an imaginative and dynamic sense of how the site could be used.

In retail, Clore was in a league of his own. He had an astute and practical awareness of what the average man in the street wanted; and he rightly saw the trend moving from shops to department stores. It was for this reason that he was so interested in the site on Wigmore Street which Selfridges put on the market several years before he acquired the store.

A number of people made a bid for the site. Lord Rayne obtained it

eventually and he remembers vividly Clore's deep interest and disappointment on losing it.

> The project was very close to Charles' heart. He resented Selfridges dispos-
> ing of a valuable asset before he was able to buy the company. His
> comment at that time was: 'The only good thing that that management
> ever did was to enable Max Rayne to make a good deal of money.' It irked
> him, but he was very generous to me about the whole incident.

Such setbacks were rare for Clore. He was constantly picking up plum
property, and frequently used Token Construction to develop the sites.
Although other developers in the 1950s saw the sense of filling both
roles, Clore was well ahead of them.

In total contrast to his approach in later years, when he was building
for charity, Clore approached construction with the eye of a financier.
He rarely felt any aesthetic interest in the buildings he constructed; so
long as a building yielded a comfortable profit, was put up by the
promised date and fulfilled its purpose, his task was done. Many of the
office buildings he developed are strikingly plain and functional. A
1,000,000 square foot site in Oxford Street, for instance, was transformed from war damaged squat Victorian shop units to a graceless,
rectangular, six-storey office building. Leonard Sainer explains: 'Clore
made no apology for the fact that in developing property he built above
all for profit. He said he "didn't believe in any great architectural
triumphs, which result in bankruptcy".'

Clore left most of the organizational details of his development to
Tovey, including the choice of architect. 'I usually had a model made. He
loved looking at them. I never knew him to say he didn't like it, once he
saw the model,' he explains.

Clore was working with a small number of architects, among them
Lewis Solomon Son & Joseph. Morris Joseph, senior partner of this firm,
became a close associate of Clore. Among the most significant sites was
St George's Court, one of the earlier lessor schemes. The eight-storey
building is still an important landmark in the Holborn area. It was
through Joseph that Clore came into contact with Sidney Kaye, the
architect who would one day design for Clore and Conrad Hilton one of
the most prestigious hotels in the world.

When Clore met Kaye, he was a young, promising architect who had
just been made a junior partner in Joseph's firm. But after the unexpected and premature death of Joseph, Kaye found the reins of the
practice pushed suddenly into his hand. He felt inexperienced and
ill-prepared for such a responsibility. He recalls: 'I was the backroom
boy who didn't know a single client, with the result that we lost a lot of

business. I was very fortunate that Clore stuck by me – although at the time I thought this was due entirely to the influence of Sainer.'

It was not the only time Clore stuck by a promising youngster. Joe Levy was still a very junior partner in the estate agents when his elder brother David died. He, too, was surprised at the loyalty of a man he scarcely knew.

Kaye's practice grew from a staff of ten to over a hundred. Clore became a major client, yet it took considerable time for Kaye to feel at ease with him.

> He was a man who put up a very brusque front and was difficult to get close to. His time was limited and in spite of the enormous volume of business our practice had with him, I don't recall being with him in his office at any time for more than five minutes. I later learned that his gruff façade was merely that, and that he took a delight in helping young people to get on in their careers.

The first job Kaye did for Clore was the development of 51–54 Fenchurch Street in 1954. Norwich Union, the tenants, were successful in obtaining a building licence which enabled Clore to proceed with the building of their offices. During the construction Kaye gained a further insight into Clore's character which contradicted the gruff and hard impression that he generally left with people. Clore had just passed the Fenchurch Street site after a meeting in the City and noticed that no one appeared to be working. He rang Sidney Kaye immediately. Kaye told him that the men were probably taking a tea-break and also pointed out that he was not the contractor and this was a matter for them. After inquiry, Kaye found there was a strike going on, apparently due to the fact that building workers had just been granted a rise in wages, and the engineering workers, who were due to make their application three months later, had decided not to wait but to claim their increase immediately.

Kaye took Clore over the site commenting on the system of wage bargaining with different dates for settlement between the engineering and building workers. To his surprise Clore gave him a lecture in favour of the workers. 'You don't realize how difficult it is for these people in the building industry, and what a helluva life they had before the war,' he kept telling the architect. It was clear that the deprivations of the unemployed during the Depression had made a very deep impression on him.

The career of Token Construction was colourful and frequently rumbustious. The managing director was Leonard Mottram, a big man with a loud voice, who was completely at his ease in the noise and chaos of the construction site. He was headstrong and impulsive and never stood in awe of the big names running City Centre Properties, as Clore's property interests came to be called in the mid 1960s. No matter whom he was dealing with, Mottram liked things done his way. If people tried to argue with him, he put on a show of losing his temper and thumped the table until he got his way. He brought a new outlook to contract management. During the building of one site, Mottram began to chafe at the slowness of the lift installation. Finally losing patience, he got on the phone to his lawyers and told them to issue a writ against the company. 'On what grounds?' was the plaintive and bewildered request. 'I don't care – you find the grounds,' said Mottram, before slamming down the phone.

Mottram's stubborness occasionally led to more serious confrontations with City Centre Properties. In 1967, immediately after the military coup in Greece, Mottram announced publicly that Token Construction had won a £150 million order from the Greek government. Without the knowledge of City Centre Properties, the firm had been competing for the contract for two years, against fierce competition from American and German firms. While Mottram was confidently saying: 'Everything is settled at the Greek end. It is now for the Export Credit Guarantee Board to say if they will cover the bill, should the Greek government fail to pay', City Centre was responding in a very different way. Exasperated at the director's bad timing and embarrassed by the political overtones now attached to the deal, it tried hard to extricate itself by issuing a statement denying that the company was about to sign a contract. Mottram refused to be associated with the statement and continued to insist that Token Construction had won the order.

Token Construction sometimes resorted to unorthodox but colourful methods to get projects built in time. The Stoll Theatre in Kingsway was pulled down and replaced by an office block and theatre below ground. Immediately behind the site was a hospital. The theatre, which had huge 100-ton girders stretching across the auditorium, was going to take a considerable time to demolish. The contractor, however, simply started cutting the girders at each end and let them fall to the ground, even though the impact and noise caused the hospital next door to be shaken to its foundations. When Kaye found out, he was horrified. That same morning, when Clore asked how the building was progressing, he voiced his concerns. Clore went down to see the foreman the next morning. To the architect's surprise he returned and said: 'It's fine. You worry too much.' 'I couldn't understand how the foreman had got away with it,' Kaye comments. It turned out that Charles had gone to the hospital matron and said: 'We can take down the girders in six days or six months. Which do you want?' He filled the hospital with flowers afterwards.

A little later the Royalty Theatre – which was later used for the 'This is your Life' programme – was opened on the site. Kaye was given no indication of what a theatre should be like and had to work it out for himself. He decided the theatre was only suitable for intimate productions with a maximum of six people on stage. The Stoll, by contrast, always had huge shows. Sam Harber, the doyen of the theatre managers, who was then running the Coliseum, had the idea of using the theatre all day, starting with fashion shows in the morning and ending with late-night plays.

Kaye decided to make provision for an orchestra of forty, rising from the pit if needed. There was a proscenium arch that could be varied for small shows, and dressing-room accommodation for fifty-six people, in case the theatre was used for small operettas. Then he found that a television company was using the old Moss Empire theatre hall as a studio. To attract the television company to a purpose-built theatre, he had it specially wired for studio work and designed sight lines for wide camera screens.

Clore was delighted with everything Kaye showed him and approved it without demur. On the opening night, however, he told him the carpet was not good enough, because his girlfriend of the day did not like it.

Alfred Lunt and Lynne Fontaine were the artists for the opening night. It was a day in June and the humidity was high. Unbeknown to Kaye, it was customary to economize in theatres by turning off the ventilation during the performance. At the end of the performance, a dinner had been laid on for the guests in one of the theatre's lounge bars. Kaye recalls the sight of '1,000 perspiring people – women's make-up was coming off'. No one knew how to turn the ventilation on.

Kaye was constantly surprised by Charles' remarkable ability to make quick decisions. When the site of what is now Moor House at London Wall came on the market, 'I wasn't with him at the site for thirty seconds before he gave me the instruction to go ahead. He just asked me what I thought of the location.'

In the meantime, the performance of Clore's shipping concerns were fluctuating seriously. Freight charges were falling alarmingly quickly and British Oil was beginning to lose money. While the company had made a modest profit of £52,000 in 1952, it made a group loss of £38,000 the next year. Clore decided to sell two tankers and could only scrape the price of £500,000, losing between £500,000 and £1 million on the deal. He issued a statement giving the poor trading situation and the uncertainty of freight rates as the reason for the sale of the tankers and said that the board was considering the future of the company.

The news of the sale of the two tankers was greeted with surprise in the shipping industry. By that time freights were on an upgrade and a further rise was expected. After some deliberation, Clore decided not to abandon the company. He took a gamble and replaced his two tankers on the assumption that freight rates would rise. British Oil took out a contract to build two tankers costing £3.5 million of borrowed money. Clore had some misgivings about the decision, so he insured himself against loss by hiring his ships out to a leading British oil group. In the meantime, his shareholders were puzzled: Clore had sold out at a market low point and then begun buying when the market for tankers was near the top. Such indecision and unnecessary losses were uncharacteristic of him.

A few people privately thought that Clore did not have sufficient time or experience to steer British Oil out of trouble. 'Clore once turned to a director of the company and asked exasperatedly, "Why haven't we any business?" He didn't seem to be fully aware of the complexity of the problems,' comments a former employee of British Oil.

Despite its poor trading performance, Clore clung tenaciously to his company. Part of the reason for this behaviour stemmed from his irrational dislike of giving up a project, once it was started. To him it was an admission of defeat. On one occasion he had bought some land in the Thames Valley for housing development. Then he received a very tempting offer from Wates, the builders. His advisers told him to take his profit now. For years afterwards, he berated them saying that if Wates could make a profit on the development, so could he have done.

He was equally stubborn with Furness once it lost its early bloom. Furness was affected severely by the crisis in the shipping industry in the late 1950s. Both shipowners and shipbuilders faced world-wide overcapacity, with consequent pressure on costs. In large tanker construction, Japan was the chief price cutter in the world's shipyards, forcing Sweden to follow suit. The bigger British companies such as Swan Hunter and Vickers Armstrong could afford to rationalize and modernize facilities. It was much more difficult for the smaller yards and Clore was slow to modernize Furness. He undertook a small expansion programme but, when world trade moved towards giant tankers, his yard was unable to compete and could only build a niche in the market for smaller ships. Belatedly, he decided to spend £3 million to build more shipbuilding berths, general offices, a steel preparation plant and a stockyard.

Although the shipbuilding industry was looking increasingly precarious, Clore persisted in pouring money into his yard, to the extent that it was humorously described as the most modern loss-making shipyard in the world. However much it was modernized, the yard continued to lose ground in the world market. Shipping was slowly slipping into recession as international competition increased. Cost margins became tighter as shipowners stopped placing large deposits and started to insist on deferred credit and large discounts. These problems might have been overcome with better management, but that was the one thing Furness lacked. It went through a succession of managing directors. Usually so careful in his choice of personnel, Clore did not have the time or knowledge to find a suitable chief executive. In one case, he had arranged to see two candidates at his home in Park Street where he was suffering from an acute attack of backache. Having interviewed the first candidate, he completely forgot there was another in the wings and told the man he had the job. Maitland Smith had the embarrassing task of explaining to the second candidate, who had travelled a considerable distance for the interview, that it was too late. In the event, the chosen candidate proved no more successful at turning round the yard than any of his predecessors.

Sir Patrick Sergeant recalls: 'Furness held Sears back. Clore kept saying: "I'm going to put a padlock on the place and leave it."' The company had been absorbed by Sears in 1954, when Clore had sold his controlling interest for £3.4 million in cash. But with Sears in the early stage of consolidation and expansion, the poor performance of Furness threatened to become a serious problem – not least because, during this period, Sears shares themselves were low on the Stock Exchange.

According to Gardiner: 'Things got worse and worse. It was very difficult to build while we were modernizing the yard. We got a contract for two sulphur carriers, but we lost a lot of money on them.'

By the early 1960s Clore had had a bellyfull of the shipping industry. He reached an agreement with Anglo Norness Shipping to absorb British Oil by exchanging his shares for 10 per cent of the Norwegian company. Characteristically, he hatched a good deal from what had seemed a poor bargaining position. Anglo Norness was a first-rate growth company and was among one of the few shipping companies to be in a healthy position. Its profits had risen elevenfold over the last ten years.

The story of Furness did not have such a happy ending. For a brief time the modernization programme seemed to bring in new life. Many of the processes were highly automated and were efficient and fast. During the last six months of 1967, the yard had an average weekly output of 750 tons. Things were humming to such an extent that someone said at the yard: 'It's like a Harold Wilson speech come true.'

Then disaster struck. Very soon after the modernization programme was completed, the world market in shipbuilding sagged yet again. To compound Clore's difficulties, the yard had been beset by labour problems. Furness was in a high wage area, which made it difficult for the yard to maintain its labour force, and forced it to pay above average wages for the industry. The final death-blow was inflicted by the Geddes

Report. This rationalized the industry and selected a number of companies to form consortia. Despite Clore's pleas, Furness was excluded from the Wear Shipbuilding Group. Inevitably it became a wallflower among the big shipyards, and between 1963 and 1968 it lost £8.5 million.

The *Observer* reported of Furness in 1968: 'Someone has blundered. It would be unfair to blame Charles Clore ... but there's no getting away from the fact that a multi-million pound clanger has been dropped and its effects are reverberating throughout the North-East.'

The newspaper went on to examine Furness' problems, including the yard's failed attempts to diversify into oil rigs. Rival yards talked of 'damn poor management' and 'classic botch-ups'. The current managing director of Furness, commented: 'I don't blame Mr Clore and I'm sorry for him. He tried his damnedest.' The *Observer* commented:

> Even rivals acknowledge this is true. They shrug their shoulders, as if to say – what can you expect when an amateur gets in on this game, however much money he has? As far as he's concerned, they say, he'll just have to write off Furness as one of those unhappy stories which began 'It seemed a good idea at the time!'

In 1967 Clore announced that the shipyard was £6 million in the red and that the parent company, Sears, 'could not afford to do anything other than close down efficiently'. He entered into talks with the Shipbuilding Industry Board and the Ministry of Technology about the future of the yard. The best solution, agreed by all concerned, was that Furness should be sold to the Swan Hunter and Tyne consortium for £2.5 million, against its book value of £6.4 million.

Gardiner recalls: 'By then we had not got enough orders to keep going. Swan got the yard for a song. We had spent a lot of money on Furness, particularly on modernizing it. It was money down the drain.'

For all that, the deal was the best possible for Sears considering the circumstances. Sears received just under 10 per cent of Swan's shares and sold them for about £1 million two years later. Although the bid meant a book loss of £3.9 million, this was covered by a provision of £5 million in the last accounts, so the cash element of the bid came unencumbered. Sears 'A' shares rose by 4.5d to 33s 6d after the news of the sale.

Domestic life in the Clore household followed a remarkably similar pattern, once the brief honeymoon period had given rapid way to a tempestuous marital relationship, with occasional highs and a predominance of lows. As his business grew in size and complexity, his marriage problems grew worse. Matters came to a head when Francine left home

Charles, aged ten

Israel Clore

With two of his brothers, Hyman (left) and
David (right)

With his family at his sister Rosie's wedding to Nat Cohen, 1920. Back row, left to right: *Hyman, Jack, Bob, Charles, Abe Davis;* middle row, left to right: *Fanny, Rose (Hyman's wife), Nat Cohen, Rosie, Israel and his wife Jenny;* front row, left to right: *Con Davis, Leon Clore, David and Bernard.*

On horseback at Ray Court

The two impresarios, Charles and Alfred Esdaile

Francine, aged eighteen, at her coming-out ball

Charles and Francine's wedding picture, 7 June 1943

Charles and Francine with Alan, 1944

Vivien and Alan, c. 1950

Checkendon

Charles relaxing in his study at Checkendon

Jack Cotton (second left) *at a Norwich Union party with Aubrey Orchard-Lisle* (second right) *and Maurice Wohl, chairman of United Real Property Company* (right)

With his right-hand man, Leonard Sainer

Two tycoons together: Clore with Sir Isaac Wolfson

Even a millionaire wants his duty-free cigarettes: with Meyer Weisgal, 1962

With Teddy Kollek at the opening of the Charles Clore Hill Gardens in Jerusalem

With Alan in the 1960s

Farmer Clore at Stype

Shooting at Stype with Vivien, Jocelyn Stevens (left) and Hugh Fraser (right)

after a blazing row. She went first to her aunt, who told her bluntly to go home, then to Claridge's and on to Paris. There was clearly some hope of reconciliation because she left her dog, which would otherwise have had to go into quarantine. The next year saw two attempts at reconciliation, both disastrous. The last time, she took the dog with her, along with her jewels. It was all she was allowed to take, she declares. 'He hoped he'd starve me into coming back.'

Accounts of the separation vary. According to Francine, for some months afterwards Charles pursued her, ringing her Paris apartment time and again in vain attempts at yet another reconciliation. Another account says that Charles was so enraged when Mena, the cook, told him of Francine's indiscretions – he had been too busy at the time to notice – that he was ready to cut her out of his life there and then. Either way, it was too late; the gulf between them had become too wide.

In October 1956 Charles filed for divorce and, to ease his loneliness and escape from the rigours of work, began to look for and enjoy the attentions of beautiful young women. He speedily became the latest recruit to the international smart set. At Monte Carlo he distinguished himself by his gregariousness and boundless energy. He was often found dancing the samba and rumba till four in the morning. He often played table-tennis on the palm-fringed edge of a swimming-pool with Hugh Fraser. The two made an incongruous sight, both in shorts but one small and stocky and the other tall and lean.

In the meantime, the divorce proceedings against Francine were unexpectedly quickened by her decision to cease contesting the charge of adultery. Her discontent with her marriage and her relationship with a French physicist, who had also escaped from the Nazis when they invaded France, were no great secret. She had met him at Headington, while he was lecturing at Oxford University. The two left for Paris, where Francine found a flat and took up permanent residence soon after the divorce became absolute.

The day after the divorce came through, Clore was at a party in Mayfair, dancing until the early hours with an eighteen-year-old, six-foot-tall, debutante. Living in Geneva alone, Francine received the news that she had been awarded a settlement of £200,000. Her reaction was predictable. She announced:

> Contrary to all that has been said, there never is, and never has been, any glamour in my life. That kind of living was my ex-husband's way. He only seemed to enjoy himself at racing or night-clubs. It is the same, and always has been, whether in New York, Las Vegas, Mexico, Paris or London.

Although 'sweet' in the early stage of the marriage, Charles 'has forgotten those days. He only lives for his self-created empire.'

Under the settlement, Francine took custody of eleven-year-old Vivien, and Charles of twelve-year-old Alan. Alan was sent to the exclusive Le Rosey school in Switzerland, where he was pampered. The children commuted between their parents. Vivien, in particular, missed her horse and grew to dislike Paris intensely.

Francine married an American stockbroker shortly afterwards. The marriage lasted almost no time before she stormed out declaring it was a drastic mistake.

Charles saw his wife only rarely; when they did meet, he invariably emerged the worse off from the confrontation. In truth, he was afraid of Francine and was certainly no match for her fiery temper and scathing tongue. Knowing how he hated allowing anyone to gain an uninvited glimpse into his private life, Francine frequently irritated and enraged him by displaying her dislike for him in the most public of places. On one occasion, while they were still married, she said loudly at a dinner, 'Charles, why must you eat like a pig?', and in later years the two had a violent argument at a large family gathering at the Hilton Hotel. Even when they chose to ignore each other during social events, other guests were aware of the thick, hostile atmosphere between the two.

Despite the bitterness and hurt between them, Charles could never fully shrug of his admiration for Francine. In many ways she remained for him the ideal image of what a woman should be: accomplished, polished, independent and beautiful. Even after the divorce he continued to be proud of Francine and her achievements.

With Checkendon sold, Park Street was an empty and cheerless place in which to spend Christmas. Clore decided to go to St Moritz, where he spent an uncharacteristically quiet few weeks. Instead of the conviviality of the ski slopes (he hated skiing), he preferred the solitude of long walks. He became a familiar figure in his beaver-collared coat and Tyrolean hat, grasping a ski stick to help him along the snow-covered roads. In the mornings he would sip lemon tea, sitting in the sun on the terrace of a mountainside café. In the evenings he would sit in the hotel bar and sometimes dance in the ballroom or play bridge.

With his private life in ruins, Clore sought even more eagerly to prove his success in business. He searched for projects which would establish him as king of British industry. The London Hilton Hotel was one such opportunity.

Clore collected a group of sites and persuaded Conrad Hilton to buy the lease. 'It was an astounding deal,' says Kaye. It took a great deal of persuasion to convince a leading hotelier, and an American at that, to agree to such an apparently risky investment. Since the 1929 Wall Street crash, investors were particularly wary of hotel properties. 'If there was one thing that became valueless quickly, it was a hotel. It took a long time for hotels to get back to their former values,' comments Kaye. In the mid 1950s major hoteliers were not supplying cash flow by taking leases. Instead, they preferred franchising as a way of making a profit.

For some time it looked as if the negotiations with the Hilton would come to nothing. The Hilton representative insisted on paying for the hotel on a percentage of profits. This, however, was of little use to Clore. Unless he could show a clear income from the building, he would not be able to persuade the institutions to provide the cash to construct it. They, after all, needed some guarantee they would get their money back. The Hilton negotiators improved their offer a number of times, but always based on the same formula.

In desperation, Charles persuaded Conrad Hilton himself to come over. He and Sainer took him out for the evening, then met him at Sainer's office the next day. The negotiations began to settle back into the same groove. Eventually Charles snapped: 'This is London, England, not Addis Ababa. And here you'll pay the rent.' Hilton stared at him for a moment, then nodded and said: 'It's a deal.' The rent would be based on the cost of building.

The agreement with Hilton was not without stringent conditions. Hilton wanted the hotel built within a tight time schedule of two years, in order to catch the summer tourist trade, and to his specifications. The annual rental would depend on the cost of the building, then estimated at £4 million. Hilton was taking no chances and put pressure on Clore to start the construction almost immediately. After all, the longer the delay, the higher the costs; and the higher the costs, the greater the rent. Even though Kaye's plans were far from finalized, the bulldozers rolled in.

'Can you imagine the quandary I was in, in case the building was over the budget?' Kaye asks. In his view, the budget was underpriced by £1 million. The Hilton management breathed heavily down everyone's neck and asked Kaye how many hotels he had built. 'None', was the reply. From start to finish, the building of London's most prestigious hotel was a stressful affair. It was a nightmare to keep to the budget with everything half decided upon. Workmen, architects and surveyors were all working under severe pressure. While the foundations were laid, adjustments were still being made to the design drawing. When excavation started, fossils of snails almost nine inches long and four million years old were discovered.

Kaye chose a cement render as the cheapest finish to the upper walls enclosing the hotel's ballroom. 'Then the contractor said to me: "Why don't you use reconstructed stone? I've got a special deal with a company." I re-did the drawings and then we got blasted for causing an increase in price.'

In spite of all the confusion, the final bill for the hotel came to £4.5 million, only marginally above budget.

The bizarre tale of the Hilton had one last twist. In order to keep to the budget, Hilton decided to install four passenger lifts, instead of the six that Kaye had recommended. He created more bedrooms by using the area of free space, which Kaye had planned to turn into lounges because of the noise generated by the lifts. Some years later Hilton, realizing he would need to spend money putting sound insulation in the bedrooms nearer the lifts, tried to make Clore pay for his own earlier penny pinching. He arranged for Clore to stay in one of these bedrooms. Although Clore contacted Kaye the next day complaining about the noise, he saw through Hilton's ploy to make him, as the freeholder, pay for the noise insulation. Guests in the rooms around the lifts continue to pass uncomfortable nights.

In 1959 Charles offered the public an interest in his private property company, which by then held one of the most impressive portfolios in Britain, built up over the previous fifteen years. He opened negotiations with the Prudential with a view to acquiring development finance. By the autumn of 1960, the Prudential had agreed to advance long-term mortgage financing totalling £13 million – the largest ever single financing arrangement between a property company and a financial institution at the time. The Prudential took 10 per cent of the capital of City & Central Investments.

Within a few days after the arrangement, the Cotton/Clore merger was announced. Suddenly, the Prudential found its original investment reduced to a 5 per cent share in the new company. In return it found itself in partnership with a world class property institution. With Clore's commercial instincts and Cotton's flair, there seemed no limits to the potential of the new company. But as Charles had learnt with his shipbuilding exploits, sometimes flair is not enough to keep a company afloat. For the property business, too, there were stormy waters ahead.

8

Clore and Cotton: Another Disastrous Marriage

'There was an entire difference in
temperament. Jack trusted everyone. Charles
trusted hardly anyone. Jack sought publicity;
Charles hated it.' Eddie Footring

If Charles had learnt anything from the failure of his domestic marriage, it did not stand him in good stead when he entered into a business
marriage. The whirlwind romance between his property company, City
& Central, and Jack Cotton's City Centre Properties was tempestuous,
the honeymoon was shortlived and the divorce unnecessarily messy.

Cotton and Clore, the two great property tycoons, merged their property operations to become the largest property company in the world in
1960, and this was also the year in which Clore started to lose his touch.
There was still great genius in the man and he would go on to other
spectacular business successes, notably Selfridges, but this was the year
he began to make serious errors of judgement. For that, indeed, was
what the merger with Cotton was. Charles had learnt over the years
that he did not work well with a senior partner. Yet he was seduced by
the glamour of the publicity-hungry and visibly successful Cotton and,
for the first time, failed to think through thoroughly the implications
of the deal before agreeing to go ahead.

Over the years, the value of Charles' property portfolio had increased
in leaps and bounds. The release of artificial restraints on property
development and on rent increases had given an enormous boost to the
property sector. Those who had seen what this would mean in terms
of property values and income and were prepared to act boldly, were
almost bound to make fortunes. Clore's portfolio had not jumped as
high, however, as that of Jack Cotton, who had seen the market valuation of City Centre Properties rise from about £500,000 in 1956, when it
was known as Chesham House (Regent Street), to nearly £25 million at
the time of the merger.

Among others who had seized the abundant opportunities were
Isaac Wolfson and Max Rayne. And quietly working away building

121

what was to become the biggest property company of them all was Harold Samuel, with Land Securities Investment. Samuel, a former estate agent, bought control of Landsecs in 1944, when it consisted of three houses in Kensington, two of which were unoccupied. By the early 1950s he had increased the asset value to £15 million and by 1967 to nearly £200 million. All made the public eye from time to time. But the property tycoons who made most of the headlines in the late 1950s were Jack Cotton and Walter Flack.

Jack Cotton was a year older than Charles, having been born in Birmingham on 1 January 1903. Like Charles, he was Jewish and had family connections with South Africa. Unlike Charles, he grew up in a well-to-do middle-class area, Edgbaston. His father's firm, B. M. Cotton & Co., was a successful importer and exporter of silver plate, and traded particularly with South Africa. Other relatives were in the jewellery and related trades. Unlike Charles, he went to a public school, Cheltenham, where he made many of the connections that were to help get his property empire off the ground.

Cotton went straight into property after leaving school. He joined a firm of estate agents, working to qualify as an auctioneer. Immediately he did so, he quit to found his own firm, Jack Cotton & Partners, managing property for clients he acquired through his middle-class and Jewish connections. His father was totally opposed to the idea, so Jack had to borrow the £50 to get started from his mother. It was a small outfit for the first six years or so – a single office in Birmingham's New Street, housing just Cotton and Ruby Frost, his equivalent of Leah Gelman, the life-long faithful and discreet secretary.

Cotton was a kind-hearted man, an easy touch and a generous employer. So one story goes, he was susceptible to good hard-luck stories from the tenants he was supposed to collect rent from. On one occasion he was so moved by a widow's tale of woe that he paid her rent himself. He believed in rewarding loyalty and it is significant that, while Leah Gelman received comparatively very little encouragement during her years of service, Ruby Frost eventually became a partner in the estate agency and was left £10,000 in Cotton's will. Years later, in the garden of his Thameside mansion, he pointed to the fishpond and explained to a visitor why he had fitted it with tunnels for the goldfish to hide in. 'The herons come from the river and eat them for breakfast. I wanted to give the fish a chance. Everything deserves a chance.' It was a fundamental part of Jack's character that he wanted other people to share in his success. This instinctive human generosity (which Clore was never able to fathom) made Cotton almost universally liked, but also made him highly vulnerable.

He married in 1927 and had four children. As his business became more established, he took on civic duties with the City of Birmingham. To his death, he had a special regard for the city of his birth and his Midlands roots. When he was a multimillionaire and a public figure, chefs at the Dorchester became used to serving him with cottage pie, which he regarded as Birmingham's regional dish. He also gave generously to Birmingham charities, once writing out a cheque for £100,000 on the spot for a Midlands Arts Centre.

Cotton's career really got going in the early 1930s, when he began to buy up farmland around Birmingham, obtained planning permission and sold it off again at a substantial profit. His connections at City Hall were beginning to pay off. The money was raised in often complex deals and he gained a reputation for always paying up on or before time.

From there he expanded rapidly, setting up his own architectural firm to keep tighter control of the rebuilding side of property management. He bought and redeveloped a wide range of sites in his native Birmingham, always basing his decision to buy on location rather than price. Major landmarks, including his first school, King Edward's, were knocked down and replaced. The project on the school site gave him the taste for large deals. Costing £1 million in all, it was largely financed by a local solicitor, Joseph Cohen. There followed other successful partnerships with Cohen and new backers that set the pattern for his later developments. Before the Second World War, the skyline of Birmingham was littered with Cotton-developed office blocks. He had also made a painful foray into luxury flat development. The flats were so hard to sell that he made up his mind never to go into residential property again. Nor did he, until the City Centre merger brought in Clore's substantial holdings in London property and the Hampstead Garden Suburb. The lesson Cotton drew was that it was far better to rent or sell a building to a small number of clients, and preferably one, than to rent or sell it piecemeal.

Even thirty years later, Cotton was able to remember the precise details of properties he had handled at that time, including who bought them and for how much.

Then, just before the end of the war, Cotton suddenly upped and left Birmingham. He spent a short period in the United States, then returned to live in England and concentrate his business interests in the Thames Valley. He set up a new home on the Thames at Marlow, and offices in a discreet suite at the Dorchester. In 1947 he bought Mansion House Chambers, which was on the verge of liquidation, and used it as a vehicle to develop a variety of properties acquired cheaply during the war. His name did not appear on any of the documents and his accountant, Freddie Lindgren, became chairman.

The move obliged Cotton to think beyond the Midlands for future developments. He had already made some purchases in London, starting with Dorland House in Regent Street, but now his ambition grew. In 1954 he bought Central Commercial Properties, which consisted mainly of high-street shops, for £2 million. Judicious improvements doubled the income from these properties over the following ten years. Then three years later, in 1957, he picked up a large portion of Tredegar Estates, in Newport, South Wales. The estate consisted of several thousand acres of properties which included docks, houses, industrials, mines and, most importantly, a substantial part of the town centre. Most of the properties there were let on long leases at low ground rents.

Almost staggering beneath the weight of the estate portfolio, Orchard-Lisle visited Cotton at his Dorchester suite. He need not have bothered with the heavy load; Cotton simply asked what was the total rent roll and the reversion dates of the most valuable section of the estate on the town centre. Then he told Orchard-Lisle to bid a twenty-years purchase and have the contract sent to the solicitors. 'This evidently cavalier attitude puzzled me at the time,' Orchard-Lisle recalls.

The Pearl Assurance supplied the finance for the deal. Two or three days before the contracts were due to be signed, Cotton telephoned Orchard-Lisle to suggest that they go to see what he had bought. Without the use of any papers, Cotton walked down the shopping streets of Newport reciting every rent and lease expiration date. Orchard-Lisle comments: 'He certainly knew what he was buying.'

Cotton's instinctive flair had resulted in a remarkable deal. The agreed price for the estate was based on a twenty-years purchase of the rent received, but the estate included large parcels of valuable housing and other land, besides other non-income-producing property, which effectively cost nothing. During the two years delay before the completion date – arising because many of the deeds had not exchanged hands for generations and were missing or incomplete – Cotton sub-sold many of the less valuable sites, leaving the valuable town centre virtually intact. By the time of the completion date, a very high proportion of the purchase price had been recovered in sub-sales.

His native Birmingham was not neglected. He had been quietly buying up great chunks of the city centre with the aim of redeveloping a major bombed site on New Street that had lain fallow for many years. But so had another company, Revenseft. Eventually the two combined forces in a massive redevelopment of the sites, which was known as the Big Top because it had once been used as a circus. The *Evening Standard*, whose City pages voted him Man of the Year in 1960, described his genius in these terms:

Mr Cotton's trick was to improve a whole district, a device which obviously had great possibilities. It is plain that a house in a 'respectable' area is far more valuable than an exactly similar house in a disreputable area. So he improved the quality of the area.

City Centre Properties, a company established in the eighteenth century, was bought in 1955 as a rationalization of his affairs. But Cotton still refused to take his rightful role as chairman. He shunned all publicity and frequently admonished his staff to have nothing to do with the press.

By the time the press discovered him in 1957 – the result of an extravagant gesture at his daughter's wedding (he laid on a special train to take guests to Birmingham) – Cotton was riding high. He was remarkably successful yet, to the public, a complete unknown. As the newspapers pursued him, the recluse suddenly found he enjoyed the publicity attached to the role of international property developer. He began to play up to it with a will. From then on, he became addicted. To a considerable extent, the pace of City Centre's growth over the next few years (at one stage there was almost one major new deal every week) was driven by his egotistical desire to have something new to announce to the press.

This obsession with self-publicity was to become his Achilles' heel. Eventually it clouded his judgement, took precedence over commercial considerations and brought about his downfall. In 1959, shortly before the merger deal was hatched, it wrecked a major development project at Piccadilly Circus. Cotton had acquired the Cafe Monico site from Express Dairies in 1954 for £500,000, and had formed a company with Legal & General Assurance to redevelop it. The purchase was a swift decision, based as always on the superb location. Planning approval took years of muddled negotiations with the London County Council, but was eventually given verbally. Then Cotton held a massive press conference to show off the new building. It was the television programme, which appeared soon after, that did the real damage. The public furore at the sight of cranes and electric signs covering Piccadilly Circus prompted a public inquiry and caused the London County Council to take fright and withdraw planning consent. It was just in time; a shortage of typists at County Hall meant that Cotton had not yet received a written consent from the Council. The contract was whipped away from under his nose. Cotton was devastated, but refused to give up. For years afterwards he spent time and money trying to convince anyone who would listen that his plans were right for Piccadilly Circus.

City Centre formed more and more partnerships with more and more people, growing so rapidly that Cotton was able to boast that there was not enough money in the world to keep pace with his expansion needs.

In particular, Cotton linked up with the insurance companies who had financed previous deals. In 1958 he sold 25 per cent of his shares to Pearl Assurance and took one of its top people, Edward Plumridge, onto his board. Under pressure from the Pearl, he assumed the chairmanship. A year later, with shares having soared from 7s 7d to 72s, City Centre was building or acquiring properties all over England and South Africa, and was looking for suitable deals in the United States. It owned sites all over London, including a large chunk of land on Park Lane, almost next door to Clore's Hilton development. It was there that Cotton, still smarting over his treatment at the Cafe Monico site, commissioned Gropius, the eminent American architect, to design the elevation of the Playboy Club.

In early 1960, Cotton formed a partnership with another property developer, Walter Flack. Flack's company, Murrayfield Real Estate Co., was strapped for cash. It had grown so fast that it had too many projects half-finished. Cotton saw an opportunity to expand his empire for relatively little effort and agreed to buy 30 per cent of Murrayfield. Ignoring the financial implications, Cotton agreed to provide the finance needed to complete the Murrayfield projects at 1.5 per cent over base rate. This open-ended commitment was later to become a drain on City Centre funds and a major cause of friction between Cotton and Clore.

Charles had watched the emergence of Cotton, the provincial developer, with amazement and not a little envy. The two men had met from time to time, via various intermediaries. Both were major customers of estate agents Healey & Baker, an old-established firm nearing its 150th anniversary. Tovey used to look after Clore's interests while Orchard-Lisle looked after Cotton's, although by no means exclusively. This arrangement worked well before the merger.

The two property millionaires had much in common. Both were emotionally vulnerable; both shared a love of fine art. Cotton had acquired Renoir's magnificent painting, *La Pensée*, for £70,000 and hung it on his office wall at the Dorchester. Like Clore, Cotton enjoyed his art treasures for their beauty as much as and more than for their cash value. 'It makes me think,' Cotton told journalists of his Renoir. Both Cotton and Clore were also men of their word. Having agreed to a deal, they would not prevaricate or change their minds, even if they had second thoughts (which neither did very often). Some years ago, Cotton's pre-war bank manager, Norman Iles, recalled an incident in 1959 for a property writer. Iles was visiting Cotton in London to discuss finance for a major deal in the United States. Out of the blue, Cotton asked him: 'What is the main quality you've supported me for over all these years?'

'You've always been a little better than your word,' replied Iles.

Cotton rang a bell to summon a young man into his office. 'Would you mind repeating what you just told me?' he asked Iles. When Iles had done so, Cotton looked pointedly at the young man and said, 'Now, get that into your head', and dismissed him from the room.

Cotton's word was rarely questioned. On the few occasions when it was, he was able to cope easily with the situation and would often emerge in a considerably better light than the doubting party. At the time when he was putting together the Monico site, Cotton agreed to buy for a considerable sum of money a long leasehold interest, then belonging to the trustees of the J. Lyons & Co. family. Contracts were exchanged and a date for completion fixed when rumours began circulating that Cotton's company was hard pressed for cash. Alarmed at the implications, the Lyons trustee, the late Sir Louis Gluckstein, QC, went to see Cotton at the Dorchester. He requested that the completion take place within a fortnight's time, instead of the agreed two months, and asked Cotton what discount he would want for the earlier completion. In his usual drawl and with great dignity, Cotton replied that the Lyons family seemed more pressed for cash than his company and, in the circumstances, he would be happy to arrange for the completion at the earlier date without discount.

Both Cotton and Clore were keen Zionists. Both gave generously to Jewish causes and, surprisingly, to London Zoo. Clore's efforts for Israel were later and more munificent, but Cotton gave practical help in establishing the new state, by organizing Jewish emigration to Palestine.

For all these reasons, here were two tycoons who had, on the surface at least, so much in common that they ought to have been natural business partners.

The deal was hatched by Charles' close friend and property adviser, Douglas Tovey. Flying across the Atlantic to view some New York property, Tovey suddenly thought how senseless it was that he and Orchard-Lisle should be competing against each other on behalf of different clients, when they both worked in the same offices. Clore and Cotton liked and respected each other and recognized the importance of size in achieving commercial clout.

That Sunday, having already obtained Clore's consent to explore the possibilities of such a deal, Tovey drove over to see Cotton, who was in bed with flu at his house in Marlow. He explained his idea, stressing how much more powerful the two rival companies would be on both sides of the Atlantic, if only they joined forces. Cotton immediately saw the possibilities. But how to sell the deal to Clore?

Tovey had given that aspect of the deal considerable thought as he drove over. 'The terms will have to be one share of City Centre for one of City & Central,' he suggested. Cotton demurred. After all, his shares stood much higher than Clore's, at 70 shillings against 55. Why should he give away so much?

Tovey went back over the arguments. It would be the biggest property company in the world – think of the prestige. He would be able to take advantage of Clore's expertise, influence and contacts in other industries. The portfolio would be more diversified. He had Cotton hooked.

'All right,' said Cotton. 'I'll agree to those terms on one condition. I must be the chairman of the new company.'

Tovey then drove to Clore's country estate at Stype and told him: 'Jack agrees. The terms are to be one for one. There's just one snag – Jack wants to be chairman, with you as deputy chairman. Otherwise, he won't agree to the terms.'

'Douglas,' said Clore, unable to repress his glee, 'for 70 shillings a share I'll be the office boy.'

Why was Charles so keen? After all, he was doing nicely, thank you, with his own property exploits and had no real need of a partner. Moreover, City & Central, with its own extensive property portfolio, could easily have absorbed City Centre. One reason was that Charles was beginning to lose interest in managing property himself. He had many other interests to pursue and was aware that he was not able to give his property interests the attention they deserved. This led the News of the World to wonder if Clore had 'lost his keenness of a few years back'.

Another reason was that he was becoming increasingly jealous of Cotton's success. In particular, he was put out by Cotton's publicity coup in acquiring 50 per cent ownership of the Pan Am Building in central Manhattan. The vast monolith above Grand Central Station had been conceived and constructed by the American developer, Erwin Wolfson. A contender for the tallest office block in the world and arguably the most prestigious in New York, the building was to be the culminating glory of Wolfson's career. Costing £35 million to build, the sixty-four-storey block would accommodate 30,000 workers and provide an annual rental of £6 million when fully occupied. Wolfson had arranged a complex financing deal with the airline, which was to take most of the office space. At the last moment, however, Pan Am stretched Wolfson on the rack, delaying signing the tenancy agreement in hopes of extracting a better deal. Ironically, this is just the sort of situation that other famous Wolfson, Isaac, dearly enjoyed creating in reverse.

The Pan Am building was an international status symbol and Wolfson, who now was desperate for cash to finish it, was far from happy at the idea of having to seek equity participation from rival US property moguls, although there were plenty who were interested. He started looking for an overseas partner. When Cotton, who was on holiday in the Bahamas, was asked if he were interested, he jumped at the chance. The commercial sense of the deal was compelling; but what clinched it was the publicity value of owning the tallest building in New York.

Jack played that publicity value for all it was worth. At the annual general meeting, at which his participation in the Pan Am project became public knowledge, he outdid the Americans themselves in the razzmatazz of the announcement. The annual lunch with the press was interrupted by a recording saying: 'Gee, that's big. Why is it so big? Because it's gotta be big. It's gotta be the biggest in the world.' The room was then filled with the sound of the CBS orchestra playing a specially recorded song. It was spectacular, attention-grabbing, larger than life – everything that Cotton wanted.

Clore was not a little envious. His only major US property buy had been 40 Wall Street. It was not, by any considerations, as spectacularly good a deal as Cotton's. The seller, Bill Zeckendorf, was a leading light among US property developers and knew the value of his property only too well. Few people ever came off best in deals with him. The building, which had previously been occupied by Chase Manhattan Bank, needed considerable refurbishment. Clore, however, was this time less interested in the property value than in the status of the seventy-storey building – one of the most prestigious in the financial centre. The Wall Street deal brought Charles to sudden international prominence. Suddenly he was *persona grata* across the United States. Luncheons, dinner parties and dances were held in his honour.

A third reason for Charles' enthusiasm was that he thought he could control Cotton, stop him from hogging the limelight, if he brought him on to the same board.

Most of all, however, Charles agreed because the financial terms of the deal seemed so good. With Tovey's help he had pulled off a remarkable coup. He was so wrapped up in self-congratulation that he scarcely stopped to look at the potential problems. Had he done so, he might well have persuaded Cotton to let him be chairman – a course which would have avoided most of the later disputes and dissension. Afraid that the deal would collapse if he insisted on this, Charles ignored his better judgement and gave Cotton his way. It was to prove a disastrous mistake.

After all, from Clore's point of view the deal seemed, in many ways, a risk-free opportunity. City & Central shares had lacked lustre, being primarily in less glamorous properties than Cotton's. The merger deal was remarkably generous. Had the roles been reversed, Clore would have demanded a two-for-one exchange of shares, given the relative share values. He could not lose in the short term. The new company would be valued at £65 million, of which Cotton's personal stake was worth £14 million and Clore's £10 million. Such was Charles' confidence that the venture would work that he brought his own building company, Token Construction, into the deal for a token sum. It was, in any case, a subsidiary of City & Central.

For Cotton, the obvious advantages were those outlined by Tovey. His better judgement was clouded, too, by the glory of being international top dog in property. The Birmingham lad made good had all the money he wanted. Now he was looking for increased prestige and social acceptance.

The two men manifestly had a great deal of admiration for each other and this undoubtedly blinded them to each other's weaknesses. There was no thought on Charles' part, for example, that Jack might be developing a drinking problem, even though Charles did take his new partner aback at their first meeting to discuss the merger details by waving away the celebratory drinks. 'Get rid of those bottles,' he snapped. 'I'm here to do business.'

With the exception of Tovey and the two principals, no one else in the Cotton and Clore camps was in favour of the deal. Their concerns were less that the two empires would not fit together easily than that Clore and Cotton would not establish a viable working relationship.

Certainly there were differences in their respective approaches to business, their style of management and in the property portfolios they had built up. Clore by now had learnt to distrust partners in any shape or form. If he took control of a property or a business, he wanted it all. He obtained his loans as cheaply as possible or, wherever practical, financed a deal out of his own cash resources. He hated to be in debt and, whenever he had to borrow, invariably paid off the loan as rapidly as possible. Cotton, on the other hand, would make partners with anybody, would attempt to work with anybody and would expect to share the rewards. This was, in fact, a serious weakness, for he lacked Clore's remarkable ability to judge the calibre of people about him. Clore would rapidly decide that someone was either highly capable and worth bothering with (in which case he would go to great lengths to involve them in his schemes – this was a prime reason for the marriage with Cotton) or would ignore them totally. The initial enthusiasm with which he embraced Cotton was a measure of the strength of his regard for the Birmingham man as a property genius. Cotton was just nice to everybody, and would have made many more mistakes had he not been fortunate (or wise) enough to have superb lieutenants who could head him off from bad deals most of the time.

Clore's property portfolio was far more staid. He was always looking mainly to the long term and had invested his money into solid properties with guaranteed returns. Among these was a residential and office estate in Mayfair. In general, he did not experience the problems that had made Cotton wary of residential property, although his acquisition of the Hampstead Garden Suburb had led to heated public debate. At issue was whether or not tenants could exercise their statutory right to acquire the freeholds of their homes. The suburb had been built as an integral community and, claimed City & Central, the environment would be greatly changed if the leaseholders were to lose control. For Cotton and Clore, the issue became academic. Well before the arguments were over, they had sold the estate on. In turning the estate, in which many of the houses were inhabited by Jewish families, into a viable business, Clore made few friends among the tenants. While he aimed to maximize income, his primary goal was to increase the asset value. It was unfortunate that the 1960s saw the rise of a number of unscrupulous landlords who used dubious methods to evict tenants and increase rents – among them the notorious Rachman. While Clore may not have been a model landlord, he did not deserve in any way to be bracketed with these characters and would have been deeply offended at such a suggestion.

In style of management, City & Central ran a meticulously tidy office, with clear routines and procedures for approving action. Clore, Sainer, Archie Sherman and Eddie Footring took a structured approach to each deal, going into great detail about the current status of each project. In between board meetings, recalls Wally Townsend, then financial secretary at Park Street,

> I used to have to show him the property portfolio every day. If it was down, he was really browned off. It took so much time to draw up that in the end I persuaded him to do it once a fortnight and eventually once a month, but he was interested in the detail all the time.

Clore's natural caution would not allow him to rush into a deal until he knew that he had the finance sewn up and that he had as exact an estimate as possible of the money to be made.

Cotton, on the other hand, could not and would not be a detail man when it came to finance. His style had always been to agree the fundamentals and then to take no more interest until the deal was clinched. 'Talk about it with Freddie [Lindgren],' he would say. His instinct for 'good' property was almost unerring and he relied upon it totally. As long as the location was right, he would agree to buy first, then begin to look for the finance, in the knowledge that his reputation was sufficient to ensure that the money would be found. It was then merely a matter of ingenuity to come up with a development plan that would provide a substantial return on the investment. Cotton thrived on the intricacy of his network of relationships with banks and insurance companies. His style of management could almost be described as shotgun. His empire was a hotchpotch of entities spread around the country. Paperwork and formal meetings were sparse. He made little secret of his lack of financial expertise, once saying: 'I have never understood money: I don't even sign the cheques myself. That's the part of it I never understand.'

Eddie Footring, who came to know both men well, describes them in these terms:

> There was an entire difference in temperament. Jack trusted everyone; Charles trusted hardly anyone. Jack sought publicity; Charles hated it – he left Sainer to do all that. Charles never interfered, Jack was the reverse. He did everything himself; he wouldn't delegate. It was impossible to keep up with him and no one knew what he was doing. Charles was the delegater supreme – everything was done for him. Jack wasn't secretive, in fact he was too talkative about the business.

The difference between the two companies can be seen as one of relative maturity. City Centre Properties was a typical entrepreneurial business, run to a large extent on flair, rather than systems. At some stage in its development the entrepreneurial business has to go through a metamorphosis, a maturing process that instils order and procedure. If it fails to do so, creative disorder gives way to destructive anarchy, as the business becomes too big to handle in an intuitive way. Charles' companies had made that transition some years before. Cotton, as is so often the case with large-scale entrepreneurs, was probably incapable of making it happen.

Until now, Charles had rarely gone into serious partnership with a friend. With the exception of Tovey, all his business relationships were just that. He would occasionally dally with the idea of some form of partnership with dining companions such as Charles (now Lord) Forte or Marcus (now Lord) Sieff. But he was reluctant to mix business and social life and he recognized that he could not be comfortable in any partnership where he could not be top dog.

The merger with City Centre broke both of these habits. In spite of the rivalry between them, Cotton was a friend. He was also the less dominant of the two. The strength of the deal, as originally envisaged by Tovey, was that Charles would moderate Jack's excesses of enthusiasm, while Jack's drive and fertility of mind would continue the expansion of the enlarged company. To work properly, the new company needed Charles in the top spot, to force the whole organization to the maturity of City & Central. The transition should have been made immediately – after all, the enlarged company was now way beyond the size that could be managed by the seat of the pants. By playing second fiddle, Charles lost the chance to instil order into the company.

Certainly, the City commentators saw the benefits of the deal in terms of organizational maturity. The *Investor's Chronicle* considered that

> the factors that brought the two Mr Cs together were the relative lack on Mr Clore's part of a wholly integrated, full-time executive board and the generous zeal on Mr Cotton's part to expand, to have the opportunity of working with Mr Clore and by so doing to conquer new property fields. Others have wondered if the speed of Mr Cotton's development called for the support of a much larger organization. Certainly, the expert way in which CCP has been built up is owed almost entirely to the creative strength of Mr Cotton's own personality and abilities, but in itself this is a weakness, judged from the long-term point of view.

In the event, instead of building on the two companies' strengths, the merger emphasized their weaknesses.

An additional warning sign emerged in the structure of the new company. Neither man was willing to forgo his own empire entirely. While there was a group board chaired by Cotton, both companies maintained their own identity and went on operating as they had done before. In fact, there were three private fiefdoms, belonging respectively to Clore, Cotton and Flack, each with their own alliances and their own team of advisers. To a considerable extent, the board was held together by the institutional shareholders. George Bridge represented Legal & General, while Cotton's old friend, Edward Plumridge, looked after the interests of the Pearl.

Typically, it was Cotton who did all the talking to the press. 'This is not a takeover,' he declared. 'It is a merger and it has been decided that an exchange of shares is the best way to achieve it.... Between us, we shall control between £175 million and £200 million of property in Britain and other countries, including America and Africa.' Charles was happy to leave him the floor as long as he was making money.

Yet from the first board meeting things began to go sour. The meeting was held in Cotton's palatial suite at the Dorchester. Jack went through all the motions. At the end of the agenda, Charles asked: 'Anything new?'

'We've bought some properties in Cardiff,' replied Jack. Clore nodded as he heard the names of the sites. His approval was checked by Cotton's next response to his questions.

'Exactly where?' Clore asked. Jack wasn't quite sure.

'Freehold or leasehold?' He couldn't recall.

'What's the income?' He didn't know.

Sainer and Clore exchanged worried glances. They recognized then that Jack's lack of attention to detail was going to be a problem. No one was questioning his instinct; years later these same sites were sold by City Centre Properties for many times their original cost. Clore recognized Cotton had made a good deal; he just had to figure how to come to grips with Cotton's style.

Before very long it became clear to Charles that the outflow of cash into Murrayfield's seemingly bottomless pit would have to be curtailed. It was increasingly questionable whether there was money to be made from some of these properties even after they were developed. Clore insisted that Murrayfield must become a wholly owned subsidiary, so that City Centre could control its activities and spending. Both Flack, who was on to a good thing, and Cotton, who hated to turn the screws on him, argued against the change. But Sainer's logic, backed up by Charles' forceful personality, broke their resistance, and news of the amalgamation was broken to the public in May 1961. The deal, which involved a £2 million exchange of shares, gave Flack a seat on the board. 'The sergeant', as he was known in the City, had arrived.

But for Flack, whose rise to riches had been even more rapid than Clore's or Cotton's, his arrival in the big league was also the beginning of the end. Born in 1917 he, too, was the son of a Jewish tailor. A failed solicitor, he had somehow found himself working as an estate agent negotiator after the war (his active service was as a cook) and had eventually left to set up his own partnership, which was only moderately successful. In character, he would today have made a very successful public relations man. Flack started buying and doing up properties with his £300 war gratuity. His meteoric rise to prominence started when he acquired Murrayfield in 1958. All he received for the £11,000 was the Stock Exchange quotation, but that was the vehicle he needed to expand. He brought into the company a few properties he already owned, then set about looking for more.

Flack's permanent problem was the need to raise finance. There was never enough for all his plans and he lacked credibility with the big banks, because his track record was so short. He solved the problem partially by bringing on to his board influential figures such as his commander in the army, Field Marshal Auchinleck, and Sir Frank Price, a former leader of the socialist party on Birmingham City Council. But he was always the newcomer and regarded as a bit of an adventurer.

He first came to wide public notice with a successful £1 million bid for a prestige block of flats in Whitehall. The financial impetus for Murrayfield's growth came, however, from a city centre development at Basildon. The deal was typical of many at the time. The local council, which owned the land, wanted to off-load all the risks of development. It approved the development plans, but insisted that the developer raise the finance for demolition and construction, and took responsibility for finding tenants for the shops and offices. Murrayfield received a ninety-nine-year lease on the site, but did not have to start paying rent until the project was completed. As there was then a sellers' market for centrally located office and shop premises, Murrayfield was able to line up tenants before it had to pay rent. For the developer in these circumstances, the only problems were raising the loan to cover the construction cost and building the premises as swiftly as possible, to minimize interest payments. Once tenanted, the income from the shops and offices far outweighed the loan interest and the rent to the council, providing a guaranteed and substantial long-term income. As an alternative, the developer could realize his asset as cash by selling it off as a going concern at a huge profit.

Sainer recalls the tale of how Flack convinced the Basildon Council to give him the go-ahead:

> He drove down in a Rolls-Royce he had hired for the day with his last £20. He clearly made an impression on the council with his presentation. Then they said: 'You have £2 paid up capital. How are you going to find the money?' He walked up and down for a moment, then turned to them and said: 'I'll tell you what. I'll give you my personal guarantee.' They accepted.

There followed a string of major town centre developments across the country, in towns such as Huddersfield and Preston, as well as in the capital. Flack gained a reputation for careful planning that would retain as much as possible of the character of the redeveloped area. For example, the first big project brought to him by Price – a multimillion pound redevelopment of central Dundee – moulded the shopping precinct around the city's ancient churches. He was also known for his disarming frankness. One of his mottoes was: 'Give it to them straight, even though they won't believe you half the time.'

Flack ventured on to the Continent, buying, among other properties, a big old house on the prestigious Avenue Foch in Paris (not far from Francine's childhood home) to turn into luxury flats. Property writer Oliver Marriott recalls how Flack kept an impressive 'English bible' listing all the details of all the British properties he was involved in.

The deal with Cotton and Clore worried some of the Labour-controlled councils Flack was building for and he had to make conciliatory trips to explain that nothing had changed, that he now simply had more resources behind him. The biggest challenge was Huddersfield, where the atmosphere as he entered the council meeting-room was tense and threatening. On the wall of a theatre he had bought as part of the redevelopment was the graffiti: 'Cotton and Clore go home.' This had given Flack an idea of how to turn the meeting to advantage. As it got under way, he kept referring to 'the other two Cs' and how they would really have been something to worry about. Eventually, the council chairman could bear it no longer.

'Who are these other two Cs?' he demanded.

'Why, Crippen and Christie,' replied Flack. 'We know what they did, but what have Cotton and Clore done that is so wrong?' The meeting collapsed into laughter and the problems dissolved.

Flack's sudden arrival in the big time went to his head. Blind to the experience of Cotton and Clore and to the quality of their portfolios, he felt he could do anything they could. But the truth was that he was not a star, merely one of the supporting cast. Had he not been rescued by Cotton, his empire would have collapsed before long. As the weakest of the three, it was inevitable that he would be the first casualty.

Relationships between the three protagonists deteriorated rapidly and were not helped by an unfortunate *faux pas* by Cotton in New York. The occasion was the formal opening of the Pan Am building. City Centre flew over a host of dignitaries from London and Europe. It was Cotton's big day, even if the building had been conceived and largely built by Erwin Wolfson, and he was not about to share the glory with Clore. When Charles found that he was seated among the rump of the diners, rather than among the principals, he was furious. To be fair, he was not actually on the board of the subsidiary that owned the building. But the slight rankled and was not easily forgotten, even though both put a good face on it. He did not, however, allow it to influence his business judgement. 'Charles would have kept Jack on even if he insulted him every morning, just as long as he was successful,' maintains Eddie Footring.

Gradually, City Centre broke up into two armed camps that disagreed with each other on everything. Plans to expand into Europe with the Rothschilds were shelved because Cotton was jealous of Clore's connections. Charles Wilson, then at Investment Registry, recalls that the board meetings were eventually so hostile that 'they used to line up on right and left. None of them were speaking to each other'.

All that, however, came after the honeymoon. The momentum of the merger carried City Centre's popularity well into 1962. In June, *Queen* magazine was warmly commending the company and its 'guiding geniuses', Cotton and Clore. In addition to the ambitious Pan Am project, City Centre had properties in 268 cities and towns. Plans for Europe included a joint property development company with Dutch electronics giant, Philips. Predicting a dividend rise from 25.5 to 40 per cent by 1964, *Queen* eulogized:

> The dynamic expansion of City Centre is far from reaching its end. Sound
> property investments have proven over the years to be among the most

rewarding investments in terms of growth of both income and capital value. The art, of course, is picking the right investments. No one has ever questioned the ability of Cotton, Clore and their associates on this score.

The deals with institutions came fast and furious. Everyone wanted to be on the Cotton/Clore bandwagon. In addition to the joint ventures with General Accident, Legal & General and the Pearl, there were deals worth more than £18 million with the pension funds of Imperial Chemical Industries, Unilever and Imperial Tobacco. The Church Commissioners, long-term supporters of Clore, grew close to City Centre, as did both Shell-Mex, BP and Woolworths.

One of the first bids launched was a £2.4 million offer for Manchester's historic Royal Exchange, one of that city's most valuable sites. The ninety-year-old city centre complex contained office blocks, shops and stores, and the air terminal. Although the directors advised against accepting the bid, the lure of Cotton and Clore was sufficient for 90 per cent of shareholders to accept the share for share offer. 'That's the attraction of our bid,' boasted Cotton. 'No one can tell what our shares will be worth in twelve months' time.' Clearly, the investors shared Cotton's conviction that the share price would continue to rise.

The list of projects went on and on and rapidly became far too long for Cotton to keep proper track of, gradually moving away from big office developments towards building hotels and shopping centres. In Reading, City Centre was engaged in developing the whole of the railway station forecourt. In Liverpool, there were £30 million plans to restore the residential nature of the city centre with a 27-acre redevelopment reaching down to the banks of the Mersey. In the Isle of Man, City Centre was bidding to build a major casino complex.

In London, there were plans to change the forecourt of Charing Cross and to build an eleven-storey office block with restaurant and bowling alley at Leicester Square. Several London clubs, including the Constitutional, the National Liberal and the Army & Navy, signed over their sites for redevelopment and were rehoused. (When, in 1965, Charles was elected to the Carlton Club, it was joked that the members only let him in to stop him knocking the place down.)

The famous Pimms House in Bishopsgate (the home of Pimms cups) succumbed to City Centre in 1963. Further West, City Centre started construction of the fourteen-storey Royal Garden Hotel, which had to be specially designed so as not to overlook the gardens of Kensington Palace. Another, smaller hotel was planned in Grosvenor Square.

Many of these ventures were the inevitable Cotton partnerships, primarily with pension funds and insurance companies, but also with private individuals. Cotton was immensely flattered at being asked to advise Earl Fitzwilliam, the proud owner of some 20,000 hereditary acres, on property management. Inevitably, the relationship led to a joint venture to redevelop several of Fitzwilliam's properties in Grosvenor Street.

Even some of the apparent failures turned to gold in the long term. Moor House, a skyscraper project in London Wall started under City & Central, drew considerable disparaging comment. The first major office block in the Barbican area, it was considered by the pundits to be too far out from the Stock Exchange and, at 5s 9d a square foot for the lease, a foolhardily expensive buy. The rent City Centre was asking – £2 a square foot – was high enough to keep parts of the block empty for months, earning it the nickname 'the White Elephant of London Wall'. Charles, as usual, had the last laugh. The last of the twelve blocks on the site went to another developer at three times the ground rent, and office rents in the area gradually rose to £9 per square foot.

By 1962 the Cotton/Clore genius for making money from property was so universally recognized that Dr Beeching, the famous (or infamous) axer of railways, consulted them over how best to redevelop railway property.

Not everyone took kindly to the idea of redeveloping their city centres. 'Can Slough keep out the Cottons and Clores?' clamoured the *Slough Observer* in alarm. Battersea Council was recalled from holiday for an emergency session to fight a City Centre plan to build private flats on surplus railway land. And Cambridge residents were up in arms at the first hint of a City Centre development in the heart of their city.

If the projects that went well were time-consuming, those that went badly were doubly so. The Piccadilly Circus saga ground inexorably on, diverting Cotton's talents from more viable projects. But two abortive projects particularly illustrate how Cotton's growing obsession with thinking big was reducing his capability of managing a complex organization – the respective bids for City of London Real Property and Stoll Theatres.

City of London (CLRP) was virtually the same size, in capital terms, as City Centre itself. Even before the share offer on the City Centre merger had closed, the new company had launched its bid for CLRP. The bid raised a good many eyebrows in the City. Had it succeeded, it would have created an enormous property group. The trouble was that Cotton had not done sufficient groundwork.

Founded in 1864 by two brothers on the profits from rum importation and sugar plantations in the West Indies, CLRP had a portfolio of solid, blue-chip office properties spread the square mile of the City, but particularly concentrated in the general area between Fenchurch Street and Eastcheap. Many of them had been rebuilt after the war. As property companies go, this long-established company was the Establishment.

While its growth was not spectacular, its gearing (the ratio of borrowing to equity) was exceptionally low. It was a safe investment for people who wanted security of income rather than rapid growth in share value. As such, it was scarcely the kind of property portfolio Cotton was used to managing. The acquisition would tie up cash, which could only be released if some of the assets were sold.

Cotton's interest was kindled when City solicitor Christopher Reeves, whose family held the largest shareholding (about 20 per cent), intimated through Orchard-Lisle that he was interested in selling up. The lure of making an even bigger company was overwhelming for Cotton. His enthusiasm evinced a cautious go-ahead from Clore, who was in the United States at the time. Initial discussions with Reeves were positive and a verbal agreement was made.

When the bid was announced, a shocked Establishment closed ranks. The other shareholders and many of Reeves' acquaintances and clients took the solicitor aside and insisted he changed his mind. Sell up by all means – but to those two interlopers, no.

Cotton, who had relied on Reeves' word and had nothing in writing, was left high and dry. The *Daily Telegraph* was kind to Cotton when it reported the events thus:

> Mr Cotton was firmly of the belief that Mr Reeves would support the takeover bid and that the rest of the board and other big shareholders would do likewise. When it was curtly rejected, he was so taken aback and affronted, that he closed his books on the whole affair.

In reality, Clore had insisted that City Centre withdraw rapidly before any further damage was done to its reputation. When he returned from the United States, a furious Clore demanded why Cotton had not paid cash for Reeves' shares on the spot, the moment the deal was agreed. Then and only then should the bid have been launched. With the largest shareholding in City Centre's hands, the CLRP board would have had little choice but to submit. The embarrassing bungle had been caused not just by Cotton's failure to recognize that Reeves might not complete the deal, but by his unwillingness to invest risk capital. Had he bought the shares and lost the takeover bid, Cotton could still have sold out again at a profit, for the bid would almost certainly have forced a revaluation of CLRP's assets.

By Sunday, the *Telegraph* had obtained a fuller account of events and remarked sanctimoniously:

> Mr Cotton may with some justice complain that he was a victim of circumstance. But it is pretty clear that had Mr Clore, and not Mr Cotton, been handling the affair, it would not have been handled in this

amateurish fashion. . . . The terms of the bid were, in any case, inadequate, as the CLRP statement promised in the next few weeks will doubtless show. But the lesson for Mr Cotton is plain enough. Look after the property and leave the bids to Mr Clore.

Cotton was already proving to be out of his depth in the world of high finance.

Equally embarrassing was the débâcle over the Stoll Moss theatre empire. Again the problem arose because of inadequate bid preparation. In November 1960, Cotton and Clore, in collaboration with Bernard (now Lord) Delfont, formed a new company to launch a bid for Moss Empires. Moss owned thirty-seven theatres and other current or former entertainment sites around the country, including the Palladium, the Theatre Royal in Drury Lane, the Apollo and the London Hippodrome. Many of these sites were ripe for redevelopment. Once again, the £5.7 million bid was launched before sufficient shares had been secured. Moss' chairman, Prince Littler, rushed about buying up all the shares he could lay his hands on, at any price, on behalf of Stoll Theatre Corporation, which already had a sizeable shareholding and of which he also happened to be chairman.

When Littler announced he had secured a majority of the shares, Clore immediately wrote an open letter, demanding evidence. Littler, who produced notarized certificates, demanded an apology. The nearest he received was a somewhat sanctimonious letter, saying:

> I, personally, would not have doubted your word, but you will appreciate that this was a matter which attracted a great deal of public interest, and it would not have been fair to the shareholders of Moss Empires to withdraw the proposed offer, which was in excess of the market price, without some formal confirmation of your claim to have gained control of the company.

The next obvious step would have been to bid for Stoll Theatres. Again, however, Clore and Cotton were blocked. Stoll's ordinary shares were outgunned by 80,000 special management shares, three-quarters of which were owned by Littler, his brother Emile and their financial adviser. No one at City Centre had thought to establish the status of the various shareholdings. Charles and Jack retreated with their tails between their legs. The price of City Centre shares dropped 5s.

Then there was the bizarre idea – wrongly attributed to Clore – of moving St George's Hospital at Hyde Park Corner to 'a healthier spot' outside London. In its stead would be erected a hotel, department store and luxury flats. The Ministry of Health was remarkably polite about the idea in the circumstances. Alastair (now Sir Alastair) Burnet, then a young writer on *The Economist*, was so taken with the idea that he penned a light-hearted article suggesting that Buckingham Palace should also be moved out, preferably to the North where it would generate much-needed employment, leaving the site to Cotton and Clore. A surprising range of people took the outlandish suggestion seriously.

The strain began to tell on both Cotton and Flack. Charles, who had other interests to pursue and had by far the toughest constitution, seemed largely unaffected. Cotton tried hard to please, continually trying to pull new rabbits out of the hat, which only compounded the problem. He saw that he had been judged by Charles and found wanting, but he was unable to do anything practical to make Charles revise his opinion, other than to increase the already excessive hours he was working. Most days he would begin work mid-morning and keep going till the early hours – and still find that he could not catch up. Part of the problem was that he not only enjoyed meeting famous and interesting people, but that he could not refuse anyone who wanted to see him. And everyone seemed to want to see him. As Price recalled: 'If you sat long enough in the reception office of Jack Cotton's suite in the Dorchester, the world and his wife would walk through. Once when I was there I saw Michael Parker, Prince Philip's equerry, and Anna Neagle and her husband'. . . . He had his bedroom next to his boardroom and lived with his work. I think that was one of the things that killed him.'

Jack started drinking more and more heavily. Unable to obtain the admiration his ego needed within City Centre, he began to look for it outside and went on an orgy of self-publicity. The schemes he proposed became wilder and wilder. When he found he could not push them through directly, he tried cajoling and wheedling, which worked no better. So he took to going ahead anyway and reporting the fact to the board as a *fait accompli*.

Charles became increasingly worried that Jack was committing the group to big transactions without the permission of the board. 'When you'd plead with Jack at least to tell the board what he was doing, he'd often just say: "Leave it to Daddio," ' recalls Footring. The problem was compounded by the absence, due to illness, of Lindgren, who had previously exerted a moderating influence on Cotton.

> For months [says Footring] we implored Jack not to run off and make transactions without taking them to board meetings, or at least discussing them with Sainer. Within minutes he'd break his promise. He'd just forget – life was running away with him all the time. After this happened time and again, we had a meeting with him to discuss ways of controlling his activities. We asked him to move from the Dorchester to Park Street, so we'd know what he was up to, but he refused. We asked various people to

speak to him, including Bridge, Plumridge and [Isadore] Kerman [a director of City Centre and Cotton's close friend]. He promised all of them he'd behave and be more orderly, but he got steadily worse. He drank more and more and wouldn't come to board meetings. He hated the constant nagging. Whenever we put the argument to him, 'what if something happened to you?', he'd give the same response – 'Leave it to Daddio.' He was just constitutionally unsuited to the merger. He was a loner; courteous, honest and fun, but he wasn't right for a large organization with public investment.

The first hints that all was not well at City Centre began to leak to the outside world. Under the headline 'Is Cotton taking on too much?', the *Evening Standard* wrote in May 1962:

With the equally ubiquitous Mr Clore behind him as a business partner, Cotton today thinks not in terms of millions but in hundreds of millions. He's building in America, France and Britain. His direct projects range from the Monico site to Sheerness Harbour and there are links with Woolworths, Great Universal Stores, Barclays DCO, Shell-Mex, BP and others.

Where will this apparently crazy property mushroom end? And how can one man – aged fifty-eight – handle so many interests?

In the City, as no doubt elsewhere, many people are beginning to wonder.

For Flack, things were going even worse. Clore regarded him as incompetent, not without reason, for he was becoming increasingly erratic as he became more and more ambitious. The problem was that, having recognized that Cotton was not able to control this extensive property empire and that Clore did not have the time to do so, Flack assumed that he was the natural person to take over. It did not occur to him that he was only in the big league on sufferance. When Cotton talked boastfully in the United States of 'Cotton, Clore and Columbus', the American continent's three great pioneers, it rankled with Flack that he was not included too. While Cotton was protecting him from Clore, Flack began to conspire to remove Cotton.

The extent to which Cotton shielded Flack was a remarkable demonstration of the tycoon's loyalty to old friends. Even when the latter's increasing erraticism came close to sinking the company's plans for grand expansion in Europe (they later foundered for other reasons), Jack stood by him. The deal concerned was with the prestigious Banque Union Européenne in Paris and would have resulted in a major trans-European property development company. Flack was to be the City Centre man on the joint venture's management committee, but after several meetings the French made it abundantly clear that they did not think he was up to the job.

During late 1962 Flack began actively to lobby the institutional shareholders, undermining Cotton's chairmanship. Although he knew what was going on, Cotton refused to take any notice. Flack was going through a bad period, Jack told himself. The poor man had been ill (he had had a severe attack of jaundice) and his marriage had just broken up. Like Jack himself, Walter had developed a drinking problem. He was living on pills and relied totally upon sleeping tablets for the few hours of sleep he did have. He had bought a much-publicized £80,000 yacht, but never had the time to enjoy it. Cotton, always wanting to give the other fellow a chance, found it exceedingly difficult to admit that, as far as City Centre was concerned, Flack was a time bomb waiting to go off.

Towards the end of 1962, however, Flack became quite blatant about his ambitions. Cotton was forced to recognize that his own survival depended on getting rid of Flack as fast as possible. Clore, who had made his own opinion of Flack clear from the beginning, was content to let the two of them fight it out.

Flack was finally ditched in January 1963. Said the *Evening News*: 'It is reported that growing differences of opinion on how the group should be run came to a head at a stormy board meeting.' The French had upgraded their expressions of disquiet about his involvement in the European venture to an outright refusal to have him chair the management committee. The board's refusal to support him was *de facto* a vote of no confidence. Flack had no choice but to resign, both from the board of City Centre and as managing director of Murrayfield. He swept out of the company, dumping all his shares as rapidly as he could, in a final gesture of contempt. Unable to understand where he had gone wrong, befuddled with drink and increasingly unwell, he was a broken man. No tears were shed by his board colleagues when he left. Severely depressed, he went on a protracted holiday in North Africa. Two months later he was dead, drowned in his own bath after taking a heavy dose of barbiturates. The coroner's verdict was death by accidental drowning, but everyone knew he had died of a broken heart.

By now the rumours of dissension between Clore and Cotton were unstoppable. Confidence in the company began to fall, as did the share price. In the end, Charles became convinced that Cotton simply had to go.

The climax occurred in June, just three months after Flack's death. A memorandum went the rounds in the company, criticizing Cotton's management. Jack was undoubtedly a fighter. But the *coup de grâce* was the withdrawal of the institutional support he had enjoyed for so long. Flack's attempts to expose his weaknesses had borne fruit – too late to do Walter himself any good – and Jack had compounded the problem by adopting the same high-handed approach towards their interests as he had towards Clore's. The institutions were also concerned about his health, which had been poor even before he started drinking heavily. If the institutions were forced to choose between Clore and himself, he was told, he would lose.

Cotton had no choice but to submit. Too ill to come up to London, he met Clore, Sainer, Bridge and Footring at his home in Marlow. 'Kerman met us there and said Jack would resign quietly,' recalls Footring. 'Jack produced a letter, on blue paper. "I hereby resign . . ." I can still see it today. It was a very miserable meeting.' Kerman had made it clear that Jack had to resign as chairman although he could be pushed upstairs to the powerless position of president. The public reason for the move would be ill-health. Jack agreed on one condition – Clore would not be allowed to become chairman.

Jack's departure was more dignified than Flack's, yet equally precipitate. He never again took an active part in City Centre. A few months later he sold all his shares, now worth £8.5 million compared to the £14 million at their peak, to Sir Isaac Wolfson and Kenneth (now Lord) Keith, less than two-thirds their value at the birth of the company. Early the following year, Jack cut off all links with City Centre, resigning the presidency, and quit England for the Bahamas. The bitterness between Clore and Cotton was too great for either to speak to the other again.

In the Bahamas, Cotton continued to drown his sorrows in drink and to give press interviews lambasting his former colleagues. His health rapidly deteriorated. 'Property,' he had said in an expansive mood at his prime, 'is my whole life. I wouldn't know what else to do.' Two minor heart attacks in 1963 were followed by a major, fatal one on 22 March 1964 – exactly a year after the death of his partner, Walter Flack.

Despite all the pressure to retire him, Cotton's acquaintances still held him in high regard and even with strong affection. Orchard-Lisle recalls:

> Jack Cotton was almost unique in his vision, genius and judgement in his prime, and rarely wrong. At the peak of his powers it was seldom that anyone questioned his judgement, and at his best he had great style and dignity. It was he that built up the immense City Centre Properties empire as his sole and personal creation. He was only sixty-one when he died, and one wonders what his fate and that of CCP would have been had not the merger or marriage taken place. I doubt whether there will ever be anyone quite like him. Business was always 'fun' to him.

George Bridge stepped in as chairman, with Footring as managing director. The company now had a full-time executive for the first time.

City Centre slowly pulled itself into manageable shape, disposing of substantial numbers of low yield property investments amassed in Cotton's acquisition spree – some £21 million worth in 1967–8 alone. 'It took us weeks to discover what Jack had been doing,' says Footring, 'and years to get the group back into streamlined order.' But by then the property boom was over. The scope for spectacular bargains had shrunk and Bridge was obliged to report that year that, 'Although many development schemes have been investigated, none of any magnitude has been undertaken in the last twelve months.'

Four years after Cotton's death, Clore, too, suddenly sold off his interests in City Centre. 'I'm emigrating from this crazy, mixed-up country,' said the *Express* cartoon of the day. 'Someone's taking over Charlie Clore.'

Even after he had effectively withdrawn from the property business, Charles retained an affection for it. When asked to describe his occupation a few years afterwards, he declared that he was not 'a West End financier', as the newspapers so often referred to him (much to his annoyance), but 'an industrialist and builder'. His main property investments now, however, were in land. The 16,627-acre Guy's Hospital Estate that he bought for £1.5 million in 1961 eventually fetched £20.5 million when sold to the Prudential in 1979.

The whole sorry saga of City Centre was one in which none of the key players came out well. Not normally one willing to admit his mistakes, Charles confided in friends that he was not proud of the events he had precipitated.

When City Centre was acquired in 1968 by Lord Samuel's Land Securities, Clore, Wolfson and the institutions received the equivalent of 80s a share in Land Securities' shares and securities. The deal created a £300 million property company. When all the dust had settled, it was the quiet man in the background who triumphed in the property stakes, rather than the much publicized tycoons.

CHAPTER

9

The High Life

'He was a madly enthusiastic farmer. Locally,
they referred to him as the "dinner party
farmer".' Jocelyn Stevens

Charles Clore never quite made his entrée into London Society while he
was married to Francine. Mr and Mrs Clore had correctly, it seemed to
them, hosted garden parties on Checkendon's rolling lawns and thrown
innumerable balls in the more sophisticated elegance of their Park
Street residence. At those events they had displayed their wealth,
possessions, good taste and Francine's family connections. But all to no
avail; attention from the right circles still failed to appear. What Francine, in particular, failed to understand was that London Society admitted outsiders by invitation only and that, unlike Paris, acceptance was
not a matter of wealth or connections, but of whether people liked you. A
long-term acquaintance of them both has said: 'Francine thought she
was the sort of person who demanded a priori to be taken up. In fact, the
social world looked at it differently. They thought she was pushy, a
social climber, and that he was a character.'

So desperate were the Clores to achieve social status that they persuaded Loelia Duchess of Westminster, now Lady Lindsey, one of the
most dominating figures in London Society, to organize a ball. Loelia was
given £5,000 to spend on arrangements and asked to put together the
list of guests from the cream of Society. Charles mugged up on all the
guests with a set-piece speech for each of them as they were introduced.
The gaucherie of the affair was a cause of merriment in Belgravia
drawing-rooms for weeks after.

Ironically, it was after Francine left him that Charles began to receive
the social recognition she had desired. 'Charlie Clore' had become a
household name and was synonymous with glamour, wealth and financial brilliance. People wanted to know this stern, aloof individual who
had made his mark upon every high-street in the country. Introvert,
enigmatic, his contrasting gregariousness and love of wild parties and
leggy debutantes made him an even more interesting character.

The aristocracy, originally offended by Clore's brashness, began to
look upon him with liking. He was uncompromising, individualistic and

146

very wealthy. He would not change his behaviour to suit the company and this naturalness delighted his hosts. To Francine's incredulity and chagrin, Clore began to enjoy the attentions of the aristocracy after he divorced her. Instead of his broken marriage becoming a social stigma, as he originally feared, it actually increased his acceptability. As an eligible single man he was invited widely. His hosts made a fuss of him. He became an object of affection. The aristocracy imitated him and told Clore stories.

One of his new-found friends was the late Duke of Marlborough. Around him gravitated dignitaries such as the Earl of Carnarvon, the Marquess of Blandford and Lord and Lady Rotherwick. Clore began to play bridge at Blenheim.

Clore had at last gained entry in the innermost circles of Society. He was consumed with admiration and envy for the confidence and polished ease of his new friends, qualities which he knew that he would never have himself. As he looked at their life-styles, he knew that he had very little to offer in return. He was determined to correct that situation.

One thing he could do was to become the gentleman farmer. A country estate and shooting weekends would supply the elegance and prestige which he himself lacked; it would also be a useful way of widening his social circle and help him to receive weekend invitations from other estates.

In 1961, Clore bought the 16,627-acre Guy's Estate for £1.5 million. Formerly belonging to Guy's Hospital, it was a huge farming property in the heart of Herefordshire with some of the most valuable agricultural land in Britain. For his personal home, he bought the Stype estate. In many ways it was a surprising choice. Neither large nor particularly impressive, it consisted of a small farm, an excellent shoot, several tenant cottages and a converted shooting lodge. Clore bought it simply because he felt at ease there.

At Stype, Clore, the gentleman farmer, began to issue weekend invitations to the favoured few, to arrange elegant dinners and to indulge himself in all the habits and pastimes of the leisurely rich. The sensation of owning land also agreed with him. It satisfied the strong streak of possessiveness in his character – a trait which had emerged so destructively in his marriage – to be able to walk around the two estates and know that the land he was treading on was his and his alone. But despite all his attempts, Clore never fully felt at ease in his new role. It was impossible for him to shed his money consciousness, and the impulsive spending of so many other wealthy socialites remained anathema to him. Because of this caution, his plan to acquire a stately mansion came to nothing.

There was certainly no shortage of choice. His daughter Vivien recalls: 'We had three choices of a new home: Ramsbury, Stype Manor, or to build a new mansion altogether. He left the choice to us, the children. Alan loved Ramsbury, but Charles felt it was "too grand for a little Jewish boy".'

Clore always regretted letting the opportunity to buy Ramsbury slip through his fingers. He never took his eyes off the seventeenth-century manor – considered one of the most beautiful in Britain – and looked for every chance to buy it should it come on the market again. In the event, another Jewish multimillionaire, Harry Hyams beat him to it and the manor never came on to the market at all. Upon hearing rumours that the owners were considering selling, Hyams strolled casually into the estate one Saturday morning. Within minutes the sale was agreed.

Unlike Clore, Hyams knew how to spend in style. He built a dazzling and ornate pool made of Italian marble. 'Clore's pool was a less grand affair and the walls were damp. He always kept quiet about it,' says a friend. When this same person stayed with Hyams, Charles plied him with questions about the pool.

With Hyams living in state close by, Clore had to be content with the rustic plainness of Stype. Although he personally liked the former shooting lodge, he was racked with doubts about whether it was smart enough for a multimillionaire.

The size of the property did not present a problem. It was a charming 2,000-acre estate on the border of Wiltshire and Berkshire, containing 500 acres of wood and 800 acres of rolling fields of wheat, barley and oats. Some modernized dairy facilities and a 5,000-bird poultry unit made up the rest of it. Best of all, the shoot at Stype was excellent and accommodated eight to ten guns and up to twelve days' shooting a year. The usual bag over the 2,000 acres ranged from 500 to 1,000 birds a day.

The estate's mansion, or rather lack of one, was a more serious problem. The original had been burnt down before the war by a thieving butler. When Lord Rootes, the previous owner, bought the estate, he converted the whitewashed shooting lodge and small, picturesque cottages into one house. The result was a slightly cramped house, with a mere ten bedrooms, a number of which were too small to contain wardrobes. It was hardly an impressive home for a tycoon.

For once, Clore was uncertain about what to do. He wanted his home to be prestigious and well-appointed and to rank with the best in the country; was renovating and expanding the lodge good enough or should he build a new house? Decisive and self-reliant in every other area of his life, he lacked the confidence to trust his own taste in these matters and was keenly sensitive to criticism.

He turned to Sidney Kaye and asked him to design a stud and a new house.

I knew nothing about horses. I did the round of all the studs. One trainer said it must be a chalk floor, another a hard floor. Some said you must have constant water. The only thing they had in common was that it was essential to have steel on the half doors to stop the horses biting.

Kaye recommended that Clore build a modern single-storey house in stone and timber to blend with the rural surroundings. The plans were almost completed when Clore changed his mind. Lord Bessborough had introduced him to an architect who specialized in designing expensive houses. Clore invited Kaye to lunch with him to meet Bessborough's architect. 'I thought I'd review the plans. In fact, I didn't – the best way to lose a client is to do his home.'

During the meeting, one of the Hilton's architects came into a room, a man highly experienced in hotel and luxury home design. Clore turned to both he and Kaye and thrust the new plans under their noses. He demanded an opinion, without naming the designer. Kaye recalls 'It was awful. I said "fine", the Hilton architect said "they're appalling, terrible". I was kicking him under the table.'

The dissent was enough to unnerve Clore. He abandoned the whole idea of rebuilding the lodge, contenting himself with renovating and expanding it. 'He was nervous of doing anything that would make him stand out from the neighbours,' says Kaye.

Building started in April. Clore came down every weekend to oversee the building of a games-room, an area for barbeques and a swimming-pool complex, which included a sauna and squash courts.

With the new manor house completed, Clore began to entertain in style, but once again he felt uncomfortable about spending money in this way. In the other areas of his life, the rules of economy reigned inflexibly. The long years of calculating and carefully allocating his resources had left certain habits from which he would never fully break free. At Stype he wavered constantly between opulence and penny-pinching. It was an odd mixture in a man with a personal fortune of several million.

'He never seemed able to throw off the guilt of spending money for pleasure,' recalls Ralph Wade, Stype's estate manager. While Clore spent lavishly on the most new and sophisticated equipment for Guy's, Stype had to make do with second-hand equipment: 'He prided himself on doing everything economically,' says Wade. A somewhat battered Land-Rover was bought for Clore's use. Although it was uncomfortable to ride in, he refused to replace it because it had a good engine.

His economizing extended even to the grocery supplies. Three weeks after moving into Stype he called his overseer and asked how much he was paying for sugar. When he heard how much the neighbourhood's high-class grocer was charging he said: 'Too much. It's cheaper at the local supermarket. Go there in future.'

His career as 'Farmer Clore', as the media dubbed him, was checkered with disasters. He started in a big way. From Lord Rootes he bought a flock of 450 Hampshire Down sheep, which later won him two show championships. Through the newly formed Stype Estate farming company he installed the most expensive herd of Aberdeen Angus cattle ever bought in Britain. In a matter of months he was set to compete against Harold Samuel, the winner of most of the leading awards for Angus cattle at the previous year's Smithfield Show.

The column writer in the *Jewish Chronicle* reported in March 1960: 'I am intrigued to notice how many of our Jewish tycoons are taking up agriculture as a subsidiary occupation – and with what zest.'

At Perth in April 1960, Clore paid £28,000 for a single Aberdeen Angus bull, a record price. The bull gloried in the name of 'Newhouse Jubilee Eric'. Like everything else in Clore's life, business or private, it had to be insured through his broker and adviser, Charles Hughesdon. The bull was insured for £30,000. A year later, they had lunch together one Friday. 'I've been talking to my agents and looked at the bull. They think the premium is ridiculously high especially since the bull is settled in Stype,' said Clore. 'There's no question about it, the bull has to be insured,' replied Hughesdon. After a few minutes Clore agreed reluctantly to reinstate the insurance. Hughesdon telephoned the agents to make the arrangements. After Sunday lunch, Hughesdon had a phone call from Clore. 'Bad news. I was watching the bull with some friends when it touched an electric fence, fell into a ditch and broke its neck.' 'It's a good thing we renewed the insurance.' 'I've just called the agents and they said the message never got through to your people.'

Clore was disgruntled about the incident, never believing that the claim would be paid. In the event the underwriters accepted, albeit reluctantly, that the verbal instructions had been fully binding, even though they never reached them until after the accident.

Also at Stype was an impressive collection of orchids, grown in a hothouse in the garden. Charles loved orchids and invested a considerable amount of money so that Stype could be ablaze with exotic colour. The beautiful displays which filled so many corners and fireplaces in the house were a lasting memory for many of Clore's friends and guests.

While Clore considered farming a hobby at Stype, the vast Hereford estate was a serious farming venture. He called it 'my little place in Hereford'. Situated between Ross-on-Wye and Hereford's Line, its 16,000 acres were split into sixty tenant farms. Clore farmed over 800 acres himself, using 500 acres for cereal crops, with the remaining acres holding 600 ewes and a herd of 100 British Friesians.

'Clore was a good landlord. The estate was becoming run down but he put a lot of money into it. What he did had beneficial repercussions all the way down the line for the tenants,' says Gordon Wordsworth, Clore's agent for Guy's. While going over the estate's accounts with Wordsworth, Clore would also give the agent some tips on the Stock Exchange.

Although there were so many tenant farmers, Clore did his best to get to know them by arranging an annual dinner party at Guy's. It was, after all, what the Lord of the Manor was supposed to do. He attended every year without fail and would never, according to Wordsworth, make a speech. 'Instead, I would take him around the tables. He was very shy; I would have to keep the conversations going.'

Clore was difficult to work for. Although his knowledge of farming was superficial and he lacked any practical experience, he believed that he knew best. He was rarely satisfied with the management of Stype, but would never allow farming considerations to interfere with the shoot. To make things worse, he insisted on listening to too many experts, which led to disaster after disaster and a long succession of farm managers at Stype. Whether good or bad, none of them lasted very long.

Clore would often telephone Wordsworth and ask, 'Why aren't we doing such and such at Guy's?' He would want to try out every new farming technique and would stubbornly cling to his ideas. Wordsworth had to argue with Clore on many occasions: 'It was fatal if you were frightened. He didn't want a "yes man".'

Most disastrous of all was the huge dairy unit at Stype. Although Clore spent a vast amount of money installing the unit, which was designed to milk 500 cows automatically, he never got it working to its full capacity. Jocelyn Stevens recalls: 'Although the "cow palace" never worked as well as it was intended to, Charles was extremely fond of it. Milking time was enforced viewing for all his guests, even after a long day's shooting. Nobody dared to ask what all the men in white coats were doing.'

Clore would pass on everything said to him at dinner to the farm manager. As a result the farm went from one extreme to another – sheep, cattle, turkeys, pigs, chickens. Stype farm lost a fortune and Vivien eventually insisted on closing down the dairy.

Clore always wanted Guy's to be the largest farming estate in Britain, as well as being the most modern. He made a bid for the adjoining farms around Guy's several times but, at the crucial moment, he would say 'too much, too much'. He could never bring himself to spend what he considered such vast sums of money. He loved to show off Guy's to friends. He would arrive at Wordsworth's office for a tour of inspection with a large group of people, all smartly dressed in suits, trilbys and overcoats. The walkaround was always timed to a second. At eleven o'clock prompt they would reappear for a gin and tonic with Wordsworth.

It also delighted him to allow his friends to fish at Guy's. The estate contained four miles of salmon-rich fishing on the River Wye, with fishing rights costing around £25 a yard. Clore had never managed to take to the sport. When he was at Guy's, his only involvement with his ghillie was to order him to prepare a beat in case any of his guests wanted to fish.

The only sport which Clore ever took to passionately was shooting. 'It was his great love, to stand there in the pouring rain and keep shooting for hours and hours,' says Wade. The trouble was, try as he might, he could hardly ever hit anything. It became a standing joke. He tried hard. He attended shooting school and was out shooting almost every weekend during the season. When Charles Wilson practised at the same school, Clore's former instructor turned to him and said regretfully: 'If only we could have got Mr Clore to stand on the right foot, he'd have hit a few birds.'

According to Stevens, Clore did not mind shooting badly: 'Charles would stand in the best place and fire off a great many shots without hitting anything. He liked shooting because he could ask his friends. As a result, he was asked all over the place, to Blenheim, for example, in return.'

Clore's reliance on his shooting instructor was viewed with amusement. It is not abnormal to have one when you are learning, but he had one permanently. Clore even took his tutor with him to Blenheim. Coming in to lunch one day, he asked, 'What about my man?' The old duke said, to Clore's amusement: 'We know he teaches you to shoot, Charles, but do you need him to teach you to eat, too?'

After one dinner, when Clore was standing knee-deep amongst a pile of spent cartridges, his neighbour said: 'Charles, I think you got one.' 'No I didn't.' A close friend comments: 'You couldn't impress him with flattery. If told that he had done well, he would reply, "You couldn't have been looking".' He would even play up to his reputation as an appalling shot. Sometimes he would order Wade to stand behind him and shoot. He would then march out at the end of the shoot and say, poker-faced, 'Look what I shot.'

It was not unusual to see Clore sitting on his stick taking a nap. His loader was old and deaf. 'They'd shout at each other and discuss the whole world,' said Vivien. Wherever he was shooting at Stype, Clore would also take his agent. If the agent shot well, Clore would turn to him and say: 'I'm not running the shoot for you, you got all my birds.' On a bad day he would say 'You're my agent. I expect you to hit something. Dreadful, dreadful.'

152

Surprisingly, he never learned a great deal of shooting lore. It was almost as if he valued his amateur status as a shot. When he saw a woodcock for the first time, he asked 'What's that?' and then said, 'Right, I'll have 200 of them.' Any serious shot would have known as a matter of course that the woodcock is a wild, untameable bird that migrates from Norway.

For Wade, running the shoot was sometimes a nightmare experience. Clore would hand him the guest list and then invite extra guests who would turn up unannounced. On one occasion, Clore turned to Wade and asked 'Who's that man?' Neither of them recognized the guest and they were eventually obliged to ask him why he was at Stype. It emerged that Clore had met the man at Annabel's and invited him to Stype on impulse.

On one occasion, Charles had rung Leah Gelman from Paris, telling her to invite the West German ambassador, whom he had just met, to shoot. On the day of the shoot, when the official car pulled up, flag waving at the front, Charles stared open mouthed at the man inside and blurted out: 'It's the wrong German ambassador.' Leah had assumed he meant the ambassador to London. After a few moments of embarrassment, Clore's hostmanship reasserted itself and he made every effort to make the ambassador feel welcome. As is so often the case, the unfortunate incident became the basis of a strong friendship.

Charles' guests at Stype included Lord George Scott, Kenneth Keith, Lord Montagu, Edmund de Rothschild, the Hon. David Montagu, the Earl of Dartmouth, the Hon. Angus Ogilvy, Charles Keith Showering, the Marques de Santa Cruz and the Spanish ambassador, some of the best shots in England. Felix Fenston came often, as well as Lord Kimberley and Charles Sweeney. Fenston, a colourful and amusing character, had a flair and genius for property. His friendship with Clore went back many years and the two frequently met socially. Fenston was born into a theatrical background and entered property at an early age. Later guests from abroad were often ignorant of both the techniques and the etiquette of shooting in England. Often in far too great numbers for safety – sometimes as many as sixteen guns – it was a miracle none was seriously injured.

No matter who came to Stype, they were expected to keep to a rigid routine. The same people were always asked for the same weekend in the year. In the winter, they were expected to arrive for dinner on Friday night. They would shoot all day Saturday and lunch at the swimming-pool. After the shoot, tea would be served also in the poolhouse. While Clore retired to his room to doze in his armchair, his guests would swim and sauna. Everyone would change for dinner. The evening would be spent talking or at games.

153

Charles himself always refused to gamble and would become irritated with those of his guests, Charles Sweeney particularly, who played for high stakes. He used to say there was no need for him to gamble: 'I've got my own gambling business, William Hill, and I always win.'

He regularly arranged a sweepstake during the day of shooting, the money going to the person who had guessed correctly what number of birds had been shot. He became quite incensed if anyone put in more than £1 a head. Even though Wade had an unfair advantage because of his knowledge of the shoot, Clore insisted that he enter. 'He liked it when I won because he felt it was "keeping the money in the family",' says the agent.

It was only at Stype that Clore could let people behind the façade of the hard-nosed businessman. When he retreated there and left London far behind him, he would relax and reveal his likes and dislikes, his sociability and good humour, and his sensitivity and concern for people, including his guests and local people. It was for this reason that Clore jealously guarded his privacy at Stype. He would never allow the media into this side of his life and was even unhappy about his guests taking photographs around the house.

Clore's own family, other than Vivien who took up shooting, were also largely excluded from this part of his life. The strict routine at Stype and the perpetual socializing were, in many ways, attempts to create a substitute family life. The severed link with Russian relatives, the early death of his mother, the succession of stepmothers and the retirement of his father to Israel, had not helped him to learn to be part of a family community. He had grown up to be emotionally and materially self-sufficient. His disastrous marriage to Francine and his stormy relationships with his children had made him even less able to express his feelings or to depend on his family.

To his friends he would show his vulnerability, albeit in his own way. A friend explains: 'He'd never put an arm round you. He showed no overt emotions. But he was a person people were drawn to. When you became a friend of his, he'd do almost anything for you. He helped a lot of people privately.'

The only time Clore would ever visit his family was on important Jewish festivals. 'Outsiders would always be invited to keep him interested and amused,' a member of the family recalls. Another adds:

> Those gatherings were always a theatrical experience for me. I felt I was in the presence of a truly remarkable man. Nearly everyone was in awe of him. He was usually the last to arrive and the first to leave. Everyone would await his appearance with bated breath. Once he arrived, the conversation would be unnaturally stilted. We were aware that he might be listening and vied with each other to sound more intelligent.

David Clore would play the role of the court jester. He would relate all
the latest gossip to Charles, knowing full well what he wanted to hear and,
of course, agreeing with every golden word that escaped his lips. There
weren't very many. Charles spoke very little, but listened intently, which
made the evening very hard going. At about 11 p.m., he would ask for his
hat and coat. An arm would be waved in the general direction of the room
and he would be gone. After he stepped into the lift, the atmosphere would
change immediately and there was an audible air of relief. The family
would relate to each other the conversations they might have had with
him, most of which were, to be honest, rather one-sided.

It seemed hard to the Clore entourage that they could not benefit from
having a tycoon in the family. Clore refused to pass on any business to
his relatives unless he believed their professional skills warranted it.
His dealings with his nephew Basil Cohen, a quantity surveyor, were
exceptional. Other members of the family tried hard to gain some
business, often to no avail. David Clore, for instance, mercilessly goaded
his son Charles to remind Clore that he was a stockbroker. After one
family gathering, young Charles desperately followed Clore to the lift
and pleaded his case. All he received was a grunt. David Clore instantly
wanted to know the results of the so-called meeting. 'I confidently lied
and said my uncle was most impressed and would be putting business
my way. Needless to say, nothing ever transpired,' Charles Jr remembers.
  While Clore refused to advise any of his friends or associates, he made
an exception with his brother David. In most cases, however, the advice
that he gave was dreadfully wrong. At the beginning of the war, Clore
said about David's house in Hampstead Garden Suburb: 'What do you
want that house for? It's wartime, you should sell it and get out of
London.' David always listened to Clore and sold it for around £3,000.
The next day the house was requisitioned by the War Office, which
meant that David would not have needed to sell it.
  David was always trying to be more independent of his brother, but
rarely with any success. When the brothers were still living at Ray
Court, David returned from London and announced that he was under-
writing £10,000 worth of shares for a new public company called Tesco
run by a man called Jack Cohen. Cohen was doing his own underwrit-
ing. Clore was furious. He was convinced that Cohen was only a market
trader and that David was throwing away the money. The brothers
argued for most of the night until David capitulated and asked Jack for
the cheque back. Years later, whenever Cohen met David, he would
delight in telling everyone within earshot how much the £10,000 worth
of shares would have been worth at the current share prices: probably
over £15 million.
  Although losing out in this instance, David none the less had good

reason to be grateful to his brother who had paid out large sums of money to cover his gambling debts since he was a young man.

In general, Clore did not believe in giving to relatives – he felt it was better for them to earn their own way. Yet for all his caution, he was generous to his family, setting up a family trust in 1955 to help any relative in need to pay school and university fees. He wanted to be a good Jew and fulfil his family obligations. Often he went beyond the measures that duty required. For instance, Israel Clore's children from his third marriage, who had emigrated to Australia, were funded through school by Charles. He paid for most major family events and he would always help if anyone was ill or in trouble financially. When distant relatives arrived from Canada or Australia, Charles would ask David to meet them, look after them and find out what they wanted. He would usually agree to their requests. The truth was that, in spite of his brusque, hard exterior, and apparent meanness, Charles Clore was a soft touch. He was a sentimentalist at heart, as his close friend Janet Milford Haven recalls: 'We'd go to films. If it was sad he'd have to dry his eyes. We'd sit there quietly while he composed himself. It was the same if you told him a hard luck story.'

Because he knew that he could not easily refuse people, Clore used either David or Leah Gelman as a buffer. He left routine family matters to Leah and allowed her to decide how much to give and when. She was far from generous with his money; his wedding present to his nephew Charles was a £200 gift, instead of the rumoured £10,000 printed in the newspapers of the day.

In many ways it was inevitable that Clore's relationship with his family would become distant. As well as being a shy man who found it hard to express his feelings, he frequently distrusted people until they proved themselves. His family never got the opportunity to do just that. The tight-knit nature of the Jewish family, whatever the faults of individual members, seemed to have no relevance or value in the world that Clore now belonged to. In the earlier years, particularly before the war, things had been different. During the time of his divorce, for instance, Clore had been under strain and was genuinely devastated by the news of Francine's affair. He had loved his wife and missed her badly when she left finally. In his loneliness, he had turned to David and his wife for support. Their son, Martin, remembers: 'When he was in-between with Francine and there was some hope of reconciliation, he would go away with my parents. He needed moral support to meet Francine.'

By the time Clore bought Stype he had long stopped sharing his concerns with his family. All they saw at each gathering was a man who seemed to have everything he wanted; who was often uncommunicative and seemingly invulnerable. Occasionally, he would unbend and show a more human face. It amused him, for instance, to relate the story of the time he gave a £1 tip to his nephew Charles, who was just about to return to preparatory school. The young boy turned to his uncle and said, 'Everybody thinks you're horrible, but I don't think you're so bad.'

Another time, Clore said to his niece, Ruth Solomons: 'If you can be quiet for two hours, I'll give you ten shillings.' He considered the money well spent when the little girl came to claim her reward two hours later.

Ironically, Clore's behaviour to his family betrayed one weak chink in his armour which he was never fully able to hide. As he grew wealthier, he could never fully shake off the suspicion that his wealth meant more to his friends and family than he did himself. Part of this cynicism and distrust stemmed from his sense of rejection and betrayal when his marriage broke down. Despite their incessant clashes, he had believed that his wife had loved him. When she left, a part of Clore shrank from close contact, and it was only the trusted friends of long years who were allowed to look behind his hard and abrupt exterior. He found it difficult to get on with children, and even his own nephews and nieces found him cold and unapproachable. When David Clore's family lived at Ray Court, no matter what the time of day, Clore would turn to the children and ask: 'Aren't you in bed yet?'

Only later, with Janet Milford Haven, did he learn to enjoy the company of children.

> If his marriage had worked he would have loved to have had more children. He adored my two boys. When they had chicken pox at boarding-school, he was the one who said 'Haven't you called them?' When they came to Stype for the day, he was the one who cried when they went back. He used to send them skiing every year with the school. He was very proud of them.

It was not that Clore disliked children, it was more that he did not know how to unbend and establish a rapport with them. He envied those people who had happy relations with their offspring. His own relationship with his children was difficult. As Alan and Vivien progressed through their teenage years, their encounters with their father became more stormy. Both children were intelligent and strong willed and vigorously resisted their father's attempts to mould them into his own image.

Alan and Vivien used to go to Annabel's occasionally when they were of age. Louis at the door would tell them: 'You can't come in. He's in there.' Clore insisted on trying to tell his children what to do and would 'go wild' if someone answered him back. Even after Vivien was divorced in her early thirties, he would still say: 'I hear you were in Annabel's last night. You're too young to be in a place like that.'

Everything his children did, no matter how trivial, had to measure up against his high standards. When Vivien failed her driving test, Clore ordered Kay to take her out in the car and tell her what she was doing wrong. 'She passed the test the next time – it had nothing to do with me but he thought it had,' Kay remembers.

'His dream for us was that we would both go to Oxford University,' says Vivien. When both children went to Oxford, they would spend their weekends at Stype. Vivien liked the country life and was an excellent shot. Alan, on the other hand, disliked most outdoor activities, to the fury of his father.

'He felt that Alan was mixing in the wrong set at Oxford. Alan was very bright, complicated, slightly grand. He didn't like business, getting out of bed in the morning, shooting – all the things dad was about. He was a very autocratic father – Alan couldn't handle it,' recalls Vivien. Clore would ask at lunchtime where Alan was. If Alan was still in bed, he would go white with temper.

Alan remained close to Francine and spent much of his time with her in Paris. He had resisted Clore's efforts to send him to Eton, saying he preferred to stay in Switzerland. When the time came to go to university, he disappointed his father by electing to read philosophy, politics and economics at Oxford's unfashionable Lincoln College. According to *Queen* magazine, he was remembered at the college for no great extravagances and for his introspection.

Clore withheld Alan's twenty-first birthday present until he heard the results of his final university exams. He said at the time: 'When my son passes his exams ... he will have achieved something. But being twenty-one ... well that happens to anyone.'

Charles had little control over Alan by that time. The children already had had a substantial settlement made upon them at the time of the divorce and this they received at the age of twenty-one. The money, which had been invested in Sears shares, had multiplied many times in value. It was customary to make settlements on children at that time to avoid death duties, but to his dying day Clore regretted giving his children financial independence so early. He told some of his closest friends that he had been wrong to take advice from Sainer, who was single and childless, about his domestic affairs.

The gift took both Alan and Vivien by surprise. Vivien never knew about the trust until Alan was called in by Lord Melchett. With trusts currently in vogue, Melchett said to Alan: 'One word of advice. Don't put your money into another trust.' Then Alan took Vivien out for lunch and passed the advice on to her.

When Vivien received her endowment, she was too terrified to spend any of it. But like Alan, she was determined to use her financial freedom. It was harder to break free than she had thought, however. She had wanted to go to the States for a long time and always been refused permission by her father. Now she decided she was going to go. He said to her: 'You'd better come with me on Pan Am.' Vivien booked herself a seat in the back of the plane. 'He made a hooha about that and had me upgraded.' He asked her: 'Where are you going to stay?' 'With a friend.' He replied: 'No, you'd better stay at the Waldorf Hotel.' With exchange controls limiting the cash private individuals could take out of the country, Vivien was unable to pay for her rooms. 'He had to pay. He had to be in control.'

After gaining his degree, Alan left Oxford and made no sign of being interested in entering business. Instead he toyed with the idea of furthering his education. Dismissing the notion, he considered opening a night-club with a friend, but then decided to start his own film production company under the banner of Alan Clore films. It was never more than a hobby. Clore watched with envious eyes as Isaac Wolfson's son Leonard entered the family business and showed every sign of being even more astute than his father.

The only area of agreement between Clore and Alan was their love of horses. Clore's stud at Stype, which was finally built in 1968, was the only place in which both liked to be. Alan became increasingly interested in breeding and racing horses and began to bid for his father at Deauville August sales. He bought his own yearlings and proved a skilful judge of horses. Clore both admired and envied his son's ability. It irked him that Alan should prove so good in an area where he had achieved only moderate success – for a multimillionaire that is.

Clore loved racing and wanted to rank among the top breeders and racers. He was never satisfied with his trainers and was always finding some new expert to run his stud at Stype. He also gave his horses to a string of successive trainers in England, France and Ireland. It was not that he could not make up his mind; just that, while he could never prove he was being cheated, he was frequently convinced that was the case. Eventually, he found a man he could trust: Tom Masson, who was said to have no peer as a horse trainer. Masson trained many of Clore's winners; Margera and French Manor both collected a number of firsts in quick succession when they started to race. Lester Piggott rode a number of Clore's horses, including Varma, a colt from France trained by Masson's son Michael. It arrived in England with a label around its neck saying: 'Too slow. Best shoot him.' In one year the horse won eight races and £18,000.

Once, after a spectacular win by a Clore horse, a leading jockey turned up at Park Street to collect his bonus. Townsend counted out the money, then asked the jockey to sign a receipt. 'Not bloody likely,' said the jockey. 'Tell Clore he can keep his money,' and stalked out.

Almost every year at Ascot, Clore would take a box, which he would fill with debs and titled friends. In the evening, he would throw a large, colourful party.

He rarely missed major events of the world's top race-tracks. Deauville was an occasion he particularly enjoyed. It was the annual grand gathering of the international set, who came to enjoy the sun and to watch the racing and the polo. Clore would stay at the Royal Hotel (one year a disgruntled Alan was refused a room because the hotel was full). He would meet with old friends, including William Hill, an avid lover of the races, and Mark Birley and his wife Lady Annabel.

It was at Deauville that the final parting occurred between Alan and his father. After many violent quarrels, Alan had ceased to talk to Charles directly and channelled all his remarks through a third person. He insisted on addressing his father to his face as 'Sir Charles'. Eventually he refused to meet him, even if they were in the same city. 'Charles was bitterly disappointed. Alan's behaviour was dreadful. Charles was always looking for reconciliation,' remarks a close friend.

Clore's relationship with Vivien was different. For a start, the two had seen more of each other: 'I always insisted on spending half the holidays with him. When I went to boarding-school in England, I was virtually brought up by him.' This in spite of the fact that Charles, who hated writing, wrote one letter only to his daughter during her time away.

Vivien was temperamentally better suited than Alan to cope with the bitter wrangles of their parents. Sensitive, impressionable and close to his mother, Alan grew up with a deep grudge against Clore. Vivien, on the other hand, was down-to-earth and practical. She understood better than Alan why her parents' marriage had come to an end and could accept her father's womanizing more easily.

The time spent at Stype established a closeness and understanding between Clore and Vivien which was never lost, even during the years of estrangement after her marriage to a non-Jew. Their relationship, although full of friction, was candid. They would clash – like so many fathers and daughters – over small things that somehow blew up out of proportion. She recalls, for example: 'He had a love of gossip and great faithfulness to his friends. I'd tell him they were sponging off him and it would annoy him.'

For many years Clore never talked to Vivien about money management or running a business. The only side of his life that he was willing to share with her was Israel. Vivien started going there with him when she was twelve.

The rift took place between them when Vivien was twenty-three. She met John Duffield, a thirty-year-old stockbroker: 'He was the first man who ever talked to me about money.' Without consulting her father, she agreed to marry Duffield. 'I just decided I wanted to get married and the best way seemed to be to go ahead and do it.'

Vivien believed that Clore, desperately trying to be accepted in the Jewish community, would be set against her marrying someone outside the Jewish faith. Without telling him she arranged the wedding. Clore was furious and refused to attend. Besides disagreeing with her choice of a husband, he was bitterly hurt by her decision not to tell him. In the heat of his emotions, he failed to recognize Vivien's unspoken appeal to him to acknowledge her independence as a grown woman. Using the pretence of a business trip, Clore went to visit the Weizmann Institute in Israel.

It was some years before the estrangement between the two ended. It was the birth of Arabella, Vivien's daughter, in 1972, which finally caused Clore to melt and swallow his pride. At first, he would not look at the baby when Vivien brought her for him to see. Then he started to take sideways glances at her. Before long he melted entirely and welcomed home the prodigal daughter. A year later, he was even more delighted when his grandson, George, was born.

With the healing of the relationship came a new depth of understanding. Clore accepted the similarities between himself and Vivien. When he recognized that she had inherited his agile mind, he began to enjoy improving and sharpening her business acumen. Stevens recalls:

> He would play business games with her to get her thinking. He always wanted her to buy Stype. He wouldn't leave it to her; he wanted her to buy it so they'd bargain over it. He loved her brain; the mutual understanding they had.

These were the skills he would have expected to pass on to his son and it is a measure of the failure of his relationship with Alan that he felt he now had, in effect, to treat Vivien as a substitute son.

With his friends and acquaintances, Clore could never be anything but himself, no matter how hard he tried. Although his wealth allowed him to create elegant and refined surroundings, he was no chameleon. He never managed to smooth the rough edges of his character and, to the last, treated everyone in the same brusque way.

'He was often rude. He didn't mean to be but it was just his way. He didn't really know what was correct. He was a good host and very generous, but he was brittle and unnatural in the role of the English gentleman,' comments a regular visitor to Stype.

His abrupt manners and domineering ways were often a shock to unsuspecting victims. He was punctual to the point of obsession: 'He'd get to the airport before the crew arrived. He was the same with trains,' comments Kay, his butler. He imposed this attitude upon all who came into contact with him. The staff at Stype were never left in any doubt that the day's timetable had to be kept to with military precision.

Dinner was especially important. Clore would suffer nothing to interfere with the evening ritual and would start dinner on time even if, as happened on some occasions, guests were late. Regardless of who or how important they were, if they failed to keep to the timetable he would show his displeasure in no uncertain terms. During a shoot the Land-Rover was the only form of transport to convey the guns to the next stud. Clore would stand impatiently by it, saying to latecomers, 'Come on, come on.' His patience would finally snap. Getting into the vehicle, he would imperiously command the driver to go. 'Leave the man – come on, drive away.' The lone figure of the stranded person against the field's horizon was a warning to other guests that in this estate, at least, punctuality mattered.

Clore always liked to be woken by Kay at 7 a.m. prompt. One morning, he received his call at two minutes past seven. No comment was passed. Three days later he was planning to catch an early morning train. Turning to Kay, he said: 'Call me at 6.30 a.m., not like the other morning when you were late.'

His manners with friends and guests could be very abrupt. Stevens recalls that in conversation, 'He would be very opinionated in what he said sometimes. There was virtually nothing he didn't know about what was going on in the business and social worlds.' When someone argued with him, he would have no hesitation in drawing the conversation to an end by saying with a wave of a hand: 'You don't know anything.'

'They always came back to him, even if they were affronted. They were drawn by his table and his money,' comments Kay.

In his own home Clore was a fascinating host. He refused to talk or do business (in contrast to dining out, when he would talk of nothing else) and had an uncanny knack of mixing people of very different temperaments and standing back and waiting for the potentially explosive results.

Jarvis Astaire was invited to stay with Clore during one weekend at Ascot. Charles had deliberately set off one woman guest who was freely airing her right-wing political views, which he knew were diametrically opposed to Astaire's own. As the argument grew heated, the woman suddenly turned to Charles and said: 'I can't bear to listen to this nonsense.' Clore turned to her and said: 'I don't know where you're going, but he's staying.'

He also had, says Vivien, 'a marvellous way of sniffing out things. In a public room full of people he'd know who the interesting ones were straight away. He'd sit at Claridge's and say: "See her over there. The earrings were given to her by X. He bought them at Mappin & Webb. He paid Y – too much".' It made him a fascinating conversationalist.

To his daughter Clore was a marvellous fount of stories. He knew who was sleeping with whom and what deal her husband was making, and would share his knowledge within his intimate circle. Outside of that circle, he was very close with information.

Another distinguishing feature was Clore's obsession with unnecessary waste. If an expensive wine was put on the table, he would know if anyone was not drinking. Before the drink was poured, he would ask his guest: 'Are you going to drink that?' It was the same with expensive Cuban cigars. He hated to see anyone light up and take just a few puffs.

Alan and Vivien were never allowed more than one glass of wine because it was so expensive. She recalls: 'We summed up the courage to ask for two glasses of something more ordinary. He told us: "You're lucky to have any Lafite at your age".'

On one occasion Kay served the after dinner coffee. 'It was made by the Italian chef. I don't know what he did with it.' After protests from Clore, Kay quickly made some instant coffee and brought in a new tray. 'Clore asked who made it. When I told him that I did, he said "You make it in future." He had instant coffee from then on.'

Clore's relationship with his domestic staff was also turbulent. He tried to select his employees according to the same rigorous criteria which he used in his business affairs. He surrounded himself with competent, reliable people who could be left to do their jobs and who were totally dependable in any circumstances, except, that is, his butlers, of whom only Kay proved reliable enough to last for any great length of time. Incompetent people were quickly weeded out. 'The butler from the Duchess of Argyll didn't last long,' says Kay. 'He called me up from Stype and said "You're my butler now" and slammed down the phone.'

While Charles had been exceptionally fortunate in finding Kay, some of his choices of butler had ranged from the unwise to the disastrous. One butler he fired stole a subsequent employer's silverware. A convicted jewel thief claimed to have been Clore's butler in earlier years. Another past butler turned out to be a psychopath, who made the headlines by murdering his employer, the Scottish MP Walter Elliot, shortly after leaving Charles' employ. For Charles it was a lucky escape, the result entirely of his attention to detail. The man had come with impeccable references and his behaviour appeared normal. Yet at a dinner party within the first few days of his employ, he served a guest from the wrong side. Charles said nothing at the time, but asked Sainer the next day to check the references, which turned out to be forged.

Clore was committed to his staff and expected high standards from them. Although normally reticent to employees, at Stype he would go out of his way to praise his staff. He always made a point of going down to the kitchen and thanking the chef after a formal dinner. Such an attitude generated a great deal of mutual respect and affection between Clore and his employees – and was one of the main reasons they stayed, some of them for thirty years and more.

Wade comments: 'Clore was a very good man to work for. He would always stand up for "my people", as he called his staff at Stype. He would tell you off privately but he always defended you to the last in front of others.'

'He never demanded respect, he just got it. Because he was a perfectionist, so were the staff. We lived life as a challenge and checked each other's jobs to get things right before he found fault,' says Kay.

Occasionally Clore won the game by catching out his staff in a rare mistake. One night Kay was laying the table for a large dinner that evening. Looking at the table he said: 'I feel something is missing.' John, the valet, could see nothing wrong. The guests arrived, were seated and about to start the meal, when Clore looked up at Kay and said: 'Can we have the serviettes?' Kay recalls: 'He laughed about it and said to me later: "I thought you'd make a mistake one day."'

Clore had a strong sense of responsibility for his staff. He was meticulous about paying small people, and once sternly rebuked one of his employees at Stype because he had forgotten to pay a small supplier. 'How do you expect him to cope if you don't pay him?' he asked.

Perhaps because he had few roots and no real home other than Stype, Clore liked having people around him whom he had known for years. Two local farmers, for instance, were invited to shoots at Stype for ten years. He hated losing an employee and would go to considerable lengths to persuade people to stay. When he first bought Stype, there were two Poles and a German who had been working on the estate since the war. Clore allowed them to stay and made special efforts to pass the time of day with them, even though he was told that the German, a quiet courteous man, had been a member of the SS.

Even when he fell out with an employee, Clore would prefer to quarrel with him rather than sack him. He had a war of silence with Speake, the head keeper at Stype, for years. One season Clore had decided that a particular wood at Stype was unsuitable to shoot. He gave instructions to Speake not to shoot there again. Next season the keeper took them to the same wood. Clore was furious that his orders had been totally disregarded. He said: 'I'm never going to speak to that man again.' He kept his word and for around eleven years he never spoke a word to

Speake. Ralph Wade, his estate agent, acted as go-between for them.

Racing and breeding horses, shooting and farming, Clore had eagerly and successfully adopted all the pursuits of the gentleman farmer. But although London Society had taken him to its bosom, there was still one important missing piece. He desperately wanted to receive a knighthood. Many of his contemporaries, who had achieved far less, had already received the office and Clore felt that the Establishment was slighting him. He seemed to come close to achieving his goal many, many times. The more he wanted the honour, the more tantalizingly it eluded him. He never forgot the time, for example, when Harold Macmillan, the Prime Minister, turned to him and said: 'Thank you for introducing me to that charming man, Mr Harold Samuel. I'm going to make him a peer.'

It seemed to many that Clore's huge donations to charity, totalling around £500,000 a year, were transparent attempts to buy his knighthood. He had contributed large sums of money to a number of highly public and prestigious projects. The name of Charles Clore could be seen on buildings, retirement homes, schools and even a mammal house at London Zoo in Regent's Park. It was Lord Zuckerman who persuaded Clore to become a generous benefactor to the zoo. Since his arrival in 1955, Zuckerman, a distinguished scientist, had done an immense amount to improve the amount of private funding for the zoo and he courted Clore assiduously. This attention paid off in 1965, when Clore donated £50,000 towards the half-built zoological gardens. Two years later he made a yet larger contribution, giving £200,000 for a new mammal pavilion. The Charles Clore Pavilion was opened by the Queen in May 1967. The new building was on two levels and housed more than 200 nocturnal animals. Simulated moonlight and sunshine meant that the sight of the animals feeding, burrowing and rearing their young, was exposed to the public for the first time.

Clore's motives were a mixture of opportunism and humanitarianism. He had inherited his father's social conscience but he was also anxious both to gain acceptance in the community of wealthy Jews and to reach equal footing with his titled friends.

But many of Clore's donations to charity were done as quietly as possible. The Freedom from Hunger Campaign, for instance, found that an unknown person had granted them free use of a former shop in Leicester Square. Months later the same person gave the charity free use of a store in Kensington to stage an exhibition. A boys' club in Haringey was given £5,000. When Clore heard the club's building fund had fallen £2,000 short of its target, he promptly paid the difference. At many high society charity raffles, a diamond brooch or gold cigarette box would have been given by Clore.

Whatever the sum involved, he insisted on checking that the money was being used wisely. When a vicar in the neighbourhood of Stype approached him for a donation to repair the church roof, Clore not only donated the whole sum but also sent his surveyor to the site to make sure that the builders were doing a good job. The vicar of the next parish heard of the donation and made a similar request. Charles did exactly the same again.

When the charitable foundations, which he financed, were being combined into one in December 1964, Clore was asked by the *Financial Times* how he planned to direct the donations. He became vague.

'Medical research?'

'You could say that.'

'Education?'

'You could say that too, I suppose.'

'Projects in Israel?'

'Yes, but elsewhere, too.' There was a long silence. 'I don't like to publicize my charities.'

The long-awaited knighthood finally arrived in 1971, yet the charity work continued and became an increasingly important part of his life. In May 1973 work started on a £2 million project for the Home for Aged Jews, Nightingale Lane, one of the largest homes of its type in the world. It provided facilities for the active aged, the semi-infirm and the infirm. David Clore, by then an outstanding worker for Jewish charities, was appointed chairman of the appeals committee. Through David's efforts, £7 million was raised during his term of office. Largely because of David's involvement, Charles gave substantial amounts, with Lord Rayne and Sir Michael Sobell also contributing heavily.

Active, popular, busy with his horses, farms and charities, Clore's life had never seemed quite so rich and absorbing. His business commitments had lessened considerably and he was at last free to enjoy his wealth. And then, suddenly, he decided to exchange the things in his life which he most enjoyed for a self-imposed tax exile which was destined to end in loneliness and regret.

CHAPTER

10

Girls, Girls, Girls

'There were those girls who were invited
socially, and those who were just invited...'
Eric Sosnow, a long-standing friend of Charles
Clore

Once Charles became the eligible bachelor owner of the Prince of Wales,
the shy young man who had to ask friends to chat up girls for him
disappeared rapidly. He became more confident, more daring and,
although his manner was still brusque and far from silver-tongued, he
developed a kind of charm that many women found attractive. There
were always enough women available to the man who could make their
theatrical careers.

At the same time there were the real women, those for whom he felt
genuine respect, who had impeccable social backgrounds. For example,
Lily Moretzki was a casual girlfriend for a period before her marriage to
Lord Sieff, although nothing came of the relationship. She was then a
divorcee working at the Israeli consulate in London, and Charles was
instrumental in introducing her to her future husband. Francine, the
French exile, was clearly another such person.

During his marriage and for some time after the separation, Charles
was by most accounts faithful. He thought he had what he wanted – a
beautiful wife for social events and the kind of stable family life for his
children that he might have had if only his mother and step-mother had
not both died.

When Francine walked out for another man, Charles was shattered
emotionally. As a child, the two most important women in his life had
deserted him when he needed them. Now Francine had done the same.
Never again was he able to let a woman come really close to him. Never
again – with one exception – did he achieve a truly stable relationship
with a woman. According to one old friend:

Francine's behaviour affected him deep down. It made him more brusque
with women. He couldn't sleep without somebody, so he always had girls
around him. He wanted to marry a real woman, someone who would be a
good wife to him for the rest of his life. He never found anyone like that.
Even if he had, he couldn't talk to them.

167

From that moment on he sought female company wherever he could find it. There were now two kinds of women in his life: the tarts and tramps, and the aristocratic or exotic. The first category was never allowed to mix with the other. He would always make sure that he was accompanied to every occasion by the appropriate class of companion. The tarts were for night-clubs and evenings; the aristocratic and exotic were for the most formal occasions or to add flavour to weekends at his country estate or for extravagant events such as first nights or Ascot.

Charles behaved towards each of these types of women in typically different ways. The tarts would be ushered in and out again with rapidity. With typical ingenuity, he had solved the age-old problem of when and how much to pay ladies of easy virtue. Neither payment in advance nor payment in arrears can guarantee satisfaction. Charles adopted the routine of writing a cheque and tearing it in two – half now and half upon satisfaction.

Finding this sort of girl was no problem. If he did not have a suitable companion for the night, he would despatch a reliable person to find one. At Rehovot, where he had a penthouse within the grounds of the Weizmann Institute, some of the drivers would willingly earn extra by doing his 'shopping'; others refused.

Charles' throughput of these young ladies was prodigious. In England he was in good company. Paul Getty shared many of his tastes and interests, not least the pleasure of a personal harem. Charles was a frequent visitor to Getty's home and took great pleasure in swapping risqué stories with the dour American. They were seen at parties together on numerous occasions and Charles was always on the guest list for parties at Getty's British mansion, Sutton Place. The society pages recorded Charles' acquaintance and socializing with other renowned womanizers, such as Douglas Fairbanks Jr. At parties he also met the then Minister for War, John Profumo, and other members of the 'Cliveden set'.

Ray Court, Charles' old home in Maidenhead, was only a few minutes away from Cliveden on the other side of the river, and he undoubtedly met Cliveden's owners, the Astors, from time to time while he was there. It was not until the 1960s, however, that he became in any way one of the Cliveden set and then only peripherally. It was, however, just at that time that the name Cliveden became synonymous with sex scandals, through its connection with the trial of Stephen Ward.

Stephen Ward's trial came about as a side-effect of a wider scandal. Ward was a mere sidelight in a grander play involving John Profumo, the Russian naval attaché, Captain Eugene Ivanov, and a 'model', Christine Keeler. Ward, a genial fifty-year-old osteopath, effectively arranged for Profumo to meet Keeler at a wild weekend party at

Cliveden and Profumo was quick to seize the opportunity. Ward had already introduced her to Ivanov. The security service was far from happy at the idea of the Minister for War sharing the same mistress as a presumed Russian spy. Warned off by the Secretary of the Cabinet, Profumo broke off the affair and all would have been forgotten if Keeler had not been brought to the attention of the press by an affray caused by another former lover. Enjoying the publicity, Keeler spilled all about her relationships with Profumo, Ivanov and Ward. The scandal led to the downfall of Profumo and a thirst by the Establishment for a scapegoat. Ward was an obvious choice, and he was charged with a variety of offences, all centred on the theme of living off the earnings of prostitution. Although the evidence against him was extremely thin, Ward committed suicide before the trial ended.

In her evidence as a witness for the Crown, Keeler made reference a number of times to a client she called Charles of Mayfair. The press could not resist fuelling speculation over the identity of 'Charles of Mayfair', although no one was ever openly named. In City boardrooms the candidates, Charles among them, were widely discussed. Keeler, who had at one stage been the mistress of the notorious property exploiter Peter Rachman, herself claimed even under sharp questioning by the trial judge that she could not remember this client by any other name than Charles. But several things point to Clore, apart from the association that both he and Ward (who, it was claimed, introduced Keeler and the mysterious Charles) had with the Cliveden set. One is the location, Park Street being a good Mayfair address. Her evidence at the Old Bailey went thus:

'Who is Charles?'
'I don't know.'
'Where did he live?'
'He lived off Park Lane.'
'Was it a flat or a house?'
'A house.'

Another is Keeler's description of how she was treated. £50 was a relatively generous fee at the time, but was Charles' normal payment. Several sources testify that he would pay off girls with this amount and send them home either by taxi or in his own car. He would not visit their establishments. Few commentators on the trial believe Keeler had truly forgotten the surname of 'Charles'. However, if 'Charles' were well known and wealthy, she had little to lose and much to gain from not revealing his name. Certainly, any rich businessman with a reputation to protect would have gone to considerable lengths to keep his name out of such an affair.

Charles had certainly dated the other key witness in the trial,

Keeler's young friend Mandy Rice-Davies. Since married to an Israeli businessman and divorced, Mandy accompanied Charles on several occasions. Given his liking throughout of 'pretty young things', it would be remarkable if Charles had not also made the acquaintance of Keeler. Writing some years later, Keeler herself placed 'Charles' roughly in Green Street, just round the corner from Clore's home in Park Street.

In the end, the main evidence is negative. Close as he was, Clore did confide in special friends, particularly in his final years. Yet all deny he ever mentioned any relationship with Keeler. So was Charles Clore 'Charles of Mayfair'? We shall probably never know, but on balance the verdict must be that he was not, that the speculation was no more than that.

This compartment of Clore's life was kept rigorously away from all others. He went to great lengths to ensure that there were no tarts around when any of his family were present. Vivien is adamant that at no time as a child did she see any of her father's women stay for the night.

The respectable ladies tended to be in their early thirties and were often married. Charles would invite them to bring along their husbands to parties and many of them did. Whenever he came to Israel, he would appear with a new one on his arm. He'd take a pride in introducing them to the country and would use them as hostesses for parties at Rehovot and as suitable companions for dinner invitations elsewhere. In most cases the relationship was one of genuine, if temporary, friendship. He knew that most of them were after his money and was content to accept the situation, knowing full well that they would not get very far. Once, as he waited for an imported girlfriend to pray at the women's section of the Wailing Wall, he remarked *sotto voce*: 'I know exactly what she's praying for. She wants the shops to be open seven days a week.'

The debs would typically be acquired at cocktail parties, and invited on to a night-club. If they proved to be particularly vacuous and lacking in conversation, he would sometimes show his loss of interest by falling asleep as they chattered. Airline stewardesses were also fair game – he once invited two at once, having met them on his homeward TWA flight across the Atlantic.

Although he could be charming, he was more often brusque and even rude to the women around him. 'Where on earth did you get those awful shoes?' he once asked a society lady at Ascot. To many women his earthy humour and direct approach – 'It'll do you no harm and do me a power of good' – was offensive. Yet to others it was attractively different.

Charles was often shameless in his flirting, often with women he had never met. Once, in a night-club at Jaffa, he was attracted by a woman and asked each of his companions in turn: 'Find out her address. I want to send her flowers.' All refused. The next day he made a point of telling them that he had got the address and sent the flowers anyway.

Vivien called these women his 'leopards', because they dressed in sleek fur coats and stalked him. She recalls: 'I was awful to them. They used to appear at Sunday lunch at Stype. I hated that. Once one went with him to take me out from school. After three hours with me there she told me she knew her relationship with Charles wasn't going to last.' It didn't.

Although many of these women, both genuine girlfriends and paid one-night-stands, must have hoped for extravagant gifts from 'the richest man in Britain' – few if any of them had their hopes fulfilled. Diamonds and expensive trinkets were never even considered. The most his society girls received was a good meal and an occasional small present. In sex and companionship, as in everything else, Charles fixed a value on a service and saw no need to pay above the odds. He once approached another industrialist, sitting in a London night-club with a beautiful Swedish girl. As always, Charles was curious to know how the other fellow had landed such a catch. 'With little touches of generosity,' was the reply. 'For example, you've just lit her cigarette with a magnificent lighter. If I were you, I'd have given it to her. With your money, you can afford to buy a dozen and just keep replacing them.' Charles thought about it for a while, but just could not comprehend why anyone should want to do such a thing. It wasn't a matter of meanness. Clore was always worried that women only liked him for his money. Had he lavished expensive presents upon them, he could have trusted them even less. 'It was more that he wanted to be loved for his own sake,' comments a close friend.

A clue to the way in which he regarded the women in his life was his refusal to talk business to them. He would take young girls out to a night-club and talk across them to other businessmen all night, without a thought that they might be bored. But only with highly successful female entrepreneurs, such as Estee Lauder, did he ever attempt to discuss business matters.

The aristocratic and exotic ladies – typically tall blondes of almost any nationality – would turn up at Stype in droves. The inducement to come was an invitation to their husbands or boyfriends to shoot.

And, of course, there was the annual event of the Miss World competition. In 1959 Charles wangled a ticket to the traditional dinner dance held at the Café de Paris after the competition. One source says the invitation came via his friend, Nigel Campbell, whose wife, the internationally famous model Barbara Goalen, was one of the judges. Eric Morley, chairman of Miss World Group, maintains that Charles became associated with the competition because he was a close friend of Carl

Heimann and Alan Fairley, the joint chairmen of Mecca, which ran the event in its early years. For each of the approximately forty competitors there was an invited escort for the evening. Campbell was lucky enough to be sitting next to one of the prettiest girls, Miss Denmark. Charles made little secret of his envy, even though he had a highly desirable young lady sitting on each side of him. Eventually unable to contain himself, he leaned across the table, interrupting the conversation and said to Miss Denmark: 'He's married, you know; why not dance with me?'

From then on he never missed a Miss World show. He often booked the winner to appear at Selfridges and sometimes opened the shop on Sundays for the contestants to shop at a discount. Eventually, he became such a part of the furniture of the event that a selection of the Misses World were invited down to the estate at Stype after the competition. Jocelyn Stevens recalls how the assembled young ladies would rise early to join the guns for a day's shooting. Dressed in their best outfits and high-heeled shoes, they would slip and slide in the mud as they trailed after the men in their wellies and shooting gear.

When Charles began to identify himself with Israel, he paid particular attention to Miss Israel, annually buying the contestant an expensive ball gown from Selfridges. One year the bill was mistakenly sent to Charles Clore Jr. A glance at the exorbitant sum caused him panic-strickenly to telephone Leah Gelman to ask what to do. She told him briskly to send on the bill and mention the incident to no one.

Charles usually preferred his girl companions to be twenty-one or under, and either blonde or brunette. 'He treated them like a combination of daughters and lovers,' says his old Israeli friend, General Ze'evi. 'He liked them to admire him and to caress him, to take care of him.'

Usually they didn't last long. He certainly had a new one every time he came to Israel and staff at Annabel's night-club in London lost count of them. The newspapers loved it. At Ascot, in June 1963, there was 'pretty German art student, Angela Munemann', who insisted she definitely was *not* a model. Angela stayed around long enough to accompany him to an Edwardian Ball at the Savoy in aid of Tibetan refugees, where he politely declined an invitation to drink champagne out of a girl's slipper on the grounds that 'My shareholders wouldn't like that at all.' In 1961, he spent Christmas in Hollywood with 20th Century Fox starlet Alena Murray, before tripping off to a lunch in his honour in Palm Springs given by socialite Lois Hawk, whom he had dated in Paris and Monte Carlo. (Lois had let it be known that there was an engagement in the air between them, but Charles made sure it stayed in the air.) Earlier that year, he had taken the Countess de Bendern to New York with him, a matter of weeks after the announcement that she would be separating from her husband, the former British golf champion. And that year's Miss Denmark, Lisa Bodie, had finally succumbed to his charms and joined him at the Oaks. (She had created an international stir shortly before by being arrested under suspicion – and subsequently cleared – of involvement in the kidnapping of four-year-old Eric Peugeot, heir to the French car company.) In Monte Carlo he was accompanied by Helga Mayerhofer, described as 'a friend of racing driver Stirling Moss'; in Paris, at the end of the previous year, by Denise Hivet, a former secretary to the Duke and Duchess of Windsor; in London by British model Jean Dawnay and American model Francine Huff.

The society gossip columns were always predicting an imminent marriage or engagement, usually without any foundation other than wistful hope. The *Royal Gazette Weekly*, a Bermudan newspaper, put it succinctly when it said:

> Charles Clore is here once more. He is much sought after by New York's glamour girls, who see in him the qualities they have been schooled to admire since kindergarten – dynamism, kindness and money. But New York gossips say Charles is looking for a bride.

Rumours spread that he had proposed to a European socialite named Jenny Wolfgang, an ash-blonde divorcee in her late thirties, who lived in Switzerland. It wasn't true, but Charles made no attempt to stop the rumours. He was beginning to enjoy the role of eligible bachelor. The more the publicity, the more women clamoured to please him.

From time to time one of these inamorata would be around long enough for Charles himself to talk about marriage. 'But no one took it seriously,' says one Israeli friend. 'He'd get half-way up the ladder to marriage, then come back down again,' recalls Kay, Clore's butler.

One near miss was a married Israeli woman with children, the ex-wife of the head of an important figure in Israeli diamond dealing. The affair ended when she insisted that he either marry her or end it. Charles backed away. An Italian hopeful couldn't believe her luck when he proposed to her in the early hours. In the sober light of day, however, he denied he had done any such thing.

Another was a gushing American blonde named Barbara, who was a frequent companion for a period in the 1970s. She was often with him, for example, at the race meetings in Deauville and at the subsequent Gala des Courses (the racehorse owners' dinner). Barbara's downfall was to assume too much, too soon. The family was first alerted to her as a potential threat when she steered Charles towards a pair of Charles Jourdan shoes. 'I'll buy the company,' said Charles grandly.

Thereafter, Barbara began to refer to 'our car' and even 'our grand-

173

children'. Suddenly Francine, Vivien and Alan, all of whom were also at the races, forgot their quarrels as they combined forces to deal with the impudent interloper. Their machinations in the Deauville casino were interrupted by a panic when a policeman, over-alert as the result of a raid and robbery a few days before, accidentally fired his pistol at the ceiling. Most of the guests dived for the floor. The Clore entourage burst into the kitchen and Barbara and Francine fought over the limited space underneath a table.

It took forty-eight hours to pack Barbara on to a plane back to the United States. As far as Charles was concerned, she just disappeared. Instead of complaining at the high-handed treatment, he blinked a bit in surprise and accepted the situation. Although he never admitted it, he was flattered and pleased that Francine still felt enough for him to save him from what would certainly have been an expensive mistake.

Towards the end, the girls became more numerous, but were largely there for decoration. 'He just loved to be escorted,' says General Ze'evi. 'They made him feel younger.'

Louis, the head waiter at Annabels, recalls the occasion when the club hosted a show of Garrard jewellery: 'The show had twelve of the most beautiful models you've ever seen. They dressed in the back of the club. Mr Clore asked for a ringside table, next to where they would come out, so he could see them really close up.' Yet it would not be accurate to portray Charles Clore as a lecher. He simply took immense pleasure in having pretty young girls around him. He needed solace in female companionship and at a pinch almost any attractive young woman would do.

The nearest Charles came to a stable relationship after his divorce was with Janet, Marchioness of Milford Haven. She was one of the many girls who had been invited to shooting parties at Stype with her fiancé, the Marquess, but was, like Francine, dark haired, instead of blonde. When they married, Charles was at the wedding. When the Marquess died, Charles telephoned from Italy to offer his condolences. Shortly after he met her at a function and invited her to be his hostess at Stype and Park Street and his companion at high society affairs. From then on, although there were streams of pretty young girls – 'He had to have *someone* to take to Annabel's,' says Janet – they were constantly seen in each other's company. Together, they travelled widely both East and West.

Travel in Charles' company plane was an experience in itself. His guests took 'more luggage than a film star', so that anyone wanting to go to the loo had to move out the suitcases first. Charles loved travel but hated sea-trips (he could get sea-sick standing on the jetty), so trips to, for example, Hong Kong could be guaranteed to harbour disaster. On one occasion he took Janet to Hong Kong for the opening of the metro. Most of the programme of events meant going on boats, to his obvious disgust. At one of the evening receptions, Charles kept eyeing the shellfish. 'That's not in your religion,' said Janet. 'Don't you tell me what to do,' was the characteristic reply. The next morning half the guests, Charles included, were sick with food poisoning. By lunchtime he was the only one to have recovered.

Another trip, on which Janet accompanied him, was to Iran. Janet and her husband, David, had been there on a number of occasions and Charles wanted to explore the commercial possibilities. After a fairly short period he had the measure of the country and proceeded to say so to the embassy official who visited him in his vast hotel suite. 'We've come too late,' said Charles. 'There's no money to be made here. This fellow will topple.' The embassy official's face went through a rainbow of colours as he made gestures towards the large, unmatching lamps hanging from the ceiling. As Charles continued to expound on the Shah's mistakes, the official started scribbling notes on a cigarette packet and tried to give it to Charles, who ignored it. Janet tried to peer over his shoulder to see what the note said. Charles promptly slapped her wrist, then suddenly dried up as he read the message – 'Don't say anything, the room's bugged!' The suite had previously been taken by Lord Kissin, and found to contain no less than eighteen bugs when the embassy staff made a routine sweep. From then on, during their stay, they pointedly made reference to how marvellous Tehran was.

That same trip Charles and Janet were taken to Persepolis to see the sights. The heat was unbearable, but Charles insisted that the best way to keep cool was to close all the car windows and turn on the air conditioning. He steadfastly ignored all pleas that the air conditioning must be out of order. The driver hurtled along the half-made road as Charles wrung out his shirt. Only when it became obvious that the car was actually on fire did Charles concede that there was something wrong, by opening the door and jumping out.

It was Janet who comforted him through his first major illness. Charles would never normally get up for her, but that night she recognized that there was something out of the ordinary in his unresponsiveness as he sat in front of the television. 'Sit down and be quiet,' he told her. 'What's the matter?' 'I've got a terrible pain in my chest and arms.' Although he would normally call Dr Sacks at the drop of a hat, this time he was scared that he might really be ill. Tests the next morning showed he had angina.

The subject of marriage came up from time to time, but never seriously. Charles would say to her, only half in jest: 'It's nice being Lady Milford Haven. It wouldn't be so nice being Mrs Clore.' Yet the relationship hovered between matrimonial closeness and platonic friendship. When Charles was absent in the United States, he would ring every other night. Leah Gelman at Park Street would put up to half a dozen people, Janet included, on hold and switch them one after the other on to his transatlantic line. When one of the newspapers printed a story of high jinks with a young model in Paris, he almost panicked in his efforts to reassure her that it was untrue.

With Janet, whom he would chide affectionately for being 'just a little Bermudan girl' whenever she disagreed with him, Charles rediscovered the pleasure of the company of young children. He established a closer rapport with her sons than he had managed with either his own son or his nephews.

In the end, however, there had only been one girl in Charles Clore's life. Whenever he came close to remarriage, he would compare the woman in question to Francine and somehow lose his determination. One friend recalls how, after the divorce, Charles made a point of taking him upstairs after a dinner at Park Street. From a drawer he pulled out an album of photographs of Francine and talked about how proud he was of her and her war record.

Moshe Mayer, a close friend from Israel, recalls how Charles would eye the women parading at the casino near Geneva. Whenever he saw a really beautiful woman he turned to Mayer and sighed: 'She's not as good looking as Francine was.' Although at times he came to hate her (Janet recalls how his knees would turn to jelly whenever Francine entered the same room and how careful he would be to avoid her in Deauville in case she embarrassed him in public), he was still never able to forget that he had once loved her. Indeed, it is doubtful if he ever really understood his feelings towards her – the line between love and hate can be very thin.

It is a fair summing up of his relationships with women that they were all more or less failures. Although he was surrounded by women, and could rarely bring himself to go out to the theatre or opera without one in tow, he could never come truly close to any of them. Not for nothing was he known as 'the lonely millionaire'.

CHAPTER

11

The Israeli Connection

'In London, I'm a Sir; in Israel, I'm a Lord.'
Charles Clore

When Israel Clore disembarked in Palestine in 1929, the State of Israel was no more than a dream to most Jews. For him, however, the dream was a powerful reality and he was determined to share in its fulfilment. He and his young wife joined the settlement at Petah Tiqva, then a cluster of single-storey dwellings a few miles from Tel Aviv.

Petah Tiqva was one of the pioneer settlements of the State of Israel. Now a thriving commercial town of some 100,000 inhabitants, it was then a primarily agricultural community, turning near barren land into fruitful fields. Israel Clore lived a mere four years at the settlement before he died.

While Israel undoubtedly wrote to his favourite son from time to time, Charles, who scarcely ever wrote, was far less communicative. The theatre, the chorus girls and the publicity he attracted would not have gone down well with the strictly religious Israel, so there was much he would not have wished to write about. While there is no evidence that father and son ever became deliberately estranged, the distance and the totally different life-styles inevitably drew them apart. Charles did visit Israel to see his father once, however. The family album shows him perched uncomfortably astride a camel.

When Charles received the news in 1933 that his father was ill, he sent him some money instantly. He asked David Dimson, the young owner of a wine shop in Cricklewood, to take Israel £2, then the equivalent of two weeks' wages and the most that he could afford. Dimson was about to go to Israel, and made a special trip to Petah Tiqva where he visited Israel and his wife in their small wooden house. The old man was confined to his bed and obviously very weak. Seven days later he died. Dimson made a second visit to the town and attended the quiet funeral on Charles' behalf. In all only twenty-five people were there.

Neither Charles nor any of the remaining family members in England had been able to afford to attend the funeral. So it was that, when Charles visited Israel again in the late 1950s, he had no idea where his

177

father was buried, other than that it was somewhere in the now thriving metropolis of Petah Tiqva.

Charles' interest in Israel had been quickened over several years by the Sieffs, the Rothschilds and, most importantly, by Isaac Wolfson, the head of Great Universal Stores, one of his principal business rivals in England. Israel Sieff and Simon Marks (the joint heads of Marks & Spencer) had been strong supporters of Zionism for many years. They had, for example, largely financed the Petah Tiqva settlement. Dr Chaim Weizmann, who later became the first President of Israel, was taken in by Marks & Spencer when he arrived in England in 1904. It was Weizmann who showed the company, in its own words, 'how technology and science could be useful to storekeepers who genuinely wanted to know they were selling their customers the best merchandise'. He set up the laboratories that were at the heart of the cycle of testing and feedback to the textile and garment factories. That cycle, in turn, formed the core of M & S' constant improvement in product quality. Weizmann's efforts for M & S were repaid when Israel Sieff put up the money for the Weizmann Institute at Rehovot, near Tel Aviv, to supersede the much smaller Sieff Institute.

The Rothschilds also had strong links with both Israel in general and with the Institute. Wolfson's generosity at the time was less obvious, but he was full of the opportunities he could see in this developing land, especially when he became chairman of the Export Bank in Tel Aviv in the late 1950s.

Clore, the self-made millionaire, held out for some time against the pull Israel exerted upon his Jewish commercial peers. He was, after all, busy enough making money in England and the United States. But two things combined to break down his resistance. One was an increasing feeling of guilt that he was not playing the part that a good Jew should in the development of the country, especially when his father had devoted his latter years to the Israeli ideal. The other factor was a mixture of envy and curiosity – he simply couldn't bear the idea of being left out of a good deal.

Isaac Wolfson, never backward in persuading other people to spend their money on his good causes, finally persuaded Charles to visit Israel for an economic conference. It was one of many being run at the time as part of a campaign to interest rich Jews in investment in Israel. The prospects did not appeal greatly to Charles at that time; after all, most of the economy was agriculture-based and there were far more exciting property markets elsewhere.

It was Wolfson who introduced Charles to the brothers Mayer, who were frequently referred to in the Israeli press as the country's richest men. From an initial fortune left to them by their father, Benjamin,

Moshe and Mordechai had built up a commercial and industrial empire that included real estate development, banking, industry, construction, department stores, investment and finance companies. These were Charles Clore's type of people. He could relax with them and speak freely of personal matters. And so it was that he enlisted Mordechai's help in finding his father's grave. Mordechai recalls:

> He didn't have business at the front of his mind at all, that first time we met. He just wanted to talk about his father. So I went to the chief rabbi of Petah Tiqva, Reuben Katz, and asked him if he had known Yitzeh Clore. Katz remembered that he used to pray in his synagogue and showed me where he was buried, in a very old cemetery. When Charles next came to Israel the first thing we did was visit the grave. Then he asked me: 'What can I do here?'

Rabbi Katz was unsure of the identity of the distinguished visitor, so when the question was translated to him, he cautiously asked Mayer in Hebrew if it would be overstepping the mark to ask for £200. When Charles' giving capacity was explained to him, he asked for a students' dormitory at the *Yeshiva* school. The dormitory was duly built.

From that year on, Israel assumed a very important role in Charles Clore's personal and business life. Unlike other frequent ports of call, such as New York, the Bahamas, Paris, Gstaad or Monte Carlo, Israel took on a special meaning for him. Over the years, as the unhappiness in his personal life increased, he turned more and more to the country and his Israeli friends for comfort. It was as if he underwent a personality change whenever he entered or left the country. Zvi Dinstein, a former deputy finance minister, explains the difference thus:

> In England, he was a tough businessman. In Israel, he was a human being. In the UK, he was uncompromising, formal, stringent, tense and preoccupied; here he was accommodating, understanding, compromising, lenient and more open. In England, he'd always find faults when he went to a restaurant. Here he could go to a second-rate one and say it was good.

Instead of the stiff suit he wore in London, he would wear casual clothes and sandals, almost like a tourist.

One reason that he could relax more easily in Israel, says Teddy Kollek, Mayor of Jerusalem and one of his close friends, is that 'Here Charles was known and respected as a benefactor; in England he was known as a tycoon.' Other observers point out that the inferiority complex he struggled with in England as a poor Jewish boy made good vanished in Israel, where that background was a social asset rather than a liability. 'This is the only place I feel I can talk about personal things, rather than about business,' he told Mordechai Mayer, who insists that while Charles' passport was British, his heart was increasingly Israeli.

This feeling of having found his roots, of wanting to share in the Israeli dream that he had rejected when his father had offered it, prompted him to unparalleled acts of generosity. While his benefactions in England could – and often were – put down to his undisguised thirst for a knighthood, in Israel his motives were almost entirely philanthropic. The first significant gesture of this philanthropy was the formation, in 1961, of the Wolfson–Clore–Mayer corporation (WCM), a commercial joint venture between the two Britons, the three Israeli brothers and the Ministry of Finance. Wolfson, Clore and the Mayers took 25 per cent shares each in the company, which had paid up capital of £2 million. Thereafter, all Charles' activities in Israel were either charitable projects or used to finance charity.

One of the first major projects was the construction of the Tel Aviv municipality building, followed by the Shalom Mayer Tower, named after the Mayers' father. The building was at the time the tallest between Milan and Tokyo. Each of the partners bought two floors in the building, Charles giving his to the Clore Foundation, which he had set up to distribute his charitable donations. Then came the Wolfson Centre construction. Gradually WCM spread out across a wide range of industrial and commercial sectors, with involvements in department stores, banking and real estate development.

One of WCM's investments was in an industrial development group, GUS Industries. The managing director was Chaim Herzog, now President of Israel, and the chairman was Isaac Wolfson. Herzog recalls how Charles' blunt statements would sometimes shock an otherwise staid board – 'he could be very forthright when he saw something stupid'.

While Charles rarely intervened directly in the affairs of WCM, he was able to bring the resources of Sears to help with various problems the companies in the WCM group encountered. The Selfridges' buyers, for example, were instructed to buy for the Israeli stores as well, giving WCM the benefit of larger bulk purchases. Charles also demonstrated his ability to judge character, in particular when he persuaded Wolfson to join him in backing a carpet manufacturing rabbi. Rabbi Shapiro, now an active politician, scarcely looked the part of an entrepreneurial businessman in his traditional black garb. But Charles recognized the managerial qualities of the man and that the financial crisis the company was going through was mainly a product of the general economic crisis of the time. In addition to financial aid, Clore helped raise the quality of the product and reduce production costs, while actively encouraging sales through his own retail outlets. Caesaria Carpets is now a flourishing business several times its original size.

As far as WCM went, Charles and Isaac were a remarkably effective team. Charles was not an executive, recalls Mordechai. He brought to the party his exceptional intuition about whether a product was good or bad for the company. Wolfson brought a shrewdness of his own. In spite of their strong personalities, they never once argued or disagreed openly over WCM business. Once the decision was made, both left the implementation to the Mayers.

It was clear to the Mayers that Charles' motivations for becoming involved in Israeli industry and commerce were very different from his motivations in the UK. When difficult commercial decisions had to be made at WCM, he always instructed Mordechai to 'do what's right for the country'. 'He didn't see Israel as another place to make money,' says Mordechai.

It was Wolfson, too, who introduced Charles to Meyer Weisgal and the Weizmann Institute. The Weizmann, now one of the foremost scientific research institutions in the world, started out as the Daniel Sieff Research Institute in 1934, after a suggestion to Rebecca and Israel Sieff by their friend Weizmann. Weizmann had a small office and laboratory on the campus, where he had managed to attract a number of Jewish scientists fleeing from Nazi Germany. It was Meyer Weisgal, a New York impresario, who took the Committee for the Sieff Institute in America and rattled its teeth, shortly before Weizmann's seventieth birthday. Instead of pussy-footing about trying to raise $1,000,000, he argued, why not aim for a really significant expansion of the institute and rename it in honour of Weizmann? He contacted Israel Sieff to ask if he would agree. Sieff asked how much he still needed in pledges. Weisgal said $1 million. 'Why don't you make it five?' was Sieff's rejoinder.

From that moment on, Weisgal was a tenacious pursuer of Jews with money. He set up home at Rehovot and drew up his shopping list of target benefactors. Once he had set his sights upon achieving a certain size of donation from someone, he would sink his teeth in and not let go until he had what he wanted. It took him three years finally to snare Charles.

Weisgal adopted his philosophy from Nicholas Murray Butler, a former president of Columbia University, who pointed out that a rich man goes through three phases in his life. The first is accumulation, when you leave them alone. The second is contemplation, when the fundraiser should 'flutter about him'. The third is distribution – 'the time to be on the spot, and deliver the kill'. As Weisgal himself describes it:

> These millionaires I used to call 'my customers'. I was selling something that they wanted to buy: some a piece of immortality, their names on a building; some the privilege of being associated with a renowned scientific

institution in Israel. Some wanted to impress their alienated intellectual children; others wanted to buy off a bad conscience. A very few didn't know what they wanted, they only knew that they should want something.

Clore's motivation was a mixture of all these, but predominantly the desire to impress his children. Alas, with Alan, it never worked. The precocious youngster disliked the country and everything about it. Although he attended the obligatory openings, he made no attempt to disguise his boredom and contempt for the proceedings. One of the few occasions that Mordechai Mayer saw Charles act as a strong father was when he cuffed Alan for refusing to go on a tour of the country, shouting at him: 'You are a Jew and this is your country.'

Weisgal sensed that Charles could be snared by offering him a sense of family, of belonging, at a time when his marriage had fallen apart. He introduced Charles to intellectuals and politicians of international standing whom Alan ought to have a natural respect for, and ensured that everything possible was done to make the youngsters feel at home. At one stage, half the administration of the institute was racing around trying to find bicycles for the Clore children to ride in the grounds. Weisgal tried hard to achieve a reconciliation between Charles and Francine and succeeded at least in blunting much of their animosity towards each other. (In later years he was instrumental in making the peace between Charles and Vivien, too.) Gradually he began to really like and feel sorry for the lonely millionaire. But he still could not get Charles to commit himself to the big donation.

In the end, Weisgal conspired with Wolfson to push Charles over the edge. The institute badly needed a students' hostel. Isaac agreed to hold a meeting with the architect in Weisgal's home at ten o'clock, when Charles had also been invited over. Isaac made great play of having it built in his name, saying loudly to the architect as Charles walked in: 'I like the sound of it: "The Wolfson Student Hostel".' Meyer took Charles aside and whispered: 'It's your last chance.' Charles started to get involved in the discussions over the design. 'Don't interfere, Charles. This project's mine,' remonstrated Wolfson. Unable to contain his frustration, Charles burst out: 'No, I'm doing it.' 'For you, Charles, anything,' said Wolfson, putting his arm round Charles' shoulders, before drifting into the background and leaving him holding the baby.

Other rich Jews succumbed to the Weisgal technique more swiftly. Abba Eban recalls travelling in an aeroplane with him: 'He was sitting next to a wealthy Jew. After six hours, the victim was so exhausted that he simply asked: "All right, how much do you want?" Weisgal replied: "How much have you got?"'

On another occasion Weisgal received a cheque for $100,000 out of the blue. He wrote back to the benefactor, whom he knew could afford more,

'Thank you for your symbolic contribution...'

Years later Charles got his own back. In tying up a deal, he brought over with him a young and not very well-off accountant, Stuart Young. Young was surprised to find himself in the place of honour at a dinner at the Institute. Meyer Weisgal went to great lengths to involve him in the conversation. Young was both flattered and bewildered at the great man's attention, especially when Weisgal put an arm round his shoulder and insisted on taking him into the study to show him the model for a new building on the campus. After a few minutes, Charles entered, trying not too hard to keep a straight face. At first Weisgal asked him not to interrupt and suggested he should make himself scarce. 'We've serious business here, Charles.' Only gradually did he realize that Young was not the young multimillionaire Charles had led him to believe. 'Young man,' said Weisgal, 'you are the first person ever to get a free meal out of me.'

The relationship between Weisgal and Clore became close. Both had an intenseness, a ruthlessness and doggedness when it came to getting what they wanted. They learnt to tease each other mercilessly – in itself a sign of the confidence and trust between them. 'Go on home to England,' Weisgal would shout at him. 'Don't come back till you've made some more money to give to us.'

When the Weizmann Institute awarded him an honorary doctorate, it was more than just a formality. It was a gesture of dear friendship. Charles, who had long been sensitive about his lack of a university education – one reason he insisted both Alan and Vivien had one – wept openly at the ceremony.

Equally close was the complex and enduring relationship between Clore and Wolfson – they were known to campus dwellers as 'the odd couple'. Isaac Wolfson had grown up in a Jewish enclave at the other end of the country, in Glasgow, and retained the strong local accent of his native city. Born in 1897, he was the son of a furniture maker who had, by coincidence, fled from the same town in White Russia as had Michael Marks, the founder of Marks & Spencer. From an early age he had shown remarkable financial genius, keeping the books of his father's business when only nine years old. Had his father been able to afford to support him, he would probably have become an accountant. Instead, like Charles, he became his father's sales rep, travelling Scotland and the North Country selling picture frames. Like Charles, he was remarkably good as a salesman, 'He would never take no for an answer,' recalled one former customer. Later in his career he was enraged to discover that one of the 2,200 shops he eventually acquired had a cellar full of unsellable picture frames that he had persuaded the previous owners to buy years before!

Isaac moved to London in 1920 and set up a shop in the City Road selling clocks, mirrors, pianos and other high-margin household products, with cash loaned by his father-in-law. There, ten years later, he met George Rose, owner of the first mail-order firm, which had just changed its name from Universal Stores by adding the word Great. By then, young Wolfson was already becoming well off in his own right. Not only was the shop doing well, but he was making a tidy income by money-lending. Rose was so impressed with Isaac's sales and financial expertise that he invited him to join the Manchester firm. Part of the deal was a share option in the company, which was just about to go public. Within a year, however, a series of mishaps caused the profits and share price of GUS to tumble. Wolfson exercised his rights to buy 40 per cent of the shares of this very solid business at a third of their former worth. He became joint managing director with Rose, quickly restoring the company's fortunes. Rose resigned two years later, leaving Wolfson in charge of a rapidly growing business.

It was during the war years, however, that Wolfson really accumulated his fortune, both within GUS and in a variety of other enterprises under his private ownership. At a time when so many other businesses were either going to the wall or were greatly undervalued, he was buying. GUS alone increased its assets between 1938 and 1948 by eight times. By the late 1960s, he owned or controlled some 250 companies.

Those who did business with Wolfson often found it a harrowing experience. He gained a reputation for personal meanness, which was not belied by his refusal to carry money around with him or the relative ordinariness of his style of living. A devout, almost obsessional Jew, who became president of the United Synagogue, he neither drank nor smoked. He claimed to be able to live, in the 1960s, on a mere shilling a day and, in terms of direct personal expenditure, almost certainly did. He would, however, admit to one vice – his charities. While a veil was always drawn over the details of his business transactions, his numerous charitable activities were always given the widest publicity. He put all his fortune into a Foundation, telling a friend that 'No man should keep more than £100,000.'

Wolfson's conversion to Zionism came after the war, when he found that his fortune and charitable activities were not enough to provide entry to the homes of the Jewish aristocrats. For all his wealth, he had not arrived socially. Eventually, Wolfson asked Sieff why he never received an invitation to his house. Sieff informed him that he was so busy that he only had the time to see people who did things for Israel. Wolfson took the hint.

While never flamboyant, Wolfson was an excellent raconteur and public performer. But his private life revolved entirely around his family and his religion.

Charles, on the other hand, was a more sombre, dapper figure, with no solid family life to fall back upon. He was also far less comfortable with Jewish tradition and frequently felt ashamed that he knew so little of what to do and say within the synagogue. On the other hand, he had an exceptional reputation for fair dealing that Isaac was never able to match. As one solicitor who knew them both well at different times recalls, once a verbal agreement was made, Charles would never attempt to change it; Isaac regarded it as the basis of negotiation and would attempt to twist out an extra advantage or two right up to the last minute.

That they were exceptional friends, who enjoyed each other's company, there is no doubt. They used to time their visits to be at Rehovot at the same time and would sit carousing together till late at night, reminiscing about old times. When the mood took them, they would sing a duet, their own badly out-of-tune rendition of 'I belong to Glasgow', finally reaching a crescendo with: 'And Glasgow belongs to me ... and Birmingham ... and Manchester ... and New York ...' – wherever they had recently made new acquisitions. At other times, there would be a tension between them, not least if Isaac let slip his feeling that he was somehow superior to the largely irreligious Charles.

On one Atlantic crossing, Randolph Churchill was Clore and Wolfson's partner in a winning ship's pool ticket. Later during the voyage, whilst his partners were at the ship's synagogue, Churchill bet on his own and lost. 'Where's your *saychul*?' (the Yiddish word for 'common sense') chided Wolfson, proceeding to draw a circle. 'It sounds like circle,' continued Wolfson, making him repeat it until the pronunciation was perfect. 'If you haven't got *saychul*, a circle's all you've got – zero.'

Because Wolfson and his wife were older than Charles (Isaac was seven years his senior), he tended to make great play of tending for them. They were, indeed, considerably less energetic. Yet at the same time there was an element of jealousy in the relationship. Charles, who referred to Isaac affectionately as 'the emperor', could not help but envy his stable family life. Isaac had a charming, devoted wife. He had a son who wanted to enter the family business after him, and was accepted as a leading figure in the Jewish community in both Israel and England. It was the perfect Jewish family.

Isaac, too, had some cause to envy Charles – not least for the attractive females he always had around him and his reputation as a ladies' man. Isaac, who had chosen to maintain an image of religious devotion, could not be seen to be having that kind of good time. He felt, with some justification, that Charles outclassed him in the takeover stakes. He also envied Charles' keen eye for art, and knew that Charles used to ridicule him for seeing art only in terms of money. He would mimic Isaac showing off his paintings: 'This one cost $100,000; that's worth $50,000', rather than 'This is a Renoir; that's a Matisse.'

At first Charles was content simply to follow Isaac's lead. He was too busy, he maintained, to get closely involved. If Isaac thought a project worth while, then he'd come in. When Wolfson–Clore–Mayer completed a showpiece residential complex in Jerusalem, Charles acquiesced graciously to the idea that it should be called the Wolfson Centre. After all, Isaac was the company's elder statesman. But the concession rankled.

While the relationship between the two tycoons never became hostile, nor even remotely unfriendly, it did add spice to their rivalry. Each was determined to outdo the other in his generosity towards Israel. In England, Charles preferred to keep a low profile on his giving, in part, at least, to avoid the embarrassment of having to refuse. In Israel, however, he felt that he had to become something of a self-publicist to prevent Isaac from stealing all the thunder. For example, he insisted that the gardens he donated to the City of Jerusalem be named with his full title: The Sir Charles Clore Hill Gardens. The motive was more than just pride at his knighthood; it was a gentle snook at Isaac.

President Chaim Herzog recalls:

> They were always watching what the other was doing. Isaac bought the Shell oil company subsidiary (PAZ) here for almost nothing – a mere £5 million for the whole company. That was the value of the oil in the tanks alone. The company had been hit very badly by the Arab boycott. It was the best deal he had done in his life. Isaac gave half of the shares to the Israeli government. Charles had to keep up. He bought a substantial interest in the Israeli oil company, Delek. Then Isaac gave all the profits from his purchase to charity; so did Charles. Sometimes it was Charles who took the lead, for example, in going into the health sector.

Isaac made massive donations to build fifty or so synagogues across the country. All of this seemed to be thoroughly unnecessary to Charles, who insisted loudly that Israel didn't need so many. While he donated money to the Great Synagogue outside the walls of Jerusalem and had great plans for restoring the Horva synagogue within the Jewish quarter, Charles was more concerned with practical projects that would have a clear social benefit. He insisted upon a strong human element in the projects to which he gave. So he responded to Isaac's synagogues by building seventy-five kindergartens to commemorate his seventy-fifth birthday. Unlike Isaac's gifts, these were not just for Jews, but for people of all races, some of the kindergartens deliberately being built in Arab areas and even, in the case of the ancient town of Acre, attached to mosques.

Charles' enthusiasm for the kindergartens stemmed partly from memories of the hardness of his own childhood and partly from his disappointment at the relationship with his own children. Several witnesses were struck by the sight of this lonely old man dancing with the small children and crying as he shuffled off into his waiting limousine.

When Isaac agreed with Weisgal to have a home built on the campus at Rehovot, it was inevitable that Charles would follow suit. But here for once, Charles did not try to outdo Isaac. The penthouse suite built for him on the roof of the building he donated is simple, if large. It is far smaller than the mansion from which Isaac's sad, slumped figure in a slow-moving wheelchair occasionally emerges to tour the grounds.

At times Charles and Isaac would sit and wrangle over who was the richer, each claiming that the honour belonged to the other. Another part of the constant game they played was always to try to make the other one pay for lunch, dinner, taxis or shared expenses. Young found himself sandwiched between these strange old men for a week. He would have to get up early for breakfast with Isaac, spend the day working with both of them and accompany Charles well into the early hours of the night. In the midst of growing exhaustion, he also found that neither of the two millionaires would admit to having any money on them if the other was present (although Charles, for one, never went anywhere without a large wad of notes). The hapless young accountant found himself paying for lunch every day.

Back in England, Clore and Wolfson rarely collaborated. Charles, who constantly bemoaned the fact that shoes he could not sell in his shops went like hot cakes in Isaac's catalogues, saw GUS as a deadly rival to the high-street retailer. The only venture on which they came together was over a dormant insurance company owned by Eagle Star. The two men agreed with Eagle Star's Sir Brian Mountain to recapitalize the company and pass much of their respective operations' insurance business through it. In return, Eagle Star provided free insurance advice.

One thing both Charles and Isaac had in common was a meanness about little things. Although he was far more relaxed in Israel, Charles would still habitually argue about the bill or the service he received in night-clubs and hotels. He was often found in the early hours, one of the last stragglers to leave the night-club at the Dan Hotel, picking over each item on the bill in detail. On one occasion, he loudly accused the hotel of adding in the date to his bill.

Both also hated the thought of not coming off best in a deal. On one occasion Isaac was in a foul temper as he was driven from the airport to Rehovot. When Weisgal asked what was the matter, he replied, 'I lost a lot of money today.' Charles arrived a few hours later and explained: 'It's not that he lost money. It's just that he had to pay more than he expected for what he wanted, even though it was still a pretty good deal.'

One thing they were radically different in, however, was the manner of their giving. Isaac was a very cautious benefactor but would show little interest in his projects once the money was given. Charles also wanted to be sure he was getting value for money. Once a project was finished, however, he would visit it periodically to check it was being well looked after and to see if there was any further help he could give. Getting additional help out of Isaac was a far more difficult matter, however, for he would prevaricate whenever the suggestion came up and would never commit himself on the spot. Yaki Shiva, who was responsible for generally looking after Charles and his family at Rehovot, puts it this way: 'When you asked him for anything, he never forgot and he'd give you a straight answer, yes or no. Unlike Wolfson, he'd never say, "We'll talk about it some other time." Clore would think about it and Saturday morning he'd call me in and say "It's all done." '

As Moshe Mayer astutely observes: 'One of the big differences was that Charles really *enjoyed* his charities. He invested in them because he got a lot of fun out of them.' Charles' donations were all his own money; Isaac was concerned to spread the load by fund-raising more widely.

Life at Rehovot rapidly gained its own routine. Charles would regularly arrive from Europe and go straight to Mordechai Mayer's office. Mayer's attractive assistant, Ora Baharav, would be the first to speak to him and she would empathize with him as he wound down into his Israeli persona. Once settled in, he would spend the working hours at the Foundation office and return to campus for the evenings and relax in a manner he could rarely manage in England. 'He didn't have to spend much time on business matters. Sainer took care of that,' says Moshe Mayer. 'Here he had the *time* to do everything he wanted.'

A large collection of music (a mixture of light and classical at first and Jewish cantors increasingly in the later years), strolls in the grounds and unhurried small dinner parties were one part of Charles' routine. The inevitable nightly visit to night-clubs and two or three major parties in the penthouse each visit were another.

At the parties would be a mixture of the famous, the rich and the clever – generals and artists, millionaires and academics. Always there would be French champagne, specially flown in along with smoked salmon and acres of orchids from the hothouse of Stype. One wag observed that the parties were remarkably full of human orchids, too. Frequently, Charles would fly in a planeload of guests for the opening of some new project and the associated entertainment. He was proud of his new-found country and wanted to show it off to internationally famous people, who did not know it. In 1964, for example, he chartered a plane to bring over thirty-two people from the United States.

One noted guest was the Duke of Devonshire. When asked what he did, he replied: 'I suppose I'm in farming.' 'Local' guests included Topol, who brought along a copy of his not yet released (and first English language) film.

As in the UK, everything about the party had to be thoroughly organized, in its place, with perfect timing. He so terrorized one not particularly bright maid who could not get things exactly right that she referred to him ever after as 'the Madman' and scurried out of sight whenever Clore appeared.

The hospitality was returned. Almost every evening there was an official event or a party at someone's house, where he would be a guest of honour. If there was no party, Clore would rib his friends until someone had one. He would, for example, say to Moshe Mayer: 'You're so rich you don't hold parties any more.' He was welcome in the homes of all the leading politicians; the newspapers were always full of his exploits. He felt, with justification, that he was more important in Israel, that he was more respected for what he was rather than for his wealth.

The penthouse at Rehovot, which was given over to other important visitors when Charles was not there, was constructed to a very modern design. Clore was at pains to furnish it with art to match. His tutor in Israeli modern art was Mrs Eban, who introduced him to all the galleries and many of the artists themselves. As usual, his impeccable taste selected a superb collection, for which he was prepared to pay almost too generously. Once out of the galleries, however, his natural financial caution reasserted itself. When Mrs Eban rang home from a shop after a sale and was charged for the call, Charles was outraged. Having just spent around $1 million, he stormed into the shop to argue over a few pence.

That collection is now worth several times what he paid for it. It was Charles' intention to move not only these paintings but his entire art collection in the UK to Israel, had he lived long enough. On his visits to New York he had been fascinated by the Frick Museum, near Central Park in Manhattan. Unlike its vulgar neighbour, the Guggenheim, the Frick is homely, tasteful and delicate. Originally the home of a wealthy connoisseur, the Frick mixes old masters with ornate furnishings, a palm court and chamber music. This refined, exquisite environment appealed so much to Charles that he was determined to build a similar home in Israel for his art and his collection of Fabergé. But this, too, was destined to become yet another unfulfilled dream.

Also important in the decoration of the penthouse was a collection of

189

antiquities. Here Charles relied upon his friend Ze'evi, who, like many other Israeli army officers, is a keen archaeologist. He explained to Ze'evi that these ancient objects somehow made him feel closer to his Jewish roots. Among the valuable items he collected were a large jar from the Talmudic period and a variety of pieces from the time of the Kings. These items were not just put on display. Charles would frequently touch them, caress them as if by doing so he could establish a link with the past. He also liked to visit the digs with Ze'evi, to learn more about the era to which these items belonged.

To co-ordinate his benefaction, Charles set up two Foundations, one in 1964 and one in 1979. He deliberately involved Vivien and Alan in the financing of the first Foundation, in the hopes (unfulfilled in Alan's case) that they would carry on an interest in it after his death. That meant that he had to come to terms with projects initiated by Vivien that he himself would not otherwise have become involved with. He could not, for example, see any point in financing a museum at the Citadel. 'He couldn't understand it at first,' says Ruth Cheshin, director of the Jerusalem Foundation, whose projects Clore's foundations have frequently supported, 'but after a few visits he admitted, "after all, it's not so bad"'. That was as near an admission that he was wrong as anyone would be likely to get. Vivien threw herself into these projects with equal enthusiasm when she travelled out to Israel with Charles, Sainer and Sainer's father, Archer, to agree a project. She referred to them as her 'three young men'.

The second was established with a relatively small sum, £100,000, but intended to take half of Charles' estate upon his death. For continuity, the signatories were Charles himself, his daughter Vivien and five other individuals as required by Israeli law. Charles retained the power to appoint the other members of the Foundation during his lifetime. Since his death the first Foundation has undertaken a wide variety of projects across the country. They have, for example, rebuilt a 500-bed hospital outside Tel Aviv. At the time of writing, the second Foundation is still waiting for the UK tax authorities to release its cash, which was frozen after Clore's death.

The requests for donations kept coming. In general, the successful requests were for big projects rather than for small ones, and for projects that would improve living conditions than for those that would provide prestige. Charles was also conscious of the debt he owed to the country he was born in. 'I have to balance my giving here with my giving in England,' he once told Eban.

Most of the major projects were ones which Charles sought out himself. Shortly after the Six Day War he paid a call on General Ze'evi, then commander of the central army district, asking what he could do to help.

Ze'evi asked for a soldiers' home – a hostel in Jerusalem for soldiers away from home. Clore rapidly became immersed in the project. Apparently unconcerned about the total cost, he wanted it to be simple but to contain all the amenities – from gym and swimming-pool to a small synagogue – that would make life more comfortable for young soldiers.

The sacrifice of the young soldiers touched Charles' sentimental heart. He surprised Ze'evi during the building of the soldiers' home by asking to visit the Jordan Valley, which was still at that time heavily fortified and subject to frequent infiltration by the PLO. It was not the sort of terrain for someone of his age and background to tramp about in, but he insisted on going from one position to the next the whole day until he had a clear picture of what was going on. 'I was impressed,' says Ze'evi. 'Most rich people prefer to read a report. But he wanted to see with his own eyes and feel with his own body.'

That visit led to a donation for a memorial to those who had fallen in the fighting in the Jordan Valley. The tough businessman stood and wept at the foot of the memorial when it was unveiled.

Other donations attracted less attention, but were equally carefully considered. There was, for example, the building of a convalescent home for cancer patients in Tel Aviv, the gift of 1,000 volumes of British parliamentary papers to Tel Aviv University; and numerous donations to the Weizmann Institute. The openness of Charles' support for Israel was bound to get him into trouble when the Six Day War broke out. Firms with a Clore connection were blacklisted by the Arab states. The Arab League declared that he had 'supported Israel's economy through lavishing loans and contributions on an abnormally large scale in Israel during the past years'. Charles described the ban as 'a whole lot of bloody nonsense'.

And so, on one level, it was. Sears shares dipped slightly and recovered as it became clear that, in trading terms, the impact of the ban would be minimal. Where the ban really began to bite was in Charles' other directorships. Some time before, Charles had relinquished his hold on Investment Registry, selling it to M. Samuel & Co. in 1964 for £500,000 in cash and 600,000 ordinary shares. This company merged a year later with another financial enterprise to form Hill Samuel & Co. The rationale for owning his own issuing house was no longer strong and he could not give the business the attention it needed, nor was he willing to make the capital investment necessary to turn it into major issues of large share placings. Part of the deal was that Charles would join the board of Hill Samuel, a position that carried the City status he was often made to feel he lacked. However, the Arab League and Arabic customers of Hill Samuel put pressure on the finance company to remove its Zionist directors. When Hill Samuel asked him to resign, Charles felt it was an unworthy way out; that at the very least the board should have asked him in person to go. He resigned formally on 17 July 1975 and never forgave the slight.

Equally troublesome was the threat of kidnap or assassination. Along with Wolfson, the Sieffs and other prominently pro-Israel Jews, Clore's name was found on an Arab deathlist. Charles affected not to be concerned, but the authorities took the threats seriously. At the launch of a new knitting machine from Bentley the entire exhibition hall was surrounded by security men, who even dismantled the telephones a Post Office engineer had been working on to make sure they did not contain an explosive device.

Charles was persuaded by Sainer to take some basic precautions. His only concession to the fear of attack was to remove the CC1 number plate from his Rolls-Royce. He refused, however, to vary his daily routine of walking or driving between the two Park Street premises at the same time each day, or of strolling to Selfridges.

Charles' attempts to invest his children with enthusiasm for the new land had mixed results. Vivien rapidly grew to love the developing country and has maintained and increased the momentum of Clore's charitable work in Israel. Alan, however, was totally unimpressed and rebellious.

The nature of Charles' complex about his Jewishness also came closer to the surface in Israel. Eban recalls:

> He was very defensive about Jews being discriminated against. He felt you had to have prickles to make people leave you alone. He liked the story of the Egyptian multimillionaire who would buy any hotel that refused him. He liked stories of Jews asserting themselves. He was obsessed with the idea that to be Jewish you had to be tough.

Hence his very hawkish views about how to behave towards the Arab governments and the Palestine Liberation Organization. He felt passionately, for example, that it was wrong to hand back any land. The contrast between these views and his compassion for impoverished Arabs within Israel never seemed to strike him. Charles' intense desire to rebuild the Horva stemmed partly from the feeling that Israel needed a rallying symbol. There had been Sephardic Jews in Israel since the 1500s and there were plenty of their synagogues within the country. But for Ashkenazi Jews, who had only come to Jerusalem in the 1800s, there was only one major synagogue and that had been destroyed by the Jordanians in 1948. An equally powerful reason was that he wanted to put one over on Isaac. After all, what were dozens of small, new synagogues against the most prestigious synagogue in the world, bar the Temple itself?

Charles had plans drawn up for a $4 million building, designed by Sir Denys Lasdun, the architect of the National Theatre in London. The arguments began immediately the plans were unveiled. While many Jews applauded the architecture, the religious conservatives insisted that the building should be restored exactly as it had been. Lined up with the conservative elements was the Prime Minister, Menachem Begin. While the argument raged, Clore entered hospital for the last time. The plan was quietly buried along with him. Now all that remains of a grandiose scheme is a modern square, Charles Clore Plaza, and a memorial arch that stands quietly over the remains of the Horva.

With occasional rare exceptions, the people who belonged in the Israel slot in his life remained in that slot. 'We'd only read about the race meetings and the yacht parties,' says Eban, 'but we were never part of them.' However, Israeli friends and acquaintances were always welcome at Park Street, not least because they provided a means of feeding Charles' insatiable appetite for local gossip and news.

Charles was also ready to help them whenever they needed influence or introductions within the UK. Zvi Dinstein remembers approaching Charles for help to establish and expand the Israeli Petroleum Institute in Tel Aviv. At the time, Dinstein was responsible for the country's oil affairs. Charles had given cash to help start the organization whilst in Israel. Now Dinstein asked him to head a Society of Friends of the Institute to raise additional finance. Charles' response was characteristic: 'Release me and I'll find the right person for you.' The man he chose was Monty (now Sir) Finniston, then chairman of the British Steel Corporation, who later joined Sears itself.

But Dinstein wanted still more. The involvement of J. Paul Getty in the project would be a major coup. Could Clore help with an introduction to his famous and eccentric neighbour? Dinstein was invited out to Charles' country home as a weekend guest. On Sunday, before they departed for Getty's home, Charles went down to the kitchen and extracted a wrapped package from the fridge. It was, he explained, smoked salmon. 'That Getty is such a miser he won't give us anything more than black coffee. If we want to eat, I have to take the salmon along with me.'

CHAPTER

12

Exile and Death

'... he had totally underestimated the
importance of being rooted somewhere.'
Abba Eban

In December 1976 Charles announced his intention to step down as chairman of Sears. He had been dithering for some time, but his mind was made up by the Inland Revenue's approval of his plan to remove his fortune from the UK. Clore would now become life president, with Sainer taking his place in the chair. The announcement was not entirely unexpected. Like his son and his daughter, Charles Clore had already gone into tax exile. It was evident to all that running a £1 billion company from a suitcase was not an efficient manner of doing business.

For two years Charles had been debating what to do. His health was not all it had been since an operation for cancer of the bowel. Moreover, he was acutely aware that, for all his wealth, he had not truly enjoyed life. The thought of a partial retirement, where he could devote more of his time to relaxing pursuits and the enjoyment of leisure, had become increasingly attractive. Alas, it was to prove a chimera.

In many ways it was a good time to step down. Charles had accomplished what he had set out to do. He had received at long last his knighthood in June 1971. While secretly gratified by the honour, he mumbled to his close friends that it was long overdue. Sears had just had one of its most successful years ever, with turnover of £793 million and profits of more than £45 million. It was now a solid, broad-based conglomerate with a steady record of growth. Over the next three years it was to double in profits and grow in turnover by more than 50 per cent. There was little more he wanted to accomplish in England; there was, he grumbled, no money to be made here – all the opportunities lay in the United States. The future for Sears was set at more of the same. Unusual for an entrepreneur, Clore had the perspicacity to recognize that it was possible to remain too long at the helm and that the business had reached a stage where a new kind of management was needed to consolidate what his entrepreneurial flair had created.

In particular there was a need to identify clearly just who was in charge of Sears. As Sainer tactfully puts it in a recent history of Self-ridges:

> He was on the phone to various managing directors and it became a little troublesome, because someone would come to me for an instruction and would then ring Sir Charles and persuade him to reverse my decision. We discussed the problem and he then decided that he would retire as chairman, although he insisted on staying on the board. To his credit, the moment he retired, he never spoke to anyone except myself and Geoffrey Maitland Smith.

Although he had been increasingly open about discussing his plans with Sainer and others, he was careful not to discuss them in front of the Sears' managers. He was concerned that premature talk of his retirement might undermine staff confidence. It was, however, common knowledge that he was looking for a successor. A string of candidates was discussed, but all either failed to make the Clore grade or were already running large, successful businesses of their own and could not be persuaded to step over.

Sainer took on the post as interim chairman, but found the problem of running both Sears and his own practice insurmountable for a man in his seventies. Obliged to choose between them, he resigned his partnership to concentrate on Sears.

The decision to go into tax exile was bewildering to most of his friends and business colleagues. While there was some reason for him to step down from active involvement in Sears (he was less and less involved in the day-to-day affairs and wanted to give Sainer a chance to run the business completely in his own way), there was little obvious need for him to go into self-imposed exile. What drove Charles out of the country of his birth was a sudden and largely irrational obsession with maintaining his fortune intact. Rather than see it dissipated by death duties, he wanted to ensure that every penny went to charity. It was only half in jest that he had responded to a newspaper request for his personal motto a few years earlier with the terse note: 'A penny saved is a penny taxed.'

Charles' exile effectively began before his retirement as Sears' chairman. He had already begun the habit of leaving England in the cold months and coming back in time for Ascot. He had also discussed his plans with Sainer and others – all of whom had advised him against leaving the country. Once his mind was made up, he would constantly rationalize his action. 'Why not simply retire and enjoy the tremendous social life he had grown used to?' asked his friends. But Charles was adamant. He had given his word to Sainer and that was an end to it.

Retirement, however, did not mean that he stepped out of business altogether. He still maintained an active control of his property assets and general investment portfolio. There were the Foundations to build up and run. Now able to devote almost all his time to these activities, he amassed a series of exceptional investments that have proven so sound that the Foundations have scarcely needed to divest any.

For a while he simply wandered the world, for all practical purposes a homeless itinerant, moving from one luxury hotel or one capital city to another. It was a bewildering and demoralizing experience for a man so used to power, influence and notoriety. It was at this time, says Townsend, that he learnt how to say sorry.

> He'd never had to before. Why should he? He was the boss. He never said thank you either, until he was in exile. He was away from people who bowed to him. Living out of a suitcase made him realize he had to behave differently towards people he did not own if he wanted them to do things for him.

Ruth Cheshin, of the Jerusalem Foundation, met him in New York in the elevator. She watched in bewilderment as the lonely little man stood outside shivering in the cold waiting for a taxi. With all his wealth, and although Sears had a car and driver, he could not bring himself to use them. She recalls: 'I kept asking myself: "Why on earth does this man have to wander aimlessly around the world?" I took great pity on him then.'

Another Israeli friend, Abba Eban, was moved in much the same manner:

> In spite of all Clore's power and wealth, one felt one needed to protect him, that he needed us more than we needed him. He gave off an air of deprivation amidst all his affluence. What made the end so sad was that he had totally underestimated the importance of being rooted somewhere.

Gerald Ronson, chairman of Heron Corporation, met him regularly every month in Paris. Charles would take Ronson and his wife Gail out to lunch or dinner and – so much out of his previous character – insist on paying. 'We'd talk about everything,' recalls Ronson. 'I used to say: "Why don't you do this deal or that?" He'd say: "I can't. I'm not living there any more. You do it. You've got the energy."'

At first Charles stayed at the Ritz in Place Vendôme. But *the* hotel in Paris at the time was the Plaza Athénée, with its bright red shades outside and elegance inside. The Plaza had – and still has – a unique atmosphere and was a place where the world's famous came to be seen. Charles ate there frequently and would regularly stop at the front desk and ask the price of a suite. 'Too expensive, too expensive,' he would always exclaim, shaking his head. One day he stopped Paul Bougenaux, the managing director, and asked yet again: 'How much do you charge for a suite or a junior suite?' Bougenaux told him and received the now familiar reply: 'Too expensive, too expensive.'

'I told him we had invested a great deal in the Plaza Athénée, that we had the best hotel staff in Paris, and that they were directly involved in a profit-sharing scheme, so they were inclined to give exceptional service,' recalls Bougenaux. 'Too expensive, too expensive,' Charles replied, pointing out that he had a discount from the Ritz.

Lost for any other argument to make, Bougenaux burst out: 'We may be too expensive, but you are too rich.' Charles looked back and started laughing (the first time Bougenaux had seen him do so) and said: 'Very well, I'll take the junior suite.' From then on the Plaza was his Paris home.

The decision may have been helped by his displeasure with the Ritz. At four o'clock one morning he was woken up by an intruder in his room. Clore frightened him off.

Gradually a routine established itself. Charles would spend most of the morning telephoning London and half the rest of the world. Then he'd have lunch and retire for an afternoon nap before spending the night at Maxim's.

The obsession with retaining his money for charity became stronger and stronger. Charles became tighter and tighter about spending money on himself. On one occasion he was at a race meet outside Paris. Sainer was there, too. Towards the end of the meeting, Charles gathered together his hat and coat and prepared to leave, explaining that he had to catch the last plane to Monte Carlo. 'But you've got six company planes,' said Sainer. The HS125 executive jets were decked out in the Clore racing colours and carried CC registration numbers. Yet it simply hadn't occurred to Charles that he could make personal use of the planes, which he had seen as a tax loss rather than as a business perk. In the end, Sainer flew him back to Monte Carlo on his own way home.

So obsessed was Charles with not spending money on himself that Janet was convinced he had given away so much money he had left himself short. It came as a great surprise to learn that there was still a vast fortune to be distributed.

Charles had fastened on two homes for his exile. One was the penthouse at Rehovot in Israel, where he knew he could relax among friends. The other was in Monte Carlo, where another penthouse was being built for him. The summer holidays he and his children had spent at Monte Carlo were golden days for Charles, but he had not realized that the summer paradise can be a winter hell. 'He just didn't know how ghastly Monte Carlo is in the winter,' comments Vivien.

While he waited for the apartment to be finished, Clore stayed at the Hotel de Paris, living out of a suitcase. Every few months Kay, his butler, would come over with a case full of clean clothes and take away the used ones.

Although he never lived in it for more than a few days, the Monte Carlo penthouse apartment provided a catalogue of mishaps and disasters. The project involved converting four apartments on the seventh and eighth floors into one large suite. Among the amenities was a magnificent swimming-pool. One of the apartments below was owned by the Slezingers, who had spent a small fortune on lavish decor and works of art to furnish it.

It was Vivien's son George who woke his mother early one morning with the news that the pool was nearly empty. At first she refused to believe him. One look at the pool sent her hastening to tell her father. 'Oh well,' said Clore, 'the insurance people will look after it.' Telling Vivien to bring her passport and those of the children and packing his own, they all went off to lunch at the Hotel de Paris. Meanwhile the Slezingers returned home. When they opened their front door, out poured a flood of water with precious antique furniture bobbing along on the tide. Making sure that he was unavailable to hear the complaints of the Slezingers and the other flat owners, Charles declared: 'I've got to get out of here, they're all after me' and took himself and the family straight from lunch to the airport.

The Monte Carlo apartment was to house many of Charles' art treasures, so he sent a security expert to look it over. Stype and 95 Park Street were already fitted with bolts and alarms to rival Fort Knox. When Charles received the security expert's report he commented wryly: 'The only way to make that place secure is to put alligators on the roof.' Ironically, all the alarms, which were (often embarrassingly) triggered off at the least excuse, failed to protect the collection after his death.

Clore returned to London frequently because he sorely missed Park Street, Annabel's and his circle of friends. But somehow London was not the same city. 'He was the saddest man I knew then,' says a close associate. 'He was very lonely. Sometimes he'd invite someone to lunch and they'd refuse. That never happened before he went into exile. People were only interested in business and he wasn't doing any.'

Selling Stype, which he visited rarely, would have made sense from a tax point of view, but Clore could not bring himself to do it. Rumours abounded among the servants that he was going to sell, but he did his best to stifle them. He once called in Stype's head keeper and Wade, his agent, and said to them in his gruff way: 'I'm not going to sever ties with you. You've been with me for a long time.' In 1978 Clore bowed to the pressure from his agents and put the estate on the market. At the last moment he changed his mind and withdrew it. A year later he went through with his resolution. 'It was a big wrench leaving Stype. He never wanted to sell,' says Wade.

As he realized that retirement was not the restful experience he had convinced himself it would be, Charles became increasingly unsure of himself. He was constantly questioning his friends and former colleagues – had he done the right thing? 'However much advice he had, he always wanted a bit more,' recalls Maitland Smith. This is in total contrast to his previous, decisive nature, where he would habitually make decisions on less than complete data, as most successful entrepreneurs do.

His relationship with Sainer changed slightly, too. In his exile, Charles began to realize just how much he owed to the quiet, hard-working lawyer who had put his schemes into practice. But, characteristically, he found it hard to make the admission publicly. Instead he would goad Sainer mercilessly, albeit with good humour. 'Do you know why I'm not a rich man?' he would suddenly ask people around him. Poker-faced, he'd continue: 'It's that Sainer. He stopped me buying Avis. And he stopped me buying...' Sainer would sit there impassively, absorbing it all in the knowledge that Charles was building up to a serious discussion on something quite different.

Wandering the world, feeling sorry for himself, it was hard for Charles not to feel resentful of Sainer, who now had all the power and glory of Sears. The decision to hand over had been entirely Charles' own, yet he found it hard to live with the consequences. While he never showed (and probably never felt) any genuine hostility towards Sainer, he began to pay less and less attention to his advice. A Jersey will, which covered his estate within the British Isles, left everything to charity. In drawing up his Napoleonic will in Monte Carlo to cover his estate outside the UK, Charles went instead to French lawyers. The will left everything in Monaco to Vivien.

Sainer and others tried to warn him of the consequences of a less than watertight will, but he refused to listen. Had he been prepared to construct the Monte Carlo will as a trust it would have cost an extra 1 per cent of the capital and that, to Charles, was an unnecessary expense. 'I'll not pay.' Advised that Alan would almost certainly contest it, on the grounds that Napoleonic law did not permit a father to disinherit a son completely, he declared: 'Just let the little bugger try.' It wasn't as if he did not understand the potential consequences (he had, after all, donated a library of Napoleonic law to England); he just didn't want to think about them.

Charles signed the new will in Monte Carlo just a few days after he had been told he needed a second major operation on his stomach. He rang Janet shortly afterwards. It was one of the few occasions in his life that he was the worse for alcohol. He was rambling and pensive, clearly not his usual incisive self.

Neither of the wills mention other relatives, friends or staff, most of whom had been provided for under various trusts. The family trust handled all the essentials of relatives in need and paid for grand-children's education. Several people, among them Leah Gelman, had already been housed for life.

Clore felt that these people's basic needs had all been provided for. None of them could be said to have become wealthy at his expense, yet none was left particularly poor. It is probable that he might have been more generous had he been in a state of mind to think of such things. Certainly he had at one stage been much taken with the idea of leaving specific items to friends who had expressed a liking for them. Sick and ill, this was just too much trouble. The Jersey and Monégasque wills are notable for their brevity compared with the previous UK wills drawn up by Sainer, which were full of small bequests.

All his life Charles had a fear of illness and death. Normally remark-ably robust, he would ring up Dr Sacks at the slightest hint of a cold. 'If he had a pimple Friday and Sacks put something on it, he'd be on the phone Saturday to complain it was still there,' wryly recalls Kay. Charles hated having anything to do with sick people, from an irration-al fear of contagion, and had never been to visit anyone in hospital himself, although he would be financially generous to relatives or close employees who were ill.

It is not uncommon for Jewish people to avoid the subject of death, or even to avoid talking about those who have died. Charles was a member of an exclusive lunch group at Claridge's. It was never a club as such. By force of habit the members would drift in on a Wednesday lunchtime and gravitate to the same table, where they would seat themselves with a mutual exchange of nods and grunts. They were all multimillionaires. As one after another died, their chairs and place settings would be removed from the circle without comment as if they had never existed. This macabre practice continued until the remaining members were so few as to make it impractical to continue.

The first time he went into hospital Charles did not even tell his close friends. Vivien and Janet Milford Haven, his permanent occasional companion, were at his bedside every day. 'I knew he had cancer then,' Janet recalls. 'At the first operation he had half his colon removed.' The second operation, not unusual in a man of his age, was on his prostate. This left him weak and depressed and a further cancer operation was postponed till after Ascot. All this time he had never even confided to Sainer that he had been suffering from angina. He was so secretive about his illness that he did not reveal to Vivien that he had cancer until very close to the end.

Charles was certainly not a model patient. He hated the hospital environment and the frustrating confinement so much that he was both petulant and demanding. He was also unwilling to let others see him in such a state. 'He just didn't want to burden us with his illness,' says Sylvia Sosnow.

When he left the Wellington Hospital after his prostate operation, Charles went to recuperate at Stype. Charles Hughesdon immediately arranged to fly down to see him there the next morning. Kay came out on to the lawn as Hughesdon's helicopter landed to explain that Clore was still asleep. Although he had an appointment in London, Hughesdon waited for half an hour, and then reluctantly turned on his engine. Kay came running out, saying that Charles would love to see him. He led him to the back of the house. In his hurry, however, Hughesdon slipped and fell over, banging his nose and making it bleed copiously. At first sight of the bedraggled figure asking him how he was while trying vainly to prevent blood gushing with a wad of tissues, Clore commented: 'I'm all right but isn't it you who should be in hospital?' Hughesdon came to call again in the evening, this time with a stitched-up nose, when Charles was sunning himself. The two sat in the evening sun sharing a bottle of his favourite Dom Pérignon together. It was the last time Hughesdon was to see Clore.

In the summer of 1979 he was persuaded by his doctors that he should have a second operation on his colon. Determined to put a brave face on it, he refused to make any concessions in his social round for the days beforehand. He visited the theatre with the Sosnows, went to a party at the Dorchester and dined out conspicuously.

Yet this time he had more than an inkling that he would not come out again. 'He took a chance and almost made it,' says Janet. The day he went into the London Clinic, 1 July 1979, he was staying at Claridge's. After lunch he fell asleep in the armchair in his apartment. Kay woke him in good time to get ready for admission at four o'clock and attempted to cheer him up by talking about what he would do when he came out of hospital. '*If* I bloody well come out,' replied Charles as tears began to run down his cheeks. Kay put his arms round his shoulders to comfort him – something that would have been unthinkable at any other time in the thirty years they had been man and manservant.

Yet, aside from such moments when he let down his guard, Charles refused to give the thought that he might die any conscious credence. His talk was all of the planned establishment of the new charitable Foundation in Israel into which half his fortune would go. When Kay came to visit him on his last Sunday, he spoke at length of his plans to acquire a second home in France, not far from Paris. 'He wasn't going to retire till God did. He was confident, making plans, everything was under control,' recalls a friend. Above all, he was determined to outlive his rival, Wolfson, on the grounds that it was totally unfair that Wolfson should have a longer as well as a happier life. He sent Kay out to buy him a record – *I will survive.*

'You won't die,' Kay told him. 'You can't take it with you, so you won't go.'

Restless at being confined to bed, Charles soon exhausted everything of interest in the hospital library. 'Get me a book,' he told Stevens, who returned the next day with a hot-off-the-press copy of *A Growing Concern* by (Sir) Nigel Broackes, chairman of the Trafalgar House group. Stevens thought the book would be of particular interest because Clore appeared in one of the chapters. On his next visit Stevens asked: 'Did you enjoy the book?' 'No,' replied Clore. 'Who wants to read a book by someone who's made so little money?'

When Maitland Smith dropped in, Charles asked him for some new slippers from Lilley & Skinner. When the slippers arrived, they were too small. 'Bloody fools,' swore Charles and sent them back.

At the last, Charles' concern was for the daughter he had lost and refound. By this time Vivien had a close relationship with Jocelyn Stevens. The last time Stevens visited the Clinic, Charles grasped his hand and told him: 'You've only got one thing to do for me. Look after Vivien.'

The day before he died, Charles told his brother David sombrely, 'The party's over.' By midday he had cheered up enough to joke with his nurse not to be long getting her lunch, because this meal would be the one that killed him. Early the next morning he asked for his newspaper. As he reached to take it, a blood clot from the operation moved and stopped his heart. Charles Clore was dead.

David Clore commented after the funeral that Charles was over-doctored. Had events been allowed to take their course, David believed, his brother would have lived several more years for his cancer was not greatly advanced. 'When he went into hospital, he looked as fit as a fiddle,' says a member of the Clore family. 'We were told that it was the shock of the operation that killed him.'

The morning news headlines on the radio announced that Charles Clore was seriously ill, but by then he was dead. Because it was a Friday and by Jewish custom the dead are buried quickly, Clore's interment was arranged for the same day rather than wait for the Monday. That afternoon the small group of relatives, close friends and servants gathered at Willesden Cemetery. Rabbi Maurice Unterman, a long-standing friend of Clore's, gave a very brief oration. Few tears were shed. The body was lowered into a grave where the headstone would later be marked with the simple words, 'His word was his bond.' Unlike almost every other headstone in the cemetery, Clore's bears no mention by name of a grieving wife or children – a poignant reminder of his loneliness and isolation.

Six years later the funeral of his brother David was a less private affair. Francine was heard to remark tersely afterwards: 'I liked David Clore much more than his brother.'

The quiet burial was a poignant comment on a man who had just a short time before been a household name, who had shaken the foundations of British commerce and industry, not once but several times. The balance was redressed to a certain extent by the memorial service a month later, where the pews were stacked with titles and industrial heavyweights. Yet even that ceremony held the seeds of grief. Sainer's oration was followed by one from merchant banker Trevor Dawson. It was one of Dawson's last public acts. Not long afterwards he committed suicide.

13

The Aftermath

Clore's dream of bequeathing most of his fortune to charities in Britain and in Israel, the two countries that he loved, was in tatters. His plans to move his world-wide assets to Jersey were thrown into confusion by his premature death; only a mere three months more and his fortune would have been irrevocably beyond the reach of the taxman.

In the event, a long and bitter fight was to ensue between members of the Clore family, the Inland Revenue and Clore's charities. It was to be a fight in which the political repercussions threatened to sully the relationship between Britain and Jersey; which brought two legal systems into conflict and in which the professional reputation of several individuals was at stake. During the wrangle, which took almost six years to settle, accusations of tax evasion, 'intermeddling' and professional misconduct were thick in the air. And it all arose because Clore failed to take into account the legal complications that would ensue if he died too soon.

'It certainly wasn't the Inland Revenue's idea to send the papers in the case to the Director of Public Prosecutions. We had never so much as breathed the words "tax evasion", or suggested that anything was illegal. It was Lord Justice Templeman who called for the papers to be sent,' comments Peter Millett QC (now Mr Justice Millett), then the Queen's Council for the Inland Revenue.

Clore's last wishes should have been relatively simple to follow. He had made two wills, the general will and the Monégasque will. The latter directed that all of his assets, other than those in Monaco, should be added to a trust fund called the Jersey Personal Settlement. This trust would provide income for Clore during his lifetime and then be used to grant discretionary funds to the now numerous charitable foundations he had established, in particular the Israel Foundation and the Jersey Foundation. Vivien and Alan were to become trustees to the trust fund. The other trustees were Chaim Zadok, a lawyer and former Israeli Justice Minister; a French-based lawyer. Nathan Mayerhass; and an Israeli accountant Joseph Kasierer. The Monégasque will bequeathed Clore's property, paintings and furniture in Monaco to Vivien.

It was the way in which Clore chose to transfer his assets, and the slowness and obvious reluctance with which he did so, that enmeshed the estate in litigation after his death. He had first set up Stype Investments, an investment company, in Jersey. The next step had been to create the Jersey Personal Settlement to which he transferred the shares of Stype Investments. He then lent Stype Investments between £30 and £40 million to buy his assets, most of which were in the form of gilt-edged securities, and settled the benefit of the debt on the trusts of the Jersey settlement.

The process was almost completed. All that remained was for Stype Investments, as Clore's nominee, to sell the Guy's Estate and Stype. These two last properties were the hardest of all for him to part with.

Then the meticulous plan began to crumble. Stype Investments contracted to sell Guy's Estate to the Prudential for £20.5 million, but before the sale was completed, Clore died. His untimely death meant he remained the beneficial owner entitled to the proceeds of the sale and, if it was proven that he was domiciled in England, the proceeds were still subject to capital transfer tax. Not only that, but his free estate outside the United Kingdom and the assets of his personal settlement would be subject to capital transfer tax.

'When we found that the money from the sale had been transferred out of the country, we knew we had a good claim for capital transfer tax. But the only defendants in the UK were Stype Investments so we had to somehow construct a claim against them,' says Millett.

It was at that point that Stype Investments should have moved all of its assets out of Britain in order to avoid any claim against it. As it was, the Inland Revenue brought the charge that Stype Investments, as a foreign company, was moving Clore's assets out of the country without proper authority. It was acting as an executor and, under the Finance Act of 1975, anyone who has taken possession of or intermeddles with property, becomes liable for capital transfer tax as if he were an executor or trustee. The Inland Revenue moved swiftly and asked that Stype Investments' British assets in the UK, totalling around £30 million, be frozen. Suddenly the investment company found itself embroiled in a controversial legal battle.

The tax dispute got off to a somewhat faltering start. The Inland Revenue's case was rejected and looked as though it had died there and then. However, the Court of Appeal froze the company's British assets in spite of Stype Investments' argument that, as the vendor, it had been bound to take the money from the sale, and that it was natural to remit the money to its only bank account, which happened to be in Jersey.

The Queen's Counsel presenting the case for the Jersey company was given a rough ride by the judge presiding in the Court of Appeal. Mr Justice Templeman was known for his outspoken manner and inclination to interrupt barristers in mid flow.

A particularly tense moment occurred during the hearing when the lawyer for Stype Investments nearly lost his temper. Lord Justice Templeman had put him on the spot by demanding suddenly: 'What are your submissions?' The barrister summarized his argument hastily. Templeman jotted them down and then read them back in a paraphrased form. Then he turned to the harassed barrister and asked in a tone clearly showing that he was unimpressed, 'Are *those* your submissions, Mr Price?' The barrister could endure it no longer. Violently banging the wooden box in front of him, he barked out: 'No, they are not my submissions and if your Lordship insists on taking down my words and changing them, you must put your name under them.'

As if the situation were not complex enough with the Inland Revenue struggling to justify proceeding against Stype Investments, Alan Clore's intervention threw the whole procedure into chaos. He entered the already crowded arena by disputing the validity of Clore's wills, both of which excluded him. Bitter, alienated from Clore even to the moment of his death, Alan was determined to flout his father's last wishes. He did exactly what Sainer and all the rest said he might do: he fought against the family by claiming that Clore was domiciled in Monaco; that the Jersey Foundation and the Personal Settlement were null and void; and that by virtue of rights under the Monégasque law of succession, he was entitled to the estate. While the Inland Revenue took its case before the High Court of Justice in Britain, Alan fought his case in the Royal Court of Jersey and Monaco. The contest was turning into a lawyer's dream. Disunity in the family's camp could only help the Inland Revenue. 'The case was becoming more and more bizarre every minute,' says Millett.

The Inland Revenue was jubilant about Alan's move to challenge the validity of the Jersey charitable trust. Calling into question the technical legality of the trust could only strengthen the Revenue's hand. According to one lawyer, however, 'Alan made a hash of his claim. He put forward a feeble argument that was very quickly torn up in Court.'

Furthermore, the hard-pressed Stype Investments found itself forced by the law to break the law. Clore had wanted to sell the estate and move the proceeds abroad. Finding a buyer proved difficult until he had the idea of setting up an overseas company to which Stype Investments could sell the estate, leaving the money outstanding on the mortgage. Meanwhile the named executor of the will applied to take out a probate but was refused. Instead, the probate was granted to the Official Solicitor. He called in the mortgage debt and sued the Jersey company for repayment. The judgment went against Stype, which then decided to pay the sum using money from its £30 million British assets. The Inland

Revenue blocked this move in a bid to force Stype to use its Jersey funds and return some of the transferred money.

'The whole thing was becoming hilarious; more and more bizarre every minute,' says Millett. 'The company had been ordered to pay, it had the money available and wanted to pay, yet the creditor wouldn't let it.'

In desperation, Stype Investments appealed. The judge refused to allow the company to use its British money. Eventually, the company capitulated and applied to the Jersey courts to remove some money from the island.

'We knew we should have to come face to face with the Jersey courts eventually,' recalls Millett. 'We were winning all along the line, but it was inevitable that at some stage we would have to apply to the Jersey court, which would refuse to assist us to recover UK tax out of assets in Jersey.'

It was a confrontation which no one wanted – two legal systems fighting over the same estate and grappling with the same issue of domicile. The issue threatened to move out of the legal and into the political arena. If the two courts reached different decisions about Clore's domicile, what would then happen? Moreover, the Jersey court had raised the question of whether a foreign court had the right to tax assets already moved to Jersey. Should the Inland Revenue present a valid claim, the tax-free status of Jersey would be seriously undermined. At worst, Parliament might intervene and a damaging political fight ensue.

The only prospect in sight seemed years of litigation stretching into the future, to the benefit of no one. 'There was never any doubt that the family and trustees would settle. Our strategy was to maintain the pressure and get all our guns out. We brought a number of cases in close succession and won each one. It was a case of wearing down the trustees,' says Millett, 'but it was essential not to lose any of the skirmishes.'

The interest from Clore's estate was steadily growing. By April 1983 the value of his free estate was around £19 million. The proceeds of the Guy's Estate retained in Jersey by the Royal Court of Jersey had amounted to £36 million. The assets of his personal estate had reached a value of £39 million.

The question of Clore's domicile was the first issue to be settled. The fact that Clore had wandered so restlessly around Europe emerged clearly from the testimonies of many of his closest friends, particularly from Lady Janet Milford Haven, Sainer, Astaire and Footring. Indeed, a rare letter from Clore to Footring particularly betrayed his loneliness and longing for England. After Clore's departure from Sears, Footring had written to him congratulating him about the manner in which he had left and thanking him for his services to the company. He had then asked Clore why he still insisted on living abroad and argued that he had done enough for his family and for his charities. He should feel free to live where and how he liked. Clore's answer was warmly honest:

> I do appreciate more than I can say your extremely kind and touching letter and the advice you gave me. In my heart of hearts I know that you are right, but as I have stayed away so long I shall see the year through. At the same time, I have already decided on a plan and will see how things work out when I return in April.

Jarvis Astaire recalled a time when he spent a weekend in Clore's apartment in Monaco. He asked Clore why he had decided to live in Monaco when all his interests were elsewhere. Clore replied that he did not know and that he was thinking of changing his mind and returning to England, regardless of the tax consequences. Continuing to call England 'home', retaining the Stype estate and plainly bored and dissatisfied with his nomadic life in Europe, the small measures that Clore had taken to change his domicile to Monaco seemed half-hearted gestures in comparison.

Amidst the confusion and contradiction, Sainer's evidence to the court was like a breath of fresh air. His candid and balanced account of Clore's indecisive wavering and unhappiness over the question of where he should reside by and large convinced the court that Clore never permanently settled in Monaco. Stepping out of his lawyer's shoes for a brief moment, Sainer indicated that he personally did not believe that Clore ever fully turned his back on Britain. 'Sainer did the right and honourable thing. His behaviour throughout the whole case was unimpeachable,' comments Millett. 'Some believed that he was behind the scheme to evade tax, but the truth was that he was a very good friend and an upright and honest man who gave Clore the right advice.'

Mr Justice Nourse, the judge at the High Court of Justice presiding over the issue of Clore's domicile, was clear in his summing up:

> On consideration, I am far from satisfied that Sir Charles ever reached the point of abandoning England.... I think that everything was in an experimental stage. Being of the make-up and disposition previously described, he could not, in my view, have committed himself to a way of life which would keep him out of England for all but ninety days in the year.

Once Clore's domicile was proved, the case for capital transfer tax was considerably strengthened. Under this additional weight, the trustees of the trust finally capitulated and agreed a compromise. After almost six years of dispute over Clore's will, the case was finally brought to an end in April 1985. The Royal Court of Jersey approved that a total of £67 million was to be paid in tax to the Inland Revenue on Clore's world-wide assets now worth around £123 million. The remaining £56 million was divided between the three charitable trusts that Clore created in Jersey and Israel.

All that was left was to sell off Clore's *objets d'art*, the last remnants of his fortune which he had so determinedly built. At first, the Clore Foundation chose to entrust the £14 million sale to Sotheby's. Then Christie's put in a submission to the trustees that it could do better – a move that would have appealed to Clore. As a result the collection was split between the houses, with the bigger share, worth about £10 million, going to Christie's.

Clore's magnificent collection of French furniture was sold at Christie's in December 1985. His illness had not deterred him from continuing to collect fine pieces – indeed it became one of his main pleasures. In 1979, he was a major buyer at a Sotheby's sale in Monaco of French furniture. The collection had belonged to Wildenstein, the dealer, and then briefly passed to Akram Ojjeh, the Saudi Arabian financier. Sotheby's had ingeniously placed Clore and Stavros Niarchos in view of one another and the two tycoons went on outbidding one another during the auction. Clore won the battle consistently and took thirteen lots, among them a Louis XVI marquetry commode by Leleu, costing £446,600, a Louis XV cabinet for £311,100, and a pair of corner cupboards by Latz for £288,900. After his death, it was discovered that the commode came from Versailles. In the Christie's auction it was sold for £1,072,934. The furniture, like everything else, was sold for the benefit of Jewish charities, most of them in Israel, and raised over £6 million.

Half of Clore's remarkable and unique collection of portrait miniatures, valued at around £1 million, was sold at Sotheby's in March 1986. It was arguably the finest to appear at auction since 1935. The 200 miniatures, painted on enamel and ivory, included works by Augustine, Bouton, Deranton, Isabey and Füger. The top price of £50,600 set a new price record for a continental miniature. The proceeds from the sale, totalling £625,515, went to his personal estate to benefit the charities that he helped during his lifetime. The rest of the collection is awaiting auction at Sotheby's.

The auction room at Sotheby's was packed for the sale. The room was cluttered casually with treasures; marble busts, huge decorative mirrors and antique French clocks littered the ornately carved tables which lined the sides of the room. Some bidders sat at their ease upon richly satined chairs and the occasional *chaise-longue*. Lining the walls of the large rectangular room were countless paintings of voluptuous, near-

naked women depicted in groups or individually. The atmosphere spoke
of decadence and wealth.

The auctioneer, a young man of crisp accent, stood on the dais, high-
lighted by the sun pouring through the skylight. Amidst muted mur-
muring from the bidders, the steady clap of the auctioneer's hammer,
and the stiff and self-conscious pose of the young boy displaying the near
invisible miniatures, the collection was dispersed swiftly piece by piece.
As the crowds drifted away, shuffling between the exhibits, it was as if
the last tide had ebbed on Charles Clore.

And yet Charles Clore is unlikely to be forgotten for many years
to come. Some of his donations while he was alive are only just coming
to fruition.

Almost his last act, while awaiting the final operation, was to approve
a £6 million donation to the Tate Gallery. At the time the Foundation
had amassed such a surplus of cash that it could fund a really large
project. Covent Garden Opera House, which was seeking funding for a
major extension, ruled itself out when Sir Claus Moser, the director,
failed to ask Vivien or her father to the fund-raising dinner. (He still
received a cheque for £200,000.) Then the Tate announced that it
wanted an extension to house the Turner collection, and Charles said to
Vivien: 'If you think it's a good thing to do, do it.'

Through Clore's bequest, Turner's last wish to exhibit all his finished
paintings in one place has finally been fulfilled. Since the artist's death
in 1851, the Turner Bequest, comprising 300 oil paintings and 19,000
drawings and sketches, has been broken up and shared between various
British museums. Construction of a new extension adjoining the Tate
Gallery began in 1982. Designed by James Stirling, one of Britain's
foremost architects and called the Clore Gallery, the L-shaped building
overlooks the Thames, which featured so prominently in Turner's life
and art. The gallery will be opened by the Queen in 1987. 'Now Turner's
vision can finally be realized; indeed, the Clore Gallery will achieve far
more than the artist ever envisaged in his will,' comments Robin Ham-
lyn of the Tate Gallery.

Meanwhile, even though the courts had not released his fortune, the
Foundation Charles set up in his lifetime had continued to fund a
number of causes on an annual income of more than £2 million. Some
are notable for their creativity; in March 1986, for instance, the Clore
Foundation announced the intention of funding a children's experience
museum, an elaborate centre which will allow children to learn through
experience by handling exhibits.

Had the will not been contested, had the Revenue not won its claim,
the estate would have been settled rapidly. But the estate was *not*
settled quickly. The bitter wrangles over the will and its uses won for

the Inland Revenue £67 million but also served to increase the cake from which the charities would eat. They also emphasized Clore's humanitarian intentions. In death, if not in life, Charles Clore proved himself to be one of this century's great philanthropists.

Conclusion

'The basic rules of business are the same whether you are in the milk business or whatever it might be. The basic requirement is always common sense.' Charles Clore, theatrical manager, retailer, financier, property developer, country squire, passionate Zionist and gentile benefactor, clearly believed exactly what he said to the reporter from *Fortune* in 1959. Yet he could have added a number of other ingredients that had helped him become a byword for big business. There was, for example, his remarkable insight into people and his willingness to delegate awesome responsibilities to those in whose competence and honesty he had learned to trust. It was perhaps inevitable that that quality would go hand in hand with a reluctance to trust anyone whom his instincts did not register as totally reliable.

Loyalty played a part, too. Although it was not a quality he was widely credited with, Clore retained the goodwill and loyalty of exceptional people by his own loyalty towards them. Having accepted, for example, that Sidney Kaye was a brilliant architect he could rely upon, it would not normally occur to him to look elsewhere.

There was, too, an element of fierce courage, of willingness to take calculated risks, when all about him were playing safe. Property bargains were available for anyone with cash during and immediately after the war years, for example. The safe thing would have been to convert everything to portable wealth and emigrate to the United States. But Charles Clore saw opportunity in adversity (both others' and his own) and was determined to exploit it to the full.

Along with courage went an understanding of the virtue of sticking to a good decision. The orthodox time to sell up his gold shares would have been when they started to collapse. But Clore recognized that cyclical businesses, by their very nature, turn full cycle, whether it takes two years or ten. Time and again, he bought in at the bottom of a cycle and profited from the upswing. Only in the case of shipping did his instinct for the cycle fail him.

An obsession with making money was also a major ingredient in his success. Charles Clore did not switch off after working hours as do so many managers and entrepreneurs. His hyperactive brain was con-

212

tinually scheming, hatching, planning new deals, new angles, new ways of shaving additional profit from an already successful operation. He would talk business at Annabel's till the early morning, across the head of the current pretty young companion, in large part oblivious to the food or the show. He lived, breathed and died with deal-making on his mind.

Most people work to earn a living. An increasing proportion do so to achieve a degree of personal satisfaction. For Charles Clore, work was what gave him most enjoyment. In his heyday, even when things were going drastically wrong, he relished the flow of adrenalin that came from putting his reputation and money on the line. As the Stoll Theatres' deal collapsed around his ears, he became almost jovial, telling a journalist who caught him at the Mirabelle, planning his contribution to an exhibition of silverware in Paris, 'I don't go in for anything unless I enjoy it.'

The 'compact line man in a blue suit' didn't know if he had won or lost the battle for the theatre group, but he was taking enormous pleasure just from being in the fray.

Clore's failure as a father was due in good measure to his obsessions with work and money. But the failure simply reinforced his single-mindedness. Only towards the end, when other interests, in particular Israel, broadened his outlook did he become seriously interested in spending rather than making money.

It was hardly surprising that he became more and more lonely, taciturn and morose as the zest went out of wheeling and dealing. When the effort became too much for an ageing man, who recognized that he had missed out on so many of the pleasures life had to offer, there was nothing else to fall back upon. One of the richest men in Britain, Charles Clore had created so little emotional capital with family, friends or lovers that he had almost nothing in that bank to draw upon.

Clore's Jewishness was also a major driving factor in his determination to win. While never an orthodox Jew like his friendly rival Wolfson, he was acutely conscious of his Jewish background. His reaction to anti-Semitic behaviour had helped shape his personality from his earliest days. Whenever he received a slight, he would attribute it to his Jewishness, which it often was. So hard did this feeling rankle, that he was driven to prove to the world that the Jewish boy from the East End was a better businessman than all his critics.

There were similar motivations behind his instinctive desire to impose his will on others, whether family, friends or business acquaintances. He did not particularly want to run their lives for them, but found it difficult to hold back when he felt he knew best. A contributing factor to this trait was his lack of height. The sight of this squat little man's head permanently at breast level of the tall blondes he danced with was a frequent cause of behind-the-hand laughter. Certainly he did not like to be reminded of his stature. Like many other small men – Napoleon and Sir Michael Edwardes are two who come immediately to mind – Charles Clore was driven to find other than physical ways of dominating others. He did so by the force of his personality, by sheer presence. Within a roomful of people he would be instantly recognizable as 'somebody'. Had Charles Clore been born a man of average height, he might have been a far less aggressive (and hence far less successful) businessman.

There was, of course, one further ingredient in Clore's business success – luck. Clore was constantly complaining about his bad luck, yet there is no doubt that his career was founded on some remarkable pieces of good fortune. Had he not gained the front-of-house rights at the Prince of Wales on a legal technicality, had he not found friends such as Esdaile and Tovey and talented associates such as Sainer, his success would have been far less spectacular. Yet Clore believed, with considerable justification, that he made his own luck. For all the exceptional breaks, there were frustrating reversals. A combination of sheer persistence and multiplicity of deals ensured that he had to come out on top at least some of the time. To Clore, luck was another word for indefatigable effort.

All these factors combined to make Clore the tycoon. What made Clore the benefactor is more difficult to divine. Certainly, there were two Charles Clore personae: one held by those who knew him closely; one held by those who knew him casually or not at all. His sharp and abrupt manner, his abrasiveness and blatant passes at women of almost any station left many people with the impression of a jumped-up, rude little man who cared only for money and had no regard for people or their feelings. It was not an entirely untrue picture. Yet, at the same time, he was recognized by those who knew him well as a generous, emotional man for whom the barrier of his gracelessness was a protection for his personal vulnerability. Charles Clore had learned early in life the pain of emotional loss and rejection; he could never bear thereafter to expose his emotions to others, for fear of rejection again.

Perhaps for this reason, his charitable works never gained the recognition in Britain that might have been expected. In the public eye, Charlie Clore was a money-grabbing Jewish upstart, an unprincipled asset-stripper, who took delight in breaking the rules of the business game, no matter what harm came to others. If he gave away any money, there had to be an ulterior motive – his knighthood, of course, then the hoped-for peerage. Yet few businessmen in his era, Jewish or Gentile, contributed so generously to charitable causes.

214

Whether history will reverse the verdict on Charles Clore the man is open to question. What is quite clear is the impact that he had upon British business. The pre-war years were really the beginning of Britain's decline as an industrial nation, the loss of its genuine world power status and the start of the slow attrition of manufacturing industry. Charles Clore's role was to hold back the pace of that decline, showing what could be achieved through imaginative management and resourceful use of company assets – buildings, people and finance. That good example on its own was not enough, however. By becoming a predator, rapidly imitated by others who saw the potential of making use of idle assets, Clore forced sleepy company managements to adopt more efficient methods, too. It is not an exaggeration to say that he was in large part responsible for the wave of consolidation and innovation that fuelled British industry and commerce during the 'never had it so good' years of the 1960s.

Unlike so many of his imitators, Clore was not looking for quick, in-and-out profits. He revelled in making successful businesses grow for the medium to long term; and grow, in almost all cases, they did.

The verdict on Clore the tycoon belongs to those 'young Turks' he identified as his natural successors and to whom he was always willing to give counsel. Once again, his remarkable instinct for people with the ability to succeed holds true. Those young men are now, in their middle age, the entrepreneurs at the head of front-line companies such as Hanson Trust and Heron Corporation.

Lord Hanson recalls that Clore

> had a vision of what could be done with companies in this country. Like Max Rayne and Max Joseph, his mastery of property gave him confidence to tackle other spheres. . . . If he were still alive, he'd be a force in property today. . . . He was only limited in achieving his ambitions because the restructuring of British industry we are doing today was not popular then. He was going against the establishment and of course they resisted. It was simply unknown for an industrialist to get the kind of media support for restructuring that exists today.
>
> He would take a great deal of trouble to explain what he was trying to do, in the thought that he was passing on some of the ambitions he himself would never be able to achieve.
>
> He was very bold. I learnt from him that if the deal is right, you should follow your convictions and go ahead. Don't have self-doubts or worry about interest rates and so on. The banks will follow. I learnt that you have to make your own mind up on what to do. Once you've done so, you are your own man.

To Gerald Ronson, Clore would talk at length about the mistakes he had made and how the younger man could avoid them. During his exile, the compulsion to pass on the torch became even greater as he finally accepted that he would never be able to hand on the business to his own son. Ironically, it was only after Charles' death that Alan showed any real interest in business. His predatory approach of buying into large companies, which are then forced to buy him out at a premium, is radically different from his father's. Charles Clore wanted to build up their lifeblood. It is unlikely he would have approved.

Sir Nigel Broackes, of Trafalgar House, describes Clore as 'probably the most original and inventive financier of the day, with the detached, cold-blooded perception to realize what a wealth of hidden treasure the British people had deprived themselves of through dividend restraint, high taxation and superfluous legislation of every kind'.

In the end, however, none of these comments fully describes the complexity of motivations and abilities that made up this extraordinary little man, with his crocodile-skin shoes and shuffling gait, his ever-present hat and coat. It is doubtful whether anyone truly *knew* Charles Clore. Many had a glimpse into one or more compartments of his life, but there were so many compartments that it was impossible to know them all. Alan French, the former Selfridges' managing director recalls:

> He was tough but he was honest. I recognized him for what he was – a man of principle. It is sad that such a man, who was essentially shy in his relations with people with whom he was not familiar, dressed himself very carefully every day with a reserve of steel armour that did not allow penetration. In the business which he controlled I believe he was one of the most misjudged men. He was respected but not liked by many of his managers and feared by too many.
>
> Only a very few who worked directly with him were able to take a different view but we never got really close to him. Work and pleasure never mixed. I suspect he got more pleasure from his work than he got from his pleasure. We would read of some of his pleasures in the society columns, but in business we only saw the business face of Sir Charles.

There were different circles for occasional and for close business contacts; for racing friends and shooting friends; for his family; for Park Street and for Israel. With few exceptions, people in one compartment were not invited to participate in another. This compartmentalization was his greatest protection against the world. As a Harley Street physician once remarked after attending a dinner with him: 'I sat right next to him, but I couldn't get near him.'

Index

Wolfson, (Sir) Isaac, 40, 65, 80, 97, 121, 144, 183–8; *see also under* Israel
Wolfson–Clore–Mayer Corporation, 180–1
Wontner, Hugh, 60–1
Woolton, Lord, 87
Woolworths, 137
Wordsworth, Gordon, 151
Works, Ministry of, 32, 49

Young, Mr (Euston Rd property owner), 108
Young, Stuart, 1, 183

Zadok, Chaim, 204
Zeckendorf, Bill, 129
Ze'evi, General, 172, 174, 190, 190–1
Zimmermann, Jack, 34, 53
Zoo, London, 127, 165
Zuckerman, Lord, 165